Praise for *Issues on My Mind*

"For over three decades, I have relied on George Shultz as a loyal friend and gifted mentor to not only identify our most difficult foreign policy and national security dilemmas but to offer sound solutions. Once again, he has risen to that challenge superbly."

—Richard G. Lugar, *US senator (R-IN), 1977–2013, former chairman of the Senate Committee on Foreign Relations*

"George Shultz draws from his remarkable life and incredible depth of experience to examine some of today's most intractable issues. His time in the Office of Management and Budget and the Treasury Department informs his positions on banking reform, while his days as Secretary of State are clear in his thoughts on diplomacy and nuclear weapons. As always, George doesn't shy away from controversy, arguing for a carbon tax and decriminalization of illegal drugs. This volume articulates lessons from one of our most esteemed statesmen, lessons that both parties should be willing to examine."

—Dianne Feinstein, *US senator (D-CA), chairperson of the Senate Select Committee on Intelligence*

"No one has the wisdom and personal memories that George Shultz brings to the wide range of domestic and global issues that we face today. The lessons of his remarkable career and of his personal experience are here to read—first summarized eloquently and then in a collection of his essays and speeches."

—Martin Feldstein, *The George F. Baker Professor of Economics at Harvard University and president emeritus of the National Bureau of Economic Research*

"George Shultz writes about a 'world awash in change,' a world with enormous potential that is also dangerously unsettled. He holds that the United States still has an indispensable role to play in rebuilding a global framework for peace and prosperity. Yet we find ourselves divided politically and ideologically, hamstrung by our own unprecedented fiscal and economic challenges.

"Drawing on his decades of experience in academic, governmental, and business life, Shultz writes clearly and forcefully about how to break through the impasse.

"Get hold of *Issues on My Mind*. Read it right now. And let's apply the wisdom of a thoughtful man who has demonstrated again and again his capacity to find sensible common ground."

—Paul Volcker, *former chairman of the Federal Reserve Board and chairman of the President's Economic Recovery Advisory Board, 2009–11*

"This volume collects some of George Shultz's most compelling analyses on topics ranging across the fields of economics, foreign policy, demography, the challenge of terrorism, and nuclear security. It is a unique record of decades of national and international service and a worthy guide for the era now unfolding. America has been fortunate to have spawned George Shultz."

—Henry A. Kissinger, *former secretary of state (1973–77) and former national security adviser (1969–75)*

ISSUES ON MY MIND

ISSUES ON MY MIND

Strategies for the Future

GEORGE P. SHULTZ

FOREWORD BY Henry A. Kissinger

HOOVER INSTITUTION PRESS

Stanford University | Stanford, California

The Hoover Institution on War, Revolution and Peace, founded at Stanford University in 1919 by Herbert Hoover, who went on to become the thirty-first president of the United States, is an interdisciplinary research center for advanced study on domestic and international affairs. The views expressed in its publications are entirely those of the authors and do not necessarily reflect the views of the staff, officers, or Board of Overseers of the Hoover Institution.

www.hoover.org

Hoover Institution Press Publication No. 636

Hoover Institution at Leland Stanford Junior University,
Stanford, California 94305-6010

First printing 2013
19 18 17 16 15 14 13   7 6 5 4 3 2 1

Manufactured in the United States of America

The paper used in this publication meets the minimum Requirements of the American National Standard for Information Sciences—Permanence of Paper for Printed Library Materials, ANSI/NISO Z39.48-1992. ⊗

Library of Congress Cataloging-in-Publication Data
Shultz, George Pratt, 1920– author.
    Issues on my mind : strategies for the future / George P. Shultz.
        pages cm — (Hoover institution press publication ; no. 636)
    ISBN 978-0-8179-1624-4 (cloth : alk. paper) —
    ISBN 978-0-8179-1626-8 (e-book)
    1. United States—Politics and government—21st century. 2. United States—Economic policy. 3. United States—Foreign relations—21st century. I. Title.
II. Series: Hoover Institution Press publication ; 636.
    JK275.S525 2013
    320.60973—dc23   2013022921

For Charlotte

&

The Future:

*My five children, eleven grandchildren,
and four great-grandchildren*

Contents

Foreword

Henry A. Kissinger

When I studied international relations, the nation was the basic unit of international politics. Its sovereignty defined the permissible range of foreign policy. The state was presumed to have the power to regulate its internal affairs and was therefore treated as an interlocutor capable of undertaking binding commitments. Aggression was defined as the use of force projected across national boundaries.

This world order is in a state of upheaval. The nation-state in Europe has recognized its limitations and is forming a European Union. But the European Union has not yet achieved the commitment of its citizens that had been characteristic of the nation-state. In other regions, the political units, even when they call themselves nations, are often composed of differing, occasionally clashing, ethnic groups thrown together by a different historical evolution than Europe's, as, for example, India and China. Or, as in Africa, they were forged by the desire of imperial powers to generate ethnic rivalries in their colonial possessions to prevent the emergence of the European-style nation-state.

These political units are seized by an internal challenge to state powers. In many regions of the world, the state faces ethnic and ideological challenges. The Islamic world is rent by ideological conflicts comparable to those of Europe in the seventeenth century. Russia is reinventing its domestic politics and its ties with the former Soviet world, while in its relations with the West it is torn between its historic patterns and its contemporary necessities. Two of the world's main classical civilizations, China and India, are emerging as modern great powers. With this, the center of gravity of international affairs is shifting from the Atlantic to the Pacific and Indian oceans. It is, as George Shultz writes in these pages, "a world awash in change."

For the first time in history, the various continents are linked by contemporaneous experience and they can be observed in real time simultaneously. Thus, two major new trends dominate the present world: first, the shift from a focus on foreign dangers to the risks produced by the international system itself; and second, the challenge this poses for domestic governance. For the generation following the Second World War, security was the dominant problem. With hostile armies facing each other across a divided continent, international order was identified in large part with military deployments and the security guarantees of the United States.

The challenges of our world are more ambiguous. The international economic system has become global, but the political structure has remained essentially national. The global economic structure is predicated on removing obstacles to the flow of goods and capital. The international political system is still largely based on the nation-state. Globalization facilitates and encourages decisions based on comparative advantage; in its essence, it ignores national frontiers. Both systems have a plausible claim to represent the popular will, one on a global and the other on a national level. The losers tend to seek their remedies within a national political system by solutions which negate, or at least obstruct, the functioning of the global system.

This dynamic has produced decades of sustained economic growth alternating with periodic financial crises of seemingly escalating intensity: in Latin America in the 1980s; in Asia in 1997; in Russia in 1998; in the United States in 2001, and then again starting in 2007; in Europe in the current period.

While each of those crises has had a different cause, their common feature has been systemic underappreciation of risk. Aided by the Internet, the role of speculative capital has magnified. With nimbleness as its essential attribute, it has often turned upswings into bubbles and downward cycles into crises, in part by the invention of financial instruments that obscure the nature of financial transactions. Lenders have found it difficult to estimate the extent of their commitments, and the borrowers to understand the implications of their indebtedness.

The global international system thus faces a paradox: its prosperity is dependent on the success of globalization, but the process produces a political dialectic that often works counter to its aspirations. The economic managers of globalization have few occasions to manage its political processes. The managers of the political processes have few incentives to risk their domestic support on anticipating economic or financial problems whose complexity eludes the understanding of all but the expertly trained. When the crisis occurs, it is often too late to close this gap.

The Internet is a neutral technology: it can help mobilize militant nationalists or religious extremists just as effectively as it brings together liberal democrats for peaceful protests. Which of these paths is followed will depend on factors which are themselves in flux across the developing and developed worlds, factors which George Shultz examines in this book: demography, economic vitality, and evolving forms of social and political organization.

In these conditions, the challenge becomes governance itself. Governments are subjected to pressures seeking to tip the process of globalization in the direction of national advantage or mercantilism. Or they face escalating demands on behalf of maximalist political or religious agendas, advanced by individuals or groups whose mobilizing power is vastly increased but who have no responsibility for the outcome.

In the West, the issues of globalization thus merge with a challenge to the nature of democracy. Many problems are better understood than executed because governments are reluctant to challenge the interest groups threatened by their insights. For the issues are technically extremely complex, thus tempting politicization and complicating serious debate.

Thus the deepest challenge, especially for Western societies, is to achieve perspective on the issues that obtrude themselves, to define their nature, and to devise solutions which the bureaucracy can execute and which the public can understand.

At the same time, the scope of the challenges impedes the capacity to deal with them with a common strategy—the ability to relate events to each other by means of a unifying perception. America has been fortunate to have spawned George Shultz. Equally at home in academia, business, and government, he has provided perspective and vision to each. Our age is awash in information, but it has not yet mastered the journey from information to conceptual knowledge, which relates tactical insights to strategic insights. Highly unusual in the American experience, George Shultz has held four cabinet posts. He has been the confidant of presidents of both political parties.

George Shultz has been able to perform this service because he has always concentrated on the big picture. In his chapter on diplomacy, he relates how, in 1985, he described before the Senate Foreign Relations Committee some of the emerging shifts in international order:

> ... we are not just observers; we are participants, and we are engaged. America is again in a position to have a major influence over the trend of events—and America's traditional goals and values have not changed. Our duty must be to help shape the evolving trends in accordance with our ideals and interests; to help build a new structure of international stability that will ensure peace, prosperity, and freedom for coming generations. This is the real challenge of our foreign policy over the coming years.

At every stage of his career, George Shultz has refined our understanding of the world—reading and traveling extensively and convening study groups and policy dialogues to analyze evolving domestic and international trends. He has applied to the changing world the best tradition of what he describes in this book as "strategic thinking—of continuously reminding ourselves of our broad objectives and of what we want to achieve in the long run." He has charted long-term objectives, from the pragmatic to the visionary, and advocates them with eloquence. A fuller appreciation of his role has been included in my laudation when Shultz was honored by the American Academy in Berlin, the text of which can be found in the epilogue of this book.

This volume collects some of George Shultz's most compelling analyses on topics ranging across the fields of economics, foreign policy, demography, the challenge of terrorism, and nuclear security. It is a unique record of decades of national and international service and a worthy guide for the era now unfolding.

Acknowledgments

This volume consists of ideas on how to address six key problem areas of current relevance: governance, economic policy, energy, drug policy, diplomacy, and nuclear weapons.

If we can handle each of these subjects correctly, then we in the United States and people in the rest of the world will have the prospect of a better future. Exceptional diplomacy will be essential and will be amply rewarded. Our economic prospects will improve, poverty will decline, and the threat of violence—particularly from the devastation posed by nuclear weapons—will diminish.

As I look back on an active life spent in association with many stimulating people in government, business, and universities, I find myself continually inspired to look forward, particularly because I now have eleven grandchildren and four great-grandchildren. Are there lessons to be culled from my past experiences that are relevant to their future? What kind of a country—what kind of a world—will these young people inhabit? These are the questions that spurred me to write this book.

Not long ago, four generations of my family gathered for the wedding of one of my grandsons. As guests assembled, another grandson provided music by playing lively tunes on his guitar. A granddaughter appeared as part of the wedding party pulling a small, red wagon holding two great-grandchildren. So first, I want to acknowledge the motivation and orientation to the future that my exciting grandchildren and great-grandchildren give to me.

My wife Charlotte is a constant source of inspiration and encouragement. My colleagues at Stanford University's Hoover Institution provide continuing challenges and ideas across a wide range of subjects. I am particularly grateful to Fouad Ajami, Michael Boskin, John Cogan, Sid Drell, Jim Goodby, Charlie Hill, Jim Hoagland, Gary Roughead, Abe Sofaer, Tom Stephenson, and John Taylor for their assistance in conceptualizing this book and their many helpful editorial and content suggestions. Adele Hayutin helped me understand the evolving demography of the world. Grace Hawes used her finely honed archival expertise to identify my past statements on key topics and to suggest photographs to accompany the text. Susan Southworth has worked tirelessly with me on this project. I thank all these friends for their encouragement and help.

George P. Shultz

CHAPTER ONE

Our Challenges

My days of public service, after two and a half years as a US Marine in the Pacific during World War II, span three administrations—those of Eisenhower, Nixon, and Reagan—and include four cabinet positions: secretary of labor, director of the Office of Management and Budget, secretary of the treasury, and secretary of state. Throughout my years in government, and continuing through my careers in business and academia, a number of vital issues have been persistently on my mind.

This book contains my thoughts about six of these central issues, including comments I have made about them in speeches and publications over the past half century.

The result is basically a how-to book. It offers thoughts on how to: do a better job of governance; get our economy back on track; take full advantage of current prospects for twin revolutions in the field of energy; take on the debilitating problems associated with addictive drugs; conduct an energetic, professional, and tough-minded diplomacy; and confront the security issues posed by nuclear weapons.

We now face these difficult issues at a particularly challenging time. We have moved *from* a period when we in the United States took the lead role in the construction of a global economic and security commons *to* a world that is awash in change. We must identify constructive ways to influence the changing world for the well-being of the United States as well as for the benefit of all.

An Economic and Security Commons

As World War II was drawing to a close, a group of gifted and creative people from the United States, Great Britain, and other Allied countries gathered to plan for the future. They reflected on the events of the first part of the twentieth century: two world wars, the first ended with a vindictive treaty and both with immense casualties (around 70 million people, civilian and military, in World War II alone), the Holocaust, and the Great Depression with the accompanying explosion of protectionism and competitive currency devaluations. Seeing this, and recognizing that the Soviet Union was an aggressive and dangerous adversary, this group realized the urgent need to construct a different kind of world.

It was in this environment that there emerged the concept of containment, the establishment of NATO, and the creation of the General Agreement on Tariffs and Trade (GATT) with its rounds of agreements lowering barriers to trade. In addition, the International Monetary Fund (IMF) was established to deal with currency issues and the International Bank for Reconstruction and Development (now the World Bank) was founded to deal with the development needs of devastated countries and, subsequently, the needs of countries with low per-capita incomes. This era also led to the formation of the United Nations to help preserve the peace and support the emergence of the European Community.

These developments resulted in what could be called a global economic and security commons in which the United States took the lead and its allies—and, eventually, its reconstructed adversaries—played strong roles. The creative contributions to these efforts by the Truman and Eisenhower administrations extended, with a few dips and valleys, through the end of the Cold War in the 1990s, at which time Russia began to take part in the global economy. China and Russia have now become members of the World Trade Organization. I was proud to play a part in this process as a cabinet member in the Nixon and Reagan administrations.

The establishment and strengthening of the global economic and security commons has been beneficial for the United States. These decades have also seen unprecedented improvement in the human condition on a global scale. Poverty has been reduced and many people enjoy better health and longer lives, due in some considerable part to breathtaking biological research and the development of pharmaceutical products and innovative medical procedures, many of them emanating from the United States.

But now we are once again living in an age of remarkable changes of enormous proportions that affect every part of the globe. This age calls for a renewed effort to understand these developments and to recreate a global economic and security commons that will benefit us as well as the rest of the world. The changes we face are real and the risks of a chaotic world are high. Serious progress must be made in addressing each of the issues discussed in the chapters that follow. The United States must once again demonstrate its capability and willingness to take the lead.

A World Awash in Change

Primary among these dramatic changes is demography, which has recently undergone stunning shifts. In almost every developed country, fertility is far below the replacement level, longevity is rising, and the labor force is shrinking in proportion to the total population. These developments inevitably affect outlook and capability. In many countries, such as Germany and Japan, populations are declining. Russia has a demographic catastrophe on its hands, with low fertility, longevity for men at around sixty years, and a declining population. South Korea, Japan, and other relatively developed countries in Asia exhibit demographics similar to those of many European nations. Of these countries, Japan now has the most rapidly aging population.

In some ways, China has the most interesting demography. With its one-child policy, fertility began falling rapidly about thirty years ago, so for a quarter century China had a growing labor pool and a decreasing number of people that labor pool had to support—call it a demographic dividend. But soon that picture will shift abruptly, almost like flipping a switch. The labor pool will start to decline and the number of older people whom the labor force must support will start rising rapidly.

The situation is quite different in other parts of the world such as the Middle East and North Africa, where fertility has declined moderately but is still relatively high, so the growing populations are primarily young. In all too many cases, however, these societies are organized in such a way that many of their youth have little or nothing to do.

Added to this demographic picture is the deep and still underappreciated impact of the information and communications revolution that allows people in nearly every corner of the world to be informed, to communicate, and to organize. This development profoundly changes the manner of governance because it sharply reduces the distance between those in power and those being governed. This shift may cause countries with representative-style governments to struggle, but these leaders are accustomed to listening to their citizens. Autocratic governments that have been in place for decades, however, will become increasingly vulnerable.

In much of the Middle East and North Africa, there is now a toxic mix: many young people are without work and, because of the information and communications revolution, they are becoming ever more aware of their plight in comparison to the lives of their counterparts in other areas of the world. Remember that the movement we might call the Arab Awakening was sparked by one entrepreneur in Tunisia who simply wanted to create a business selling fruits and vegetables. As the regime's corrupt police officers to whom he refused to pay bribes squashed him, he asked, "How do you expect me to make a living?"[1] A fundamental lesson from this incident is that the future stability of these societies will depend more on economies that can put people to work than on the barrel of a gun, because work links people to reality and can provide them with positive incentives, confidence in the future, and the dignity that comes from knowing they have earned what they have been paid.

Our world today is also plagued by the unpredictable violence that we call terrorism, much of it emanating from some strain of radical Islam. The United States and many other countries are paying a heavy price in their efforts to counter this phenomenon. They must identify less costly and more effective methods of addressing this serious threat.

Changes in the nature of the state system present another challenge. Ideally, we think of the world as being composed of states, each able to exert sovereign power within its domain and interact constructively on the world stage. These days, however, there are large areas of the world where lines have been drawn on a map and a name placed inside the lines, but where no real sovereign authority exists.

1. Bob Simon, "How a slap sparked Tunisia's revolution," CBS News, February 20, 2011.

Sovereign capacity is severely limited in many other countries. Then there are the individual nation-states of Europe, which are also part of a community with headquarters in Brussels. Most are also members of the eurozone with headquarters in Frankfurt. This dispersion of authority diminishes each state's sovereign power and sense of responsibility, and is one of the reasons that nations of the eurozone, in particular, are struggling with severe financial crises.

Added to these sources of change are the economic and financial problems so evident in Europe and the United States. The impact of these problems goes beyond their economic effects and leads to doubts about competence and the applicability of the Western model of free markets and open politics. The United States must get its house in order. Then it can reestablish leadership as it helps to reinvigorate the global economic and security commons that has effectively served the United States and countries throughout the world over the past half century.

How can this be done? Leadership is the first requirement. The United States has historically played this role. Its leadership involves working constructively with other nations, and such work can best be done when the United States is strong, prosperous, and confident. On such a foundation, we will be able to confront problems and conduct an effective, strategically based diplomacy. Today, important opportunities are ripe for development in the field of energy. The United States can also do much better in handling the devastating issues involving addictive drugs: fighting their use more proficiently, relieving burdens on our criminal justice system, and improving the lives of citizens in our hemisphere.

Creative diplomacy will be an essential ingredient in making our way to a safer world. And priority must be given to addressing the global threat posed by nuclear weapons. Progress has been made but much needs to be done.

The chapters and the appended speeches and publications that follow highlight six pressing issues with a how-to objective in mind. If we successfully address each of these issues, we will be able to ensure that future generations of Americans—and future generations around the globe—will have a more secure and prosperous world in which to live.

The final reflections in this book contain observations on opportunities and problems ahead, while the epilogue emphasizes the importance of freedom.

The points that I make in the following chapters are based largely on my personal experiences, many of which are put in story form. For example, one of the most compelling and instructive experiences in negotiations[2] came in the form of a domestic issue, a battle to bring greater fairness to education. Its critical lesson, which is widely applicable in any setting, is that successful diplomacy requires strong, credible, legitimate representation on all sides to work effectively on sensitive problems. With strong representation, arguments are brought forward in a clear and straightforward way so that solutions will be accepted with the belief that the interests involved were fairly defended and will thereby receive the support needed for implementation.

President Nixon gave me the assignment, beginning in March 1970, of chairing the process of desegregating the schools in seven Southern states. There we were, a decade and a half after the *Brown v. Board of Education* decision, with these schools still segregated by race. With strong support from Presidential Counselor Pat Moynihan, Special Counsel Len Garment, and Ed Morgan, a savvy former advance man for the president, I formed biracial committees in each of the seven states. We determined, with the president's agreement, that politics should have nothing to do with the selection of the people for these committees. We wanted equal numbers of blacks and whites who were truly representative of their constituencies. And so, with great care, we chose strong, respected leaders from each of these states.

We brought each of these committees to the White House for intense discussions designed to engage them constructively in this sensitive and potentially explosive issue. At the end of a day of substantive exchanges of ideas on implementation, I brought them to the Oval Office for a meeting with President Nixon. The president spoke to them with great conviction and considerable emotion. Looking around the room, he said, in essence:

---

2. I included this story, reprinted more fully in the appendix, in a discussion about Palestinian representation with Israeli Prime Minister Yitzhak Shamir.

Here we are in the Oval Office of the White House. Think of the decisions that have been made here that have affected the health and the security of our country. But remember, too, that we live in a great democracy where authority and responsibility are shared. Just as decisions are made here in this office, decisions are made throughout the states and communities of our country. You are leaders in those communities, and this is a time when we all have to step up to our responsibilities. I will make my decisions, and I count on you to make yours. We must make this work. By the time the president finished and committee members were ready to leave, they were charged up to put their energy into making sure the school openings and subsequent operations of the schools proceeded as smoothly and constructively as possible.

The school openings in September 1970 were peaceful, much to the amazement of almost everyone. The community leaders had done a fine job by fulfilling their responsibilities. Strong people were the key to success in negotiating this difficult and sensitive situation.

Each of the following chapters highlights an issue of critical importance that has been on my mind for many years. I hope that my observations on how to approach these concerns—based on the insights I have gained though personal experiences—may be useful.

CHAPTER TWO

Better Governance

If you are able to confront problems effectively and take advantage of opportunities fairly, you will be able to govern. So the issue of governance is an appropriate starting point for this exploration of how to achieve a better future.

Let's begin by recognizing that good governance requires top-notch, highly accomplished people—the A team. These talented individuals then need to become part of a process and organizational structure in which they can work together constructively.

The second important element of governance is the ability to identify and understand the issues inherent in leadership. These issues are often daunting. These days, especially, vast technological changes providing wide availability of information and rapid communication have to be taken into account. Leaders must realize the difficulties posed as well as the opportunities available to convey important points to their constituents.

Of course, the most important ingredient for success in governance is leadership itself—the ability to create an environment conducive to learning and to involve people as active participants in the process. An atmosphere of trust is essential, as are standards of performance and accountability.

When these three interrelated elements of governance, each of key importance, interact, high performance will be the result.

How to Attract Top Talent to Government Service

Remember the historic touchstones: duty, privilege, and the opportunity to serve the common good, keeping in mind the constitutional process for governance that has stood us in good stead for more than two centuries. These days, however, this process is widely ignored, making it difficult to recruit the A team for many key positions where policy is developed and high-quality execution is needed.

The constitutional process starts with the election of a president, vice president, and members of Congress. Then the government functions through a variety of cabinet departments and agencies in the executive branch, authorized and funded through budgets appropriated by the Congress. So, in the executive branch, the president presumably governs through a fairly large number of his appointees who serve only after the Senate has given its advice and consent and who can be called to testify.

This line of accountable executive authority is being broken and it must be restored if we are to have effective governance. Today, someone who accepts a presidential appointment must submit to an extensive vetting process, including endless questionnaires. This laborious process gives prospective appointees the impression that the government assumes there must be something wrong with them if they are willing to serve. It is as though the government is saying that its job is to discover and expose any skeletons, large or small, relevant or not, to public view. A candidate who passes this screening goes before a Senate committee and is subjected to additional questions. Sometimes the Senate acts promptly and votes for confirmation. In all too many cases, however, some senator puts a hold on the vote for reasons that have nothing to do with the candidate, who becomes a hostage to be released when the senator gets what he or she wants. As I put it in the *Wall Street Journal* on April 11, 2011:

> The situation has been worsened by the difficulty of getting presidential nominees to cabinet and subcabinet positions approved and in place. The White House vetting process has become exhaustive, with potential appointees required to fill out extensive questionnaires on such things as foreign travel and personal acquaintances, let alone financial matters. Mistakes are potentially subject to criminal penalties. The result is a drawn-out and often disagreeable process from the time a person agrees to a job to the actual nomination, and then to confirmation, should it be granted by the Senate.

Once finally confirmed, the candidate often reports mainly to a White House aide the president has chosen to oversee the policy process. This means that policy is not as good as it could be because cabinet officers and their staffs, who bring real talent to the table and have access to the impressive capabilities and storehouses of knowledge of the career people in their departments, do not communicate directly with the president.

Under a much better process, the president would designate key areas of policy and execution, form an appropriate group of cabinet officers and their associates, and look to them, in effect, as his staff for policy development. This process would produce better policies and more effective follow-through by the departments that ultimately execute the policies. It would also offer an enhanced ability to see that all relevant points of view and areas of experience are represented in the policy process. As I continued in my *Journal* op-ed:

> To return to a more effective and constitutionally sound use of cabinet members and their departments in helping the president formulate policy, cabinet secretaries could be grouped into important functional categories—national security and foreign policy, economics, natural resources, human resources, the rule of law, education, health, and others. All of these subjects involve more than one department. Sometimes the natural convener is obvious; in other instances the leading role might simply rotate.
>
> With the help of staff coordinators in the White House, cabinet members might convene by themselves and then with the president. This would involve the departments and, at the same time, ensure that a presidential, rather than a departmental, point of view would prevail. Policy execution would be improved, as would support for legislative initiatives.

Using the method I recommend also leads to the construction of a more accountable and constitutional governmental process because the people closest to the president will have been confirmed by the Senate and can be called to testify. Another benefit is a more complete interaction of relevant views since a policy group can be formed, including all the departments with an interest in, and experience with, the issues involved.

The present process, with its debilitating appointment ordeal and too many unaccountable parts, has evolved over time and could be set straight by an understanding between the president and the leaders of the Senate. Here's an example of how an outstanding public servant was appointed in the early 1940s.

I had the privilege of being associated with Paul Nitze when I was secretary of state. He was a great man and a superb public servant. In his autobiography, Paul described the way his federal government service began. He was an accomplished, financially successful person who was a partner at Dillon Read, an investment bank. His senior partner, James Forrestal, had been persuaded by President Franklin Roosevelt to come into the White House because Roosevelt, who could see the war clouds gathering, had no confident contact with the business or financial communities. Paul tells of doing some work for Dillon Read in Louisiana when he received a cable from Forrestal saying, "I want you here Monday morning." Paul dropped what he was doing and showed up. Forrestal told Paul that he had an office with two desks, an assistant who seemed to know everything and could help them both, and a rented house in Georgetown with an extra room for Paul. Paul would have to stay on the Dillon Read payroll, Forrestal said, because there was no money to pay him, but he should get to work right way. So, relates Paul, "In this wholly illegal fashion my career in Washington began."[1]

There could be no more distinguished public servant than Paul Nitze. I am not recommending that we adopt the total lack of process used for Paul, but a careful check of FBI and IRS records would flush out any real problems, particularly when coupled with the admonition that if a candidate has major skeletons in the closet, they will almost certainly surface. With today's vetting process, it is doubtful that Paul Nitze could be attracted to take a post in the federal government. But we need the Paul Nitzes of this world to work on resolving the tough problems we currently face.

Somehow we must balance a sensible vetting process with the assumption—common during the days when Paul Nitze was recruited—that people who are willing to serve are honorable and want to serve honorably. That is how we can get the A team on the job.

---

1. Paul Nitze, with Ann M. Smith and Steven L. Rearden, *From Hiroshima to Glasnost: At the Center of Decision—A Memoir* (New York: Grove Weidenfeld, 1989), 7.

The Setting

The values embedded in our Constitution and Bill of Rights cover a country of immense and continually evolving diversity. In this vast land, conditions vary greatly from one part of the United States to another, from city to city, and from suburban to rural settings and productive farmland areas. As a nation of immigrants with continuing large inflows of people from other nations, the population of the United States represents a great variety of races, religions, ethnicities, languages, and countries of origin. Representatives of every nationality can be found among the US population. As President Ronald Reagan awarded me the Medal of Freedom in 1989, he expressed his belief in the importance of this diversity:

> I think it's fitting to leave one final thought, an observation about a country which I love. It was stated best in a letter I received not long ago. A man wrote me and said: "You can go to live in France, but you cannot become a Frenchman. You can go to live in Germany or Turkey or Japan, but you cannot become a German, a Turk, or a Japanese. But anyone, from any corner of the Earth, can come to live in America and become an American."
>
> Yes, the torch of Lady Liberty symbolizes our freedom and represents our heritage, the compact with our parents, our grandparents, and our ancestors. It is that lady who gives us our great and special place in the world. For it's the great life force of each generation of new Americans that guarantees that America's triumph shall continue unsurpassed into the next century and beyond. Other countries may seek to compete with us; but in one vital area, as a beacon of freedom and opportunity that draws the people of the world, no country on earth comes close.
>
> This, I believe, is one of the most important sources of America's greatness. We lead the world because, unique among nations, we draw our people—our strength—from every country and every corner of the world. And by doing so we continuously renew and enrich our nation. While other countries cling to the stale past, here in America we breathe life into dreams. We create the future, and the world follows us into tomorrow. Thanks to each wave of new arrivals to this land of opportunity, we're a

nation forever young, forever bursting with energy and new ideas, and always on the cutting edge, always leading the world to the next frontier. This quality is vital to our future as a nation. If we ever closed the door to new Americans, our leadership in the world would soon be lost.[2]

The United States governs over diversity, not an easy task. But the ideas we glean from our own history can guide us in gaining strength from diversity. The basic principle, on display in the United States over the years, is the right balance between decentralization and cultivation of common themes. In the governmental sphere, this means federalism and development of effective state and city governments. In San Francisco, for example, Chinatown embraces an ancient culture but, with fluent English spoken by almost all second-generation Chinese Americans, US culture is pervasive as well. San Francisco now has a Chinese American mayor who governs over a city of great diversity with all its attendant problems and opportunities.

In the economic sphere, the best "decentralizer" is the marketplace. You work, you deserve what you earn, and you spend your money on goods and services of your choice. Of course, markets must be kept competitive and real educational opportunity must be available to every child. As I put it to students at the International House, University of California–Berkeley:

> In places where economic activity is organized along market lines, deci-sions about economic welfare get made on economic terms and methods of organization are such that they promote growth. You have a bigger pie and the division of the pie is decided by factors that are, if it's working right, essentially nonpolitical in nature. In countries where that is so, there is a better chance of working successfully with ethnic diversity. The more the state controls the economy, the greater regional and ethnic resentment of the political center, particularly the resentment of those parts that don't think they're getting a fair turn.

2. President Ronald Reagan, remarks at the presentation ceremony for the Presidential Medal of Freedom, Washington, DC, January 19, 1989.

Thomas Jefferson, arguing for the separation of church and state and for tolerance of religious differences, said that we should adhere to the maxim, "Divided we stand."[3] So decentralization can help, as with our federal structure and city governments. After all, these levels of government are closest to the people and therefore in most intimate touch with their problems and apprehensions. All this, of course, requires an atmosphere of reasonable tolerance for differences, a willingness to find areas of consensus, and a recognition of the importance of the common good.

In my remarks at International House, I added:

> Somewhere in this mixture of how to deal with diversity is the element of tolerance. It doesn't mean being tolerant of everything. It does not mean not standing for something and having one's own ideas. But it does mean learning to have some respect for a different point of view, a different culture, a different outlook, a different set of values, and seeing that they can be legitimate and learning to live with it.

Every department of government has a variety of constituencies, so it is necessary to know how to manage diversity. When I became secretary of labor in 1969, I had many subcabinet appointments to make so I needed to identify a group of people with a variety of points of view and areas of experience. I sought the best management person I could find. I wanted a genuine labor leader, a top lawyer who knew the law of the labor market, a person who really understood manpower training, someone who had worked in the field of racial discrimination, and a top statistician. I assembled a diverse group and managed to bring them together to work as a team and to gain strength from their diversity of experience.

Of course, governments at any level need to operate smoothly if their respective functions are to be carried out effectively. Unfortunately, all levels of government in the United States are now in serious trouble. The debt of the federal government, when all unfunded promises are counted,

3. Thomas Jefferson, letter to Jacob De La Motte, September 1820, Manuscript Division, Papers of Thomas Jefferson (Princeton, NJ: Princeton University).

is staggering. As summarized in a June 2012 report by the National Center for Policy Analysis:

> Other obligations of the federal government including accrued Social Security and Medicare benefits, which are conceptually similar to accrued federal pension and benefit liabilities, should also be considered federal liabilities. Including a conservative estimate of these commitments— accrued benefits payable to current participants who have reached the age of eligibility—raises total federal liabilities in 2011 to $30.3 trillion or almost 200 percent of GDP.[4]

Many state and city governments are facing acute fiscal problems. I recently served on the State Budget Crisis Task Force, which carefully examined six states in great detail. Chaired by former New York Lieutenant Governor Richard Ravitch and former chairman of the board of the Federal Reserve System Paul Volcker, the group concluded:

> There can be no doubt that the magnitude of the problem is great and extends beyond the impact of the financial crisis and the lingering recession. The ability of the states to meet their obligations to public employees, to creditors, and most critically to the education and well-being of their citizens is threatened.... The storm warnings are very serious.... The costs, whether in service reductions or higher revenues, will be large. Deferring action can only make the ultimate costs even greater.... The existing trajectory of state spending, taxation, and administrative practices cannot be sustained. The basic problem is not cyclical. It is structural. The time to act is now.[5]

Effective and courageous leadership in many states and cities shows that the problems are solvable, but only with a strong tough-love effort. Certainly, our federal government has dealt successfully with many hard problems before. A key ingredient in regaining fiscal sanity at all levels

4. National Center for Policy Analysis, "Policy Report No. 338," June 2012, 13.
5. Report of the State Budget Crisis Task Force, July 2012.

of government is a return to strong noninflationary economic growth, an issue addressed in the following chapter.

These days, governance takes place in an atmosphere that has been sharply changed by the information and communications revolution. Before the advent of the Internet and social networking, those in authority had a major advantage in access to information and in the ability to organize. Now, anyone who tries can get the information he needs, and people can easily communicate and organize to support a point of view.

A study by New York University Professor Paul Light[6] sheds light on this phenomenon and reveals some startling statistics. The information and communications age has shortened the distance between leaders and those they govern. Top executives understand the front lines of their organizations' work. Businesses have recognized this development and many layers of middle management have been eliminated as a result.

The US government has gone the other way. Professor Light's study reveals that, from 1960 to the present, the number of layers in the typical cabinet department increased from seven to eighteen. Instead of layers being cut, they have been added, and the average number of executives at each level has increased from 451 to 2,600. This development has led to startling problems because officials with top responsibility in government are far removed from people on the front lines of work, so they have a hard time getting a real feel for what is going on. That's no way to run a railroad.

The information revolution has led to a change in the atmosphere of governance. It is now more important than ever for leaders to put information into realistic perspective and impart the stability that goes with clarity of strategy. As I said in a 1986 address in Paris:

> The information age poses profound *political* challenges to nations every-
> where. . . . The information revolution is already shifting the economic

6. Paul C. Light, "Perp Walks and the Broken Bureaucracy," *Wall Street Journal,* April 27, 2012.

balance between East and West. The leaders of closed societies fear this shifting economic base, and for good reason. First, they are afraid that information technologies will undermine the state's control over its people—what they read, watch, hear, and aspire to. In most of these countries, familiar means of communication like the mimeograph machine and photocopier are already kept under lock and key. The specter of direct broadcast satellites alarms their leaders even more.[7]

The information and communications revolution places a special strain on regimes governed by long-time autocrats, as we see in the Arab Awakening and in the protests in Russia, China, and elsewhere. But this revolution can give rise to fundamentally constructive developments: a better-informed electorate, the increased possibility of greater decentralization of decision making, and less temptation for corruption. The process of governance has already been profoundly affected by the rapid increase in access to information and the ability to communicate instantaneously across the globe.

Some Ideas about Leadership

I have had the privilege of working with some outstanding leaders in government, business, and academia. I have also had the privilege and opportunity of leadership myself. Styles of leadership undoubtedly vary, reflecting individual talents and experience, but I have learned that there are some fundamental principles that all leaders should observe.

Leaders must set standards for performance and clear goals and then hold people accountable for their actions. In my case, I absorbed the importance of accountability from participating in sports. Whether you are part of a team or play an individual sport such as golf or tennis, your actions have consequences. A sport holds you accountable in a relentless way.

7. George P. Shultz, "The Shape, Scope, and Consequences of the Age of Information," address at Stanford University Alumni Association's International Conference, Paris, March 21, 1986.

Here you are on the green. There is the hole. There is the ball. You stand alone and you hold the putter. You hit the ball and when the ball stops rolling, the result is unambiguous. Americans love golf and other sports because of this relentless accountability. There is no room for the I-can-get-away-with-it approach.

I came to an early appreciation of how important it is for leaders to foster an environment in which workers are continually learning. I realized how much people enjoy learning and I felt that if I could create around me an atmosphere in which everyone, myself included, were learning something, I would have a hot group.

This helpful insight first occurred to me as the result of an accident. I had come to football practice in my senior year at Princeton all set to make the team and play well. But in a pre-season scrimmage, I was clipped— blocked across the back of one of my knees—and I was out for the season. Since I was well versed in the offense and defense systems at Princeton, I was asked to coach the freshman backfield. We had a talented group, but I gradually came to understand that the lessons I was teaching were not always sinking in, so my style of teaching had to reflect that reality. What mattered was what the players learned and could apply. When you are learning, you are almost always a participant, so you have the empowerment and sense of responsibility that come from genuine involvement.

I also observed that if a leader demonstrates trust in people, they will almost always reciprocate that trust. An organization will perform far better if it is based on trust. This is one reason that I fought so hard against the managerial use of lie-detector tests when I was secretary of state. I was appalled by the arguments of those who advocated the practice. They agreed with me that lie-detector test results were often wrong, but they promoted the use of these tests because fear, not trust, was their motivational tool for management. They assumed that nobody could be trusted. I argued that we needed to restore the culture of trust in governance.

Advocates of using lie-detector tests convinced President Reagan to sign an executive order for their program while I was on a lengthy trip abroad. When I returned, I was asked if I would take the test. I said, "Yes, I'll take the test once, but then I'm out of here. If you ask me to take the test, you are saying that you don't trust me. If you don't trust me, I don't belong here." All hell broke loose but, in the end, the president rescinded the executive order. My relationship with the CIA never fully recovered. I believe that Americans are basically patriotic, decent, want to do the right thing, and can be trusted. Of course, anyone who proves to be untrustworthy should be relieved of his or her post. As President Reagan put it, "Trust but verify."

One of my favorite stories about trust comes from a skit performed at a Gridiron Club roast of President Eisenhower shortly after he took office. His views on many topics were obscure and members of the press had been frustrated in their efforts to find out where the president stood on various issues. What they did know was that Ike loved to play golf, so in the skit, reporters were reduced to interviewing his caddy. "Where does the president stand on antitrust issues?" they asked. The caddy replied, "There ain't an ounce of 'anti' in that man. He trusts everybody." I have always thought that trust was part of Eisenhower's magic.

Some Rules for Leadership

Many of these ideas about leadership are reflected in the following six rules that I discussed at an event honoring the late Elliot Richardson, a great public servant who held cabinet positions in the Nixon and Ford administrations.

1. The first rule is to be a participant. Excellence in government depends on the willingness of talented people to get involved. Back when I was working with Ronald Reagan, long before he was elected president, he gave me a tie carrying the words "Democracy is not a spectator sport."

2. Public service is more of a privilege and an opportunity than a duty. But public service is effective only if, in the tensions of these high-pressure jobs, you are true to yourself. In other words, you cannot want the job too much. You need to hold fast to your principles and be willing to resign rather than remain as an integral part of a team supporting a crucial policy with which you disagree.

3. In my book, the best congressional strategist ever to hit Washington was Bryce Harlow. He had a complex web of intense relationships with people who were sometimes on his side and sometimes not. He was constantly forming and re-forming coalitions to work on particular subjects. He believed that people had to know that you were a tough adversary and would fight hard and skillfully for your point of view. Harlow had a number of simple rules: Return calls promptly, deal straight with members of Congress, and never agree to do anything unless you know that you can get it done. One of Harlow's most important maxims was, "If you give your word, then you'd better deliver." That way you develop trust. As he said, "Trust is the coin of the realm."

4. As secretary of labor, I persuaded Joe Loftus, a premier labor reporter who had worked at the *New York Times* for twenty-five years, to join me as spokesman for the department. Joe had seen press spokesmen come and go and he told me, "The spokesman has credibility only when reporters know that he is on the inside." As spokesman, he would have to know what was going on, be welcome to attend any meeting, and be well informed. That way, he would never be blindsided. He would conduct himself in accordance with "Loftus's Laws" and he expected me to live by them, too:

   • Don't lie. Don't mislead. Credibility is precious; it can never be misused. Once destroyed, it cannot be recaptured.

   • Respond to questions directly. Don't be afraid to say, "No comment."

   • Never call a news conference unless you have some news. "Why not, even if just for the sake of dialogue and accessibility?" I asked. "Because," Joe said, "reporters make their living by getting their byline in the paper, preferably on the front page. When you call a news conference, they expect a story. Disappointed, they try to create one by goading you into saying something stupid."

   • Help reporters get their facts straight. The press is an important way to communicate with the public. Don't act as if reporters are your enemy, however tempting that may be at times.

   • Get on top of breaking stories. Be part of the original story because nobody reads the reaction story. So be quick and don't hold back.

In practice, this means a constant tug-of-war between the spokesman and officials who are often reluctant or slow to provide needed
information.

5. Competence is the name of the game in leadership. I had a revealing—
even initially embarrassing—experience on this score shortly after
Richard Nixon nominated me to be secretary of labor.

I quickly began the process of filling the many political appointee jobs.
For under-secretary, I wanted the most experienced and best management person in the labor field that I could find. Everyone said, "That's Jim
Hodgson, a vice president at Lockheed, but you'll never get him." I talked
to Jim and he accepted. I also wanted somebody who really understood
manpower training programs. My friend and colleague Arnold Weber
had the best experience and he agreed to come on board. We wanted
someone who understood unions through experience in representing
workers, negotiating contracts for them, and selling the contracts; we
found Bill Usery. We wanted the best statistician to head the Bureau
of Labor Statistics and we found Jeff Moore of the National Bureau of
Economic Research.

I was told to clear all appointments with a designated person in the
White House and with the senior Republican senator on the Senate Labor
Committee. I went to work and got people lined up reasonably quickly.
The president-elect was pleased and suggested that we meet with him
in his headquarters at the Pierre Hotel in New York City. I would then
introduce my team to the press.

The meeting went well and I went to the press room and introduced
Jim Hodgson. He was asked a series of searching questions and everyone
concluded that he was a real pro who knew what he was doing. At the
end of the session, a reporter in the back of the room raised his hand
and said, "Mr. Hodgson, are you a Democrat or a Republican?" That was
a question I had never even thought to ask. Jim said, "I'm a Democrat."
Next up was Arnold Weber. His performance was dazzling. At the end,
the same reporter asked the same question and Arnie answered, "I'm a
Democrat." And so it went. The last man up was Jeff Moore, head of the
National Bureau of Economic Research and a statistician's statistician.

When he got the same question, he paused and thought about it. Finally, he said, "I guess you'd say I'm an Independent." I could have killed him!

When I got back to my hotel room, the phone rang off the hook with Republican senators asking me if I understood that there had been an election—and the Republicans had won. I said that I had cleared all the names with the White House and with the ranking Republican, Jacob Javits of New York. Senator Javits was not their favorite Republican.

All the people I recruited performed at an extraordinarily high level. Some of the senators who had been critical of my choices later told me they appreciated my nominees. I was succeeded as secretary of labor by Jim Hodgson, who later became ambassador to Japan. Bill Usery became secretary of labor a few years later. Arnold Weber went on to start the management side of the new Office of Management and Budget and then to a successful presidency of Northwestern University.

The lesson is that competence matters. My years as secretary of labor would have been much more difficult if I had ruled out all of these competent people because they were registered Democrats.

6. Finally, give the people on your team responsibility and reward them for exercising it.

The future belongs to coming generations. The efforts of today's youth will give us a better country and better governance. Take, just as one impressive example, Teach For America, a national corps of outstanding recent college graduates who make two-year commitments to teach in urban and rural schools. Corps members go above and beyond traditional expectations to improve the lives of children in low-income communities. More than 10,000 corps members will have taught 750,000 students in the 2012–13 school year. This demonstration of readiness to serve by so many gifted young people is a great boon for the future.

We must come to grips with the serious problems of governance now at hand, attract the best people, and limit the excessive layers of management that exist in all too many government organizations. Then we will be able to resolve important problems in a much more effective way. With people in charge who have creative instincts and the confidence to grapple with pressing domestic and global problems, constructive solutions will be found and the United States will once again be the shining city on the hill.

The appendix to this chapter includes two of my earlier writings on governance. The first expresses my conviction that the federal government is not organized in a way that can produce the best results, but with strong leadership in the executive and legislative branches, urgently needed change can be attained. The second is an address I gave in Paris in 1986, "The Shape, Scope, and Consequences of the Age of Information," on the growing revolution in information technology and its transformative impact on governance. The influence of this ongoing revolution is apparent not only in the Arab Awakening but also in pressures on governance everywhere, most notably in countries with authoritarian regimes.

I also had the privilege in 1986 of addressing the annual meeting of that famous writers' group, PEN, a somewhat unusual setting for a secretary of state. The theme of my remarks, the centrality of freedom as a principle for successful governance, resonated with writers, who are particularly concerned about freedom of expression. Following is an excerpt from my speech:

> Let us remember today those writers who exist in states where the typewriter and mimeograph are regarded as dangerous weapons, where writers have no independent right to publish, and where a free press has no free access. Let us work to support the solitary writer in a suppressive society. Let us take heart that many governments and their censors have found that it is not so easy to stop all the writers, every last solitary individual with a pen and paper or typewriter and friends who will smuggle out what he or she writes.
>
> The writer will be the last to be stifled. The writer will always be with us, testing the limits and expanding the horizons of his society.
>
> I am optimistic about the future. As the world gets smaller, the importance of freedom only increases. The yearning for freedom is the most

powerful political force all across the planet. You are among its champions. You can be proud of what you have done for that cause.

And don't be so surprised by the fact that Ronald Reagan and I are on your side.[8]

The issue of freedom of speech is central today as we witness protests against arbitrary authority in many parts of the world and efforts to suppress those protests, sometimes by use of military force. We must never give up supporting those who speak up. Let freedom ring.

---

8. George P. Shultz, "The Writer and Freedom," address at the Poets, Playwrights, Essayists, and Novelists (PEN) International Conference, New York City, January 12, 1986.

CHAPTER THREE

Return to a Vibrant Economy

As a teenager in the 1930s, I was acutely aware of the tough economic conditions in the United States and the government's efforts to improve them. The New Deal, I could see, represented a massive intervention in the economy but it did not seem to help. I also recall that some of this intervention was declared unconstitutional by the Supreme Court and that President Roosevelt's subsequent court-packing plan, through which he sought to fill newly created seats with justices who shared his views, was blocked by Congress. I recognized that the strongly negative reaction to Roosevelt's move was an affirmation of the importance citizens attach to the system of distributed power—the checks and balances produced by three independent branches of government.

While I was a Marine in the South Pacific in World War II, I was conscious of the high degree to which the US economy was mobilized for the war. When I returned from active duty to study economics, a key question was how the government could disentangle itself from the war effort and reconstitute a normally functioning economy. We all hoped that lessons learned from the Great Depression—and the protectionism and competitive currency devaluations that aggravated and accompanied it—could lead us to institute more sensible policies. We wanted prosperity without inflation, an open-trade regime, and a workable exchange rate system. Despite periodic recessions, bouts of inflation, and threats of protectionism since the end of World War II, those objectives have been achieved. But wide shifts in the policy road over the years have produced obvious consequences, both positive and negative.

As I think about the tensions underlying the current economic debates, six important ideas come to mind. Paying attention to these concepts will contribute to good economic policy.

The **first** involves the time horizon that governs actions. When orientation is short, intervention can be precipitous and can result in many unintended—and mostly negative—consequences. The adoption of longer time horizons is often difficult, however, particularly for political reasons.

Second, a sense of strategy is critical because economics is essentially a strategy science. Inputs usually produce outputs, frequently with a lag. I have learned that, all too often, an economist's lag can become a politician's nightmare. In my estimation, however, our economic strategy should be guided mainly by long-term consequences, not short-term fixes.

Before moving on to my remaining points, I offer some stories drawn from my own experiences that highlight the importance of paying attention to time horizons and maintaining a sense of strategy.

As director of the Office of Management and Budget in the early 1970s, I worried about the growing atmosphere favoring wage and price controls. We had the budget under control and the Federal Reserve Board had a sensible monetary policy in place. Unemployment was too high and prices were rising too fast, but the rates of change in both were coming down. Long-run thinking suggested that we should stick with these policies. I set out to convince people that the proper course was "steady as you go," an approach I advocated in a speech in April 1971:

> The basic strategy of economic policy and its current tactical implementation are generally on course and economic policy can benefit from application of the old nautical phrase, "Steady as you go" . . . .
>
> A portion of the battle against inflation is now over; time and the guts to take the time, not additional medicine, are required for the sickness to disappear. We should now follow a noninflationary path back to full employment. . . .
>
> Those of you familiar with sailing know what a telltale is—a strip of cloth tied to a mast to show which way the wind is blowing.
>
> A captain has the choice of steering his ship by the telltale—following the prevailing winds—or . . . by the compass.
>
> In a democracy, you must keep your eye on the telltale, but you must set your course by the compass. That is exactly what the president of

the United States is doing. The voice from the bridge says, "Steady as you go."[1]

Unfortunately for the economy, the voice from the bridge changed its tune and hit a different note. I lost the battle. When President Nixon imposed wage and price controls, the move proved to be wildly popular at first. But, in the end, it produced a massive infusion of government regulation with the dire consequences that economists had predicted, including the very inflation the controls were intended to target. The president had violated the injunction to "think long" and the country paid the price in the form of a poor economy in the 1970s. Not until Ronald Reagan took office in 1981 did the United States get back on a sustainable economic track.

President Nixon's decision to impose wage and price controls was triggered by the reality that he was forced to close the gold window, ending the US guarantee that it would buy gold at thirty-five dollars per ounce. There were more dollars out there than gold in Fort Knox, so it was clear that a run on the federal depository was coming. Closing the gold window was bound to lead to an overdue change in the value of the dollar compared with the currencies of other major countries, a devaluation that would make imports more expensive. As a result, it was argued, we would have significant inflationary pressure. I thought these pressures were being overestimated, but the argument of others prevailed.

(When I became secretary of the treasury, I found that the wage and price control system, then in effect for over a year, was in my direct line of responsibility. In collaboration with the two men in charge, Don Rumsfeld and Dick Cheney, I was in the process of dismantling the controls. Against my strong advice, President Nixon decided to re-impose them in full. I resigned, telling him that he needed a new secretary of the treasury. I was eventually succeeded by my deputy, William Simon.)

By the time I became secretary of the treasury in June 1972, the international exchange system was in disarray and there was no US plan to restore

1. George P. Shultz, "Prescription for Economic Policy: 'Steady as You Go,'" address before the Economic Club of Chicago, Chicago, April 22, 1971.

stability. I set out to create a plan that we could propose at the annual meeting held by the World Bank and the International Monetary Fund, always attended by the world's top finance ministers and bankers. I was convinced that the United States and the world would be better off if the exchange rate system were more flexible. But I knew that many throughout the world, particularly in Europe, preferred a system in which exchange rates were more fixed, with par values for various currencies set and not expected to change. So, out of a conversation I had with Milton Friedman, the idea emerged of a floating exchange rate system in the clothing of par values. All countries had reserves and, in the system we devised, major changes in reserves would automatically create changes in exchange rates.

I spent the summer of 1972 working through the idea of a floating exchange rate system with my government colleagues. My undersecretary, Paul Volcker, pulled the laboring oar with great skill and wrote a series of memoranda supporting our plan.

On the Sunday before the Bank-Fund meeting began, I took the unprecedented step of inviting the finance ministers of the major countries to meet with me individually, review the speech I would deliver at the meeting, and offer suggestions. This process was the start of long-lasting friendships with Valéry Giscard d'Estaing of France, Helmut Schmidt of Germany, Tony Barber of the United Kingdom, and, eventually, Takeo Fukuda of Japan. None of them requested substantive changes to the basic US plan contained in my speech, but each offered valuable suggestions that probably contributed to widespread receptiveness to it.

With that, the world heaved a sigh of relief, not because every country agreed with the US plan but because the United States was now back in the game with sensible ideas. Eventually, through a series of larger meetings involving some twenty countries and extensive private discussions among the finance ministers in our little group that had gradually formed, the world found its way to the present system of loosely managed floating exchange rates. Problems have cropped up along the way, of course, but the system has worked reasonably well over the years, remaining fundamentally consistent with the recognition by the post–World War II statesmen that competitive devaluations of currencies, like protectionism in trade agreements, are a bad idea.

Lessons from this experience stood me in good stead when I was secretary of state because the process had deepened my understanding of how international agreements might be forged. It had also given me the opportunity to develop genuine personal friendships with leaders of other major countries. The experience helped me see not only what could be done but also how to make something happen.

Almost a decade after my "Steady As You Go" speech, the Reagan administration pursued a steady approach to the economy, and the results show the wisdom of that course. I chaired President Reagan's Coordinating Committee on Economic Policy during his election campaign and through the first eighteen months of his presidency. Before his inauguration, my committee sent the president-elect a memo containing a series of recommendations. Here are the key points from that memo, as applicable today as they were in 1980:

Sharp change in present economic policy is an absolute necessity. The problems of inflation and slow growth, of falling standards of living and declining productivity, of high government spending but an inadequate flow of funds for defense, of an almost endless litany of economic ills, large and small, are severe. But they are not intractable. Having been produced by government policy, they can be redressed by a change in policy.

The essence of good policy is good strategy. Some strategic principles can guide your new administration as it charts its course.

- *Timing and preparation are critical aspects of strategy.* The fertile moment may come suddenly and evaporate as quickly. The administration that is well prepared is ready to act when the time is ripe.
- *The need for a long-term point of view is essential to allow for the time, the coherence, and the predictability so necessary for success.* This long-term view is as important for day-to-day problem-solving as for the making of large policy decisions. Most decisions in government are made in the process of responding to problems of the moment. The danger is that this daily fire-fighting can lead the policy maker farther and farther from his goals. A clear sense of guiding strategy makes it possible to move in the desired direction in the unending process of contending with issues of the day.

Many failures of government can be traced to an attempt to solve problems piecemeal.

- *Consistency in policy is critical to effectiveness.* Individuals and business enterprises plan on a long-range basis. They need to have an environment in which they can conduct their affairs with confidence.

  The fundamental areas of economic strategy concern the budget, taxation, regulation, and monetary policy. Prompt action in each of these areas is essential to establish both your resolve and your capacity to achieve your goals.

Our committee went on to comment on specific policy areas.

- Your most immediate concern upon assuming the duties of the president will be to convince the financial markets and the public at large that your anti-inflation policy is more than rhetoric. Get the budget under control.
- Your tax proposal should be presented early in the new administration in tandem with other key elements of your economic program. We consider that the key ingredients should be your proposals for the Kemp-Roth cut in personal income tax rates, simplification and liberalization of business depreciation, and a cut in effective taxes on capital gains.
- The current regulatory overburden must be removed from the economy. Equally important, the flood of new and extremely burdensome regulations that the agencies are now issuing or planning to issue must be drastically curtailed.
- Many of our economic problems today stem from the large and increasing proportion of economic decisions being made through the political process rather than the market process. An important step to demonstrate your determination to rely on markets would be the prompt end of wage and price guidelines and elimination of the Council on Wage and Price Stability.
- A steady and moderate rate of monetary growth is an essential requirement both to control inflation and to provide a healthy environment for economic growth. We have not had such a policy.

- With these fundamentals in place, the American people will respond. As the conviction grows that the policies will be sustained in a consistent manner over an extended period, the response will quicken and a healthy US economy will restore the credibility of our dollar on world markets, contribute significantly to smoother operation of the international economy, and enhance America's strength in the world.[2]

These ideas were consistent with positions President Reagan had taken during his election campaign. He followed through on implementing them and the long-run results were spectacular. President Reagan showed courage as he held a political umbrella over Paul Volcker at the Fed, despite warnings from political advisers of a recession and political losses in the midterm election. He took the view that inflation must be dealt with and he accepted a short-term hit in order to achieve long-term gains for the economy. By early 1983, inflation was under control, tax-cut incentives had kicked in, and the economy was taking off.

Along with a sensible time horizon and a sense of strategy, a **third** important element of economic policy is reasonable predictability. Those in authoritative government positions should operate according to known rules so that people in the private sector will know what to expect. A significant fact, established by extensive research and common observation, is that the behavior of consumers, investors, and business managers is influenced by permanent, rather than temporary, economic policies. Milton Friedman called these temporary policies "transitory" in his classic work, *A Theory of the Consumption Function.*[3]

Think of economic policy in terms of a sporting event. Players need to know the rules before they play and they must be confident that the rules will be fairly enforced and will not be changed in the middle of the game. In economic terms, it is essential to have reasonable, stable policies with clearly defined regulations that are not subject to arbitrary change by regulators.

2. "Economic Strategy for the Reagan Administration," report to President-elect Ronald Reagan from his Coordinating Committee on Economic Policy, November 16, 1980.

3. Milton Friedman, *A Theory of the Consumption Function* (Princeton, NJ: Princeton University, 1957).

A **fourth** important issue affecting economic policy is the inadequate understanding of the function of prices. Most people think prices represent the cost of things, and they almost always wish that prices were lower. But for economists, prices are signals that help to allocate resources correctly and keep the economy attuned to changing opportunities. Efforts at price control ignore the reality that prices are signals, even though most people don't perceive them that way. They may applaud the forced cut in the price of a manufactured product, only to be upset by a shortage when the price turns out to be lower than the cost of production. Suppression of the prices of goods by decree will inevitably lead to fewer of those goods. Care must be taken immediately to ensure that price controls do not negatively affect the future quality and quantity of US health providers.

Fifth, fairness is a key element of good economic policy. Every effort must be made to ensure that all citizens have access to equal opportunities.

Fairness starts with equal access for all students to high-quality K–12 education, but the United States is not keeping up in this essential area. Not only are we falling behind other countries but we are also tolerating vast differences in the quality of education available to our children. Abundant examples show that we have the know-how to make dramatic improvements in our educational system. We must insist that high-quality educational opportunities are available to every student in the United States.

Fairness seems to imply an economy in which income is distributed relatively equally. The key is education. When there are large numbers of people who lack common labor force skills, there is bound to be a commensurate inequality in the distribution of income. But trying to cure the problem with overly strong redistribution policies causes a detrimental impact on efficiency. Often, the fairness argument is considered in immediate terms, whereas the efficiency argument requires a long-term perspective. Of course, improved efficiency enlarges the pie to be distributed.

Fairness obviously extends far beyond economic arguments. Take, for example, discriminatory policies in hiring. Workers should be treated equally and judged on their merits regardless of race, sex, ethnic origin, or religion. I had first-hand experience with the issue of discrimination during my career in labor relations, so I was alert to the problem when I became secretary of labor.

I found that discriminatory policies against blacks were rampant in the skilled building trades. In Philadelphia, for example, despite the existence of perfectly capable black workers, there were none to be found in the hiring halls of the skilled construction unions. With strong support from my assistant secretary, Arthur Fletcher, I set out to change this situation by insisting that the unions set an objective for hiring more black workers and create a timetable for attaining that objective. This effort, which came to be called the Philadelphia Plan, immediately became highly controversial. It took the form of a bill on which hearings were held and a vote taken in the Senate. During the course of those hearings, I was verbally assaulted for trying to establish a quota system. I replied, "No, I am trying to obliterate one. There has been a quota system in effect for a long time; the number is zero." Eventually, the issue went to the Senate floor. This was my first big Washington battle and I believed that I was on the right side of the issue. I went to the Senate gallery to observe the vote. After it was taken, Senator Hugh Scott of Pennsylvania, the Republican leader in the Senate, gave me his tally sheet. It showed that we had won by a margin of ten: there were 39 ayes (16 Republicans and 23 Democrats) and 29 nays (13 Republicans and 16 Democrats). One of the champions on my side was Senator Ted Kennedy. Over the years, we became real friends and he continued to offer valuable support on many issues in the Senate when I was secretary of state.

I am glad to say that since my days in the Labor Department the United States has made great strides in advancing fairness. I hope the Philadelphia Plan contributed to this progress.

A **sixth** influence on economic policy is the urge to intervene in crises. An important aspect of each of the five preceding issues is political visibility. Political leaders frequently want to take charge and show that they are getting something done, knowing that voters often reward action. By contrast is Adam Smith's famous idea of "the invisible hand," which tends to cause the pursuit of self-interest by many individuals to produce the common good.

I have seen many economic situations misjudged at critical moments, often leading high federal officials to feel compelled to intervene. Here are three examples from my own experience.

When I was sworn in as secretary of labor on January 21, 1969, I inherited a longshoremen's strike on the East and Gulf coasts. President Johnson had declared the strike a national emergency when it started the previous October. The Supreme Court, hearing an appeal on the fast-track process provided for in the Taft-Hartley Act, agreed with the president. By the time I took office, the injunction procedures of Taft-Hartley had been exhausted and the strike resumed.

What to do? What to recommend to the president? From my professorial days, I was on record as believing that government intervened too much, thereby subverting the process of collective bargaining. I also believed that the possible crises resulting from strikes were vastly overrated. The clear willingness to intervene by officials in the Kennedy and Johnson administrations led labor and management representatives to exploit this tendency to overestimate the dangers of strikes, duck their own responsibilities, and save their best offers until they got to the White House. I told a group of lawyers, "If the president hangs out his shingle, he'll get all the business."

My analysis was that the longshoremen's strike fit this pattern. Yes, it was disruptive to many businesses and employees, but it was not a national emergency. In fact, the disruptions themselves would put strong pressure on the parties to settle their dispute. I told President Nixon, already preoccupied with the war in Vietnam and disinclined to become enmeshed in a labor dispute, "Your predecessor was wrong and the Supreme Court was wrong in judging that this strike will create a national emergency. We should make clear to labor and management that we will not intervene beyond providing mediation services." The president agreed. We rolled the dice and, after about six weeks, we had made our point. We stuck with that view as the months and years unfolded. As a result, responsibility and accountability returned to unions and management, where it belonged.

I had this experience in mind when I became involved in the battle over whether to bail out the large and failing Penn Central Company in June 1970. I had just taken the reins as director of the newly created Office of Management and Budget and the argument was in full swing. A reluctant David Packard was about to authorize, on behalf of the Pentagon, a Defense Department loan guarantee to Penn Central. I found myself arguing with my friend and mentor, Arthur Burns, over whether the financial markets could stand up to such a massive bankruptcy. He was deeply concerned and pushed for what I regarded as a bailout. I contended that this would set a bad precedent and that financial markets could hold up under a large bankruptcy. I wondered what I, a labor economist, was doing disagreeing with the chairman of the Federal Reserve Board on an issue involving financial markets. I'll never know how President Nixon would have decided the case because at a critical moment his canny political adviser, Bryce Harlow, provided crucial information and a clear assessment: "Mr. President, Penn Central, in its infinite wisdom, has just retained your old law firm to represent them in this matter. Under the circumstances, you can't touch this with a ten-foot pole." Suddenly, the expected signing of a guarantee was canceled. Burns did a masterful job of maintaining liquidity in the financial marketplace. To my relief, and to the relief of everyone else, no dominoes fell. The management of Penn Central was held accountable for its mistakes and the message delivered to financial markets was a healthy one: no bailouts, even if you are big. I also noted another important message: markets are often much stronger than they are perceived to be.

A somewhat different illustration of the issue of accountability was provided by the bankruptcy of Orange County, California. We are familiar with the notion that, if California were a country, its gross product would make it the eighth largest in the world. Orange County itself has a gross product larger than that of Portugal, Israel, or Singapore, among other countries.

Risky investments had provided the Orange County government with handsome returns over a period of years. Taxpayers were delighted, but after a time the investments turned sour in a big way—so big that the county could not meet its immediate financial commitments. Once again the question was raised, this time to California's governor, Pete Wilson: will you intervene and bail out this unit of government? Once again a chorus of concern arose about the potentially devastating impact on the system of municipal finance. Governor Wilson stood up to the pressure and Orange

County was forced to file for bankruptcy in December 1994. The system of municipal finance did not fall apart as a result. On the contrary, the outcome was healthy. Government units all over the country were cautioned to review their investment practices, become more conscious of undue risk (the pension and health-care costs had not yet surfaced), and tighten up on supervision: in short, to take responsibility and accountability.

What have I learned from these examples? Marketplaces in the United States are strong. They can distinguish good performances from bad, and dominoes will not fall if they are firmly based. The free market system is one of accountability; accountability will work relentlessly against bad performance but will reward the good. Intervening in this system of accountability will inevitably change it and can easily result in moving responsibility to the intervener, usually the government and the taxpayers. The basic players will quickly sense the change and realize that risk profiles have been altered; they can take more presumed risk since they can expect to be bailed out if the risks materialize. Government policy makers must watch out for these presumably unintended consequences.

Of course, I am not arguing that intervention should be ruled out. But individual private companies, no matter how big and interconnected, are not the problem. The problem is how to protect the system, as Arthur Burns did in the aftermath of the Penn Central bankruptcy.

I would favor putting on the books a new form of bankruptcy for large and complicated financial institutions—a Chapter 14 process as described and analyzed in *Bankruptcy Not Bailout,* edited by Kenneth E. Scott and John B. Taylor. In the process, debtors and creditors would negotiate within clear rules under judicial review and a firm's operations would continue while bankruptcy proceeded. Failure would always be an option and the idea of being too big to fail would be obsolete.

Experience has also taught me that a major bias that favors action inevitably confronts the government official who is faced with a critical situation. The official, often the president or a cabinet member, who acts is seen as taking charge, avoiding something harmful, and defending the public interest. The alternative—allowing market forces to work and letting a rule-of-law bankruptcy occur—seems passive. In the long run, however, the passive, essentially strategic, approach usually will produce the best results. We need officials who will confront immediate issues with a far-reaching, strategic point of view.

The importance of taking a long view brings to mind a cartoon that made the rounds during the Eisenhower years. His secretary of state, John Foster Dulles, seemed to be in constant motion, traveling the world as a supercharged diplomat. The cartoon depicted Ike, his hands on his hips, saying, "Damn it, Foster, don't just do something; stand there." Some situations call for that good advice.

The value of strategic thinking and the difficulty of seeing it through in the face of pressure to take action are summed up by an observation made by President Eisenhower as he successfully handled a crisis with China: "The hard way is to have the courage to be patient."[4]

Before closing, I want to emphasize a point made earlier in this chapter: education is the key to a healthy economy. Eric Hanushek, a senior fellow at the Hoover Institution, and I have worked together on K–12 education, a critical part of any effort to attain long-term growth in our economy and reasonable balance in the distribution of income. Our 2012 *Wall Street Journal* op-ed, "Education Is the Key to a Healthy Economy,"[5] highlights the strong correlation between educational attainment and higher real economic growth. A wide gap in educational achievement leads to broad disparity in the distribution of income, with all the tensions that accompany such imbalances. Currently, the United States is not performing well in either of these vital areas. The need for improvement in our educational system is gaining increased recognition, and impressive efforts to address this critical issue are under way in many states. Nevertheless, the United States has essential work ahead to improve the quality of K–12 education.

As Hanushek and I pointed out, current US students—the future labor force—are no longer competitive with students across the developed world. In the Programme for International Student Assessment (PISA) rankings for 2009 published by the Organisation for Economic

---

4. Jean Edward Smith, *Eisenhower in War and Peace* (New York: Random House, 2012), 657.

5. George P. Shultz and Eric Hanushek, "Education Is the Key to a Healthy Economy," *Wall Street Journal*, April 30, 2012.

Cooperation and Development, the United States was thirty-first in math—on a par with Portugal and Italy. In advanced performance in math, sixteen countries produced twice as many high achievers per capita as the United States did. If we accept this level of performance, we will surely find ourselves on a low-growth path.

This does not have to be our fate. Imagine a school-improvement program that would make us competitive with Canada in math performance (which would mean scoring approximately forty points higher on PISA tests) over the next twenty years. As these Canadian-skill-level students entered the labor force, they would produce a faster-growing economy with stunning results. Improvement in GDP over the next eighty years would exceed a present value of $70 trillion, which is equivalent to an average 20 percent boost in income each year for every US worker over his or her entire career.

The drag on growth is by no means the only problem produced by our lagging educational system. As mentioned earlier, greater inequity in education leads to greater disparity in income distribution. If we fail to reform our K–12 education system, we will lock in problems of inequality that will plague us for decades, if not generations, to come.

Examples abound of dramatic improvements that can be made in our K–12 system. The essence of reform is giving every student the ability to attend the school of his or her choice and making every school responsible for attracting students by the quality of education it offers. By not insisting on immediate, widespread reform, we are forgoing substantial growth in our standard of living. The problem is obvious, the stakes are enormous, and the solutions are within our reach.

Added to the distressing implications of the poor quality of K–12 education in the United States is the impact of high and prolonged unemployment and underemployment on our youth. Unemployment rates for young Americans between the ages of sixteen and twenty-four are approximately twice the national average; among young blacks, the rate is closer to 30 percent. These are the years when basic labor force skills and habits are learned, so the level of success achieved by Americans in this age group is often a clear precursor to subsequent achievement in the US economy.

At the other end of the age scale, changes in demography must lead to changes in policies affecting older Americans.

Demographic changes contain distinct messages about the future. As per-capita income grows and as women assume more consequential roles in the labor force, fertility tends to fall and longevity increases. Improved health is typically accompanied by longer life spans. If present systems of compensated retirement and health benefits stay in place, it is obvious that the arithmetic will not work because fewer and fewer workers will be responsible for supporting a growing population of retirees. This phenomenon is already apparent in exaggerated form in many states where pension and health-care promises are crowding out spending on other vital functions such as law enforcement and education. The federal government also faces escalating costs of pensions and health care. Some states have started to rein in these costs, but future arrangements are key to the long-term outlook.

Creative thinking and action are in order. Changes in the US Social Security system are necessary, but they need not be drastic. For example, the calculation of benefit levels for workers under fifty-five years of age could be changed from wage indexing to price indexing, and the age of full benefits could be indexed to changes in longevity. If these two simple adjustments were made, the Social Security system would be fiscally stable in the long run at the present level of payroll tax rates. The benefits paid to those fifty-five years of age and older would be unaffected, and the benefit levels of younger workers would be fully protected in real terms.

Another change could be made in payroll taxes. For example, if a worker were declared to be "paid up" after paying forty years of payroll taxes, no further payroll deductions from that worker or payments from his or her employer would be required. The worker's take-home pay would then sharply increase and the employer would have a less costly employee. Such incentives would have the positive effect of increasing participation in the labor force by workers who might otherwise choose retirement.

In conclusion, here is a summary of how to get our economy back on the track of growth without inflation:

- Think long.
- Make economic policies predictable.
- Beware of the urge to intervene.
- Leave prices to the marketplace.
- Keep federal government spending within the revenue generated by the tax system at high employment.
- Keep the regulatory system clear, simple, and easy to administer, and then live with it.
- Keep tax rates as low as possible and keep the tax system as simple as possible.
- Expect the Federal Reserve to follow predictable, rules-based policies.
- Maintain a global system of open trading arrangements and exchange rates that adjust reasonably to changing conditions, thereby avoiding the dangers of the protectionism and competitive currency devaluations that plagued the 1930s.
- Make major improvements in the K–12 system of education.

With these policies in place, the US economy will respond and once again be a model for all the world to see and try to emulate.

Of course, there are always factors that lie completely outside the scope of politics and economics. Pope Paul VI taught me this lesson in a dramatic way when I was secretary of the treasury.

In early 1974, frantic worry about the financial system, initially precipitated by the Arab oil boycott, was at its height. Oil prices had been rising steadily in an ominous fashion and the global flow of money was changing radically. In January 1974, finance ministers of the world met in Rome. I attended as the head of the US delegation. During the course of the meeting, my wife and I had the privilege of a private audience with the pope. When we arrived at the Vatican, we were escorted to a holding room and told that our audience would be limited to ten minutes, followed by two minutes for photographs. In the course of our conversation with the pope, I was impressed by how well informed he was about the oil crisis and how perceptive he was about who would be most negatively affected by it. We had a substantive and animated discussion that continued far beyond our allocated ten minutes. Then, without actually saying so, the pope indicated that the audience was about to end. Realizing this, I decided to conclude our lively conversation on a humorous note: "This has been a wonderful discussion. I've enjoyed it, and of course all of us attending the finance ministers' meeting would agree that this winter's mild weather has done more to solve the energy problem than any measures we've been able to suggest. We thank you for your intervention." The pope did not laugh, but he looked at me and said, with a slight twinkle in his eyes, "Mr. Secretary, you may be sure it will continue." As it happened, we had another mild winter the following year.

CHAPTER FOUR

A Better Energy Future

I took a leave of absence from the University of Chicago to become President Nixon's secretary of labor in 1969. In March of that year, I received a letter from Edward Levi, president of the University of Chicago. The letter read, "Dear George, I see you have reformed the Job Corps and now you are taking over the oil import control system. What would you like to teach next fall?"

Levi's letter was prompted by President Nixon's announcement that I would head the Cabinet Task Force on Oil Import Control. The importance and sensitivity of the assignment is evidenced by the members of my task force, which included the secretaries of state, treasury, defense, interior, and commerce, as well as the director of the Office of Emergency Preparedness. I also had official advisers, including the director of the Bureau of the Budget, the chairman of the Federal Power Commission, the assistant attorney general, a representative of the Council of Economic Advisers, the Special Representative for Trade Negotiations, and the head of the Office of Science and Technology Policy. It was a high-powered group with a daunting assignment.

I managed to persuade Phillip Areeda, a distinguished professor of law at Harvard, to be the executive director of the task force. He recruited an impressive staff. Given the political sensitivity of the energy issue, our task force decided on an unusual procedure. Rather than hold hearings or invite people to come in privately to give us their views, we published in the *Federal Register* an extensive list of questions that we thought were relevant to our work. We encouraged anyone who was interested to make a written submission, and all submissions were put on file for public review. When someone wished to talk to us, we assented and told them that an account of the meeting would be placed on the public record. After a reasonable period of time, we conducted what we called a rebuttal round, inviting people to challenge any of the submissions that, in their view, needed to be corrected.

I was amazed at how well this process worked. The task force received some excellent material, including more than 10,000 pages of letters, memoranda, and other written submissions. This productive process was also much less expensive than it would have been if public hearings had been held in various locations.

President Nixon agreed with me in advance that our task force report should be published. When it was released, I was stunned by the intensity of the response it received in congressional hearings and from the press. Our report called for a sharply improved management system for the energy program in order to keep up with the many facets of the supply-and-demand situation in the United States, North America, the Middle East, and elsewhere around the world. Discussing our report with the Senate Judiciary Committee, I said:

> Our conclusion is that the most serious contingency is not military but political and arises out of Arab-Israeli tensions in the Middle East and North Africa. Accordingly, we have focused our security analysis on a denial of all Arab supplies to all free-world markets, varying the model to include interdiction of Iranian supplies as well and extending the crisis beyond one year to two and even three years.
>
> The plan the Task Force proposes would draw the bulk of our imports from Canada and other acceptably secure Western Hemisphere sources, and would strictly limit Eastern Hemisphere imports to a maximum of 10 percent of US demand.
>
> We also look at certain pre-crisis investments that could be made to increase domestic emergency supplies—through conventional and underground storage, production from synthetics, and the creation of strategic reserves.... If pre-crisis trade flows from uninterrupted sources were to continue without diversion, the Western Hemisphere could survive comfortably without any rationing whereas the rest of the free world would be beyond relief even with tolerable (10 percent) rationing throughout the free world.[1]

1. George P. Shultz, excerpts from "Statement of Honorable George P. Shultz, Secretary of Labor, and Chairman, Cabinet Task Force on Oil Import Control, before the Subcommittee on Antitrust and Monopoly of the Senate Judiciary Committee," Washington, DC, March 3, 1970.

This task force work came rushing back to me in October 1973 when, as secretary of the treasury, I had a principal role in coping with the Arab oil boycott, launched in response to a US decision to resupply the Israeli military during the Yom Kippur War and administered in such a way as to cause our allies to pull away from us. For example, the United Kingdom and France had hardly any interruptions in oil supply, no doubt as a reward for refusing to allow the United States to use their airfields in our effort to resupply Israel.

When the price of crude oil quadrupled, the reaction in the United States took unusual forms. Many state governments asked their citizens to forgo Christmas lights. Oregon went further, banning all commercial lighting, and many politicians called for a national gas rationing program. The president requested service stations to voluntarily suspend the sale of gasoline on Saturdays and Sundays. The 90 percent compliance with his request resulted in long lines at gas stations on weekdays.

I reflected on President Eisenhower's notion that importing more than 20 percent of the oil the United States used would be asking for trouble in national security terms, and I said to myself, "Ike had a point." Of course, as treasury secretary I was also distressed about the economic impact of our dependence on foreign oil.

The oil crisis sparked a surge of interest in alternative forms of energy. I thought the effort was worth encouraging, and a number of interesting ideas were presented. But even I, a non-expert, could see that it would be years before these developments could produce enough energy to substantially reduce our need for imported oil.

By 1975, the embargo was over and the price of oil had subsided. At the same time that the nation heaved a sigh of relief, I was disappointed to see that interest in alternative forms of energy and research that might advance these ideas had practically disappeared.

The Arab oil embargo was followed by other, less intense disruptions of our oil supply. During the Iranian Revolution in 1979, for example, there was a temporary reduction in supply, prices rose, and interest in renewable energy sources revived. Interest waned once again, however, when the oil supply returned to normal and prices went down.

All these episodes have caused me to be deeply concerned about the national security and economic aspects of the US energy picture. Security issues now loom larger than ever, as we see the military's need to have more energy produced where it is used. The vulnerability of the US electricity grid to natural or hostile disruption means we also have a civilian stake in more distributed energy. And environmental concerns have gradually claimed more and more of the public's attention. Some effective efforts have been made, resulting in cleaner air and water. As yet, however, we do not have a level playing field for energy producers because pollution costs vary greatly and currently are not included in the prices of their products. But with global warming upon us, the United States and countries around the world have daunting tasks ahead. For example, the emergence of a new ocean in the Arctic region has huge implications, including border questions, navigation rights, and access to valuable resources. Among other necessary actions, we must ratify the Law of the Sea Treaty so that we will have a seat at the table where these and many other issues will be sorted out.

This chapter concludes with my own views on appropriate energy policies.

New Options on the Scene

Today we see new opportunities of global significance developing in the field of energy. We have a chance to leave behind the roller-coaster policy dilemma that began in response to the disruptions of 1973. We are on the cusp of important advances that may shift the security and economic dimensions of energy in our favor. Other developments are in progress that will contribute to improving our environment by addressing global warming issues and providing cleaner air and water. These desirable outcomes can be achieved if we use thoughtful strategies and sensible energy policies.

Two key developments are at the forefront of the conversation on energy these days. One is the hydraulic fracturing, or "fracking," technology that has rapidly and radically changed the availability of natural gas in the United States, with a consequent decline in price and the prospect of greatly increased supply here and elsewhere. Using the well-developed technique of horizontal drilling, this technology involves the injection of highly pressurized fracturing fluid into shale or sandstone formations. The fracturing of the rock creates channels for the release of oil and gas. Fracking is already being used in North Dakota and south Texas to develop tight oil from fields that were previously inaccessible. Many in the industry predict that this technology will dramatically change the oil picture, just as it has the natural gas situation.

Developed in the United States, fracking technology is now being introduced in other parts of the world. The result may be a massive re-arrangement of the global geopolitical power structure. From the stand-point of the United States, the prospect of near energy independence for North America with a strengthened base within our borders is now in sight. And energy imported from Canada or Mexico does not need to go through the Strait of Hormuz or any other choke point.

Debate on the use of fracking must be based on science and expe-rience. Potential environmental risks associated with this technology, including methane leaks and groundwater pollution, led the Department of Energy to convene a special panel in 2011 to study the process and create a regulatory structure to ensure that it does not result in harmful unintended consequences. Much of the effort to regulate this industry should be done at the state level, as conditions can vary significantly. In addition, the Environmental Defense Fund (EDF) has identified problems associated with the technology as well as ways of dealing with them. EDF has made five sound recommendations for shale gas management: (1) transparency in operations, (2) high-quality well construction and maintenance, (3) attention to the water cycle, (4) effective management of methane emissions, and (5) engagement with the communities where operations take place.

The stakes are high, so responsible use of this new technology is essential. It behooves the fracking industry to use proven techniques with great care. In addition, effective regulations must be put in place and strictly enforced.

Strategy for the Long Run

The second major development is the emergence of impressive work on a wide variety of alternative sources of energy by highly talented scientists and engineers. Solar and wind energy are close to being economically competitive with grid electricity. Batteries for electric cars, already far superior to those available only a decade ago, are being further improved. Also at hand are biofuels as well as long-term and reasonably scaled storage technologies that will alleviate problems associated with solar and wind power fluctuations. Energy-saving techniques are coming into play, with real progress being made in the construction of more energy-efficient buildings. These research and development efforts are currently financed—though by no means as well as they should be—by private as well as public resources.

The civilian effort toward energy efficiency is mirrored by work being carried out by the US military. Each branch of the armed services realizes that war-fighting capabilities can be sharply improved by developing alternative ways of producing and using energy and by being able to create more energy at the point of use. Attacks on US military convoys carrying oil to the troops in Afghanistan underscore the vital importance of this effort. It is clear that there should be a focus on more distributed, secure, and adaptable energy alternatives for civilian as well as military activities.

Here are my ideas for the policies that will capitalize on present opportunities for a better energy future—a future that bolsters our national security, helps our economy to flourish, and improves our environment.

First, let's put in place sensible, clear standards and appropriate regulations so that fracking technology can proceed confidently. We will gain handsomely in terms of greater security of supply, lower and more stable prices, and movement toward greater reliance on natural gas, the most benign of fossil fuels. The United States will also attract manufacturing activity and jobs as use of this technology increases.

Second, the roller-coaster history of energy policy suggests that greater availability of oil and natural gas will divert funding from the innovative activities now under way to seek cleaner alternatives to fossil fuels. The result would be a serious setback for the development of alternative forms of energy that can operate at scale and have a beneficial effect on our environment. It is imperative that we engage in a major political effort to produce substantial and sustained funding for energy research and development. I am confident that such support will be greater if the government leaves funding for commercial enterprises to the marketplace.

Third, we should rearrange the policy mix so that different forms of energy can compete on a level playing field. For example, we should mandate that new cars with internal combustion engines have a flex-fuel feature so that alternative fuels can compete effectively for use in these vehicles.

Fourth, the cost of capital required to deploy an energy technology ought to be structured on the basis of a level playing field. Currently, coal, oil, and gas have access to low-cost private capital through master limited partnerships (MLPs). All forms of energy should have access to these financing developments.

Fifth, the playing field will be leveled only if each source of energy bears the full cost of its use, including its effect on the environment. The solution I advocate is a revenue-neutral carbon tax, and the most efficient way to impose this tax would be to collect it at the point of production. Revenue neutrality comes from distribution of the proceeds, which, of course, could be done in a great variety of ways. On the grounds of ease of visibility and application, I advocate for having the tax collection and distribution administered by the IRS or the Social Security Administration. The principle of transparency should be observed. Money collected should go into an identified fund and the amounts flowing in and out should be clearly visible. The Social Security Administration could make payments, identified as "Your carbon dividend," in equal amounts to each current recipient of Social Security or to everyone either paying in to the system or receiving benefits from it.

I have been conducting an energy experiment of my own since having solar panels installed on my house on the Stanford University campus several years ago. By now, the savings from my lower electricity bills have exceeded the cost of those solar panels. And as I commute to work in my electric car, I am driving on sunshine that is plentiful—and free—in California.

In summary, the massive energy industry is entering a period of radical change and great opportunity. We need to think strategically about these potential changes and develop policies, research, and investments in order to take full advantage of the vast and promising prospects for a better energy future.

CHAPTER FIVE

Drugs: The War with No Winner

I share the commonly accepted belief that drug addiction is harmful to the health and well-being of individuals and has widespread adverse societal effects. Unfortunately, the war on drugs that the United States has waged for decades has proved to be a losing battle, so I see the urgent need for an effective program to deal with this problem.

As I have thought about this pressing and highly charged issue over the years, my attitude has become considerably more insistent that drug abuse should be treated as a health problem. We should carefully study the experiences of other countries with decriminalization—as distinct from simple legalization—of drugs. And the time has come to have an open, informed discussion and debate about the issues and possibilities associated with this daunting problem.

I have been concerned about the drug issue since I became secretary of labor in 1969, my first cabinet position in the Nixon administration. There was growing worry back then about the damage inflicted on individuals and society by the use of addictive drugs, so an informal effort was started to keep these drugs out of the United States. The late Senator Daniel Patrick Moynihan, a friend of mine who was then counselor to the president, worked diligently on this problem. I was concerned but skeptical about the effectiveness of this approach to the issue, which focused on stopping the flow of drugs into the United States while seeming to overlook the growing demand for drugs from within our country.

One day Pat and I were driving together to Camp David, where I was to make a presentation to the president and some of his advisers. As I studied my notes, Pat, who was in a state of exuberance, kept interrupting me. "Shultz, don't you realize that we just had the biggest drug bust in history?" "Congratulations," I replied, going back to my work. "Come on," he insisted, "this was a huge bust in Marseilles. We've broken the French connection!" "Great work," I replied unenthusiastically. After a pause, Pat said, "Shultz, I suppose you think that as long as there is a big, profitable demand for drugs in this country there will be a supply." "Moynihan," I said, "there's hope for you."

Two decades later, shortly after I left the office of secretary of state, I made some informal remarks on the drug issue to an alumni gathering at Stanford University. Somehow, those remarks made it into the *Wall Street Journal*:

> These efforts wind up creating a market where the price vastly exceeds the cost. With these incentives, demand creates its own supply and a criminal network along with it. It seems to me we're not really going to get anywhere until we can take the criminality out of the drug business and the incentives for criminality out of it. Frankly, the only way I can think of to accomplish this is to make it possible for addicts to buy drugs at some regulated place at a price that approximates their cost. When you do that you wipe out the criminal incentives, including, I might say, the incentive that the drug pushers have to go around and get kids addicted, so that they create a market for themselves. They won't have that incentive because they won't have that market. . . .
>
> I find it very difficult to say that. Sometimes at a reception or cocktail party I advance these views and people head for somebody else. They don't even want to talk to you. I know that I'm shouting into the breeze here as far as what we're doing now. But I feel that if somebody doesn't get up and start talking about this now, the next time around, when we have the next iteration of these programs, it will still be true that everyone is scared to talk about it. No politician wants to say what I just said, not for a minute.[1]

The reaction to this report in the *Wall Street Journal* was profuse, predictable, and striking. Nearly everyone who responded supported my view, but a large proportion of them admitted their reluctance to express their views openly. The taboo on frank debate about the drug issue was clearly evident in their responses.

1. "Shultz on Drug Legalization," *The Wall Street Journal*, October 27, 1989.

I had another exposure to the misplaced unwillingness of the drug bureaucracy to face reality when I helped Nancy Reagan with her speech at the United Nations in 1988. Her "Just Say No" campaign emphasized the importance of persuading people not to take drugs, and she was determined to discuss this effort at the United Nations even though the bureaucratic drug warriors tried to talk her out of it.

On October 25, 1988, I accompanied Nancy to the United Nations, where she would speak on behalf of the administration about the problem of illegal drugs. She had fought a battle over the text of her speech, particularly her emphasis on the obligation of the United States itself to do a better job of curbing the use of drugs. Those opposed argued that such a statement would only complicate our efforts to persuade other countries to fight against drug suppliers. I disagreed with them and took Nancy's side. President Virgilio Barco of Colombia had told me, "The profits to be made from selling drugs in the United States are staggering, and those profits are fueling what amounts to another government in my country."

Nancy insisted that we arrive early for the UN session she was to address, saying, "If I want people to listen to me, I should come in time to listen to them." When we arrived, well before her announced time to speak, the large room was nearly empty. She took the delegate's seat and I sat right behind her in the seat assigned to the US alternate. Nancy surveyed the sea of empty seats and then turned apprehensively to me. "George," she said, "doesn't anyone want to hear what I have to say?" I reassured her: "People know when you are scheduled to speak and the room will be full by then." By the time she spoke, the room was jammed and the atmosphere expectant.

Nancy surprised the delegates with her candor:

> If we cannot stem the American demand for drugs, then there will be little hope of preventing foreign drug producers from fulfilling that demand. We will not get anywhere if we place a heavier burden of action on foreign governments than on America's own mayors, judges, and legislators. You see, the cocaine cartel does not begin in Medellin [Colombia]. It begins

in the streets of New York, Miami, Los Angeles, and every American city where crack is bought and sold.[2]

After Nancy's speech, delegates from all parts of the world came over to congratulate her. The critics of her speech had been dead wrong: delegates said that her candor encouraged them to be even more resolute in their efforts to combat the production and trafficking of illegal drugs. Nancy had spoken the simple truth, a trademark of her husband.[3]

The war on drugs that has been waged in the United States for over forty years now has failed, just as our national experiment with the prohibition of alcohol failed. Drugs are still readily available and their use in the United States is no lower than, and sometimes surpasses, drug use in countries with very different approaches to the problem. Every activity related to illegal drugs has been formally criminalized in the United States and a large bureaucracy has been created. Incarceration rates are high and a massive, costly, and sustained effort has been made to keep drugs out of the United States.

How costly is this war on drugs? A good friend of mine, Nobel Laureate in Economics Gary Becker, and his colleagues estimated in 2005 that the direct costs are over $100 billion annually in police services, court time, effort spent on offenders, and imprisonment—a minimum of about $40,000 per year per prisoner. Becker notes that this estimate does not include "intangible costs, such as the destructive effects on many inner city neighborhoods, the use of the American military to fight drug lords and farmers in Colombia and other nations, or the corrupting influence of drugs on many governments."[4]

In a blog he wrote in 2010, Becker looked beyond these direct costs to consider the effects of our drug war on other countries. He noted, "Mexico is engaged in a real war, with advanced military equipment used by the drug gangs. Often the gangs have better weapons than the army

2. Nancy Reagan, statement at the United Nations, New York City, October 25, 1988.

3. George P. Shultz, *Turmoil and Triumph: My Years as Secretary of State* (New York: Charles Scribner's Sons, 1993), 1134.

4. Gary Becker, "The Failure of the War on Drugs," *The Becker-Posner Blog*, March 20, 2005.

does. The casualties have been huge [around 50,000 in the last five years]. Major cities like Monterrey are hollowing out. No one has estimated the social cost of American drug policy on Mexico, Colombia, and other countries, but it has to be immense."[5] These costs are clearly staggering— probably in excess of Becker's earlier estimate of $100 billion. For the sake of round numbers, let's call the total a cool quarter-trillion dollars a year, not including the incalculable cost of the losses in human lives and the debilitating effects on individuals of a prison record because of drug use.

Despite these stunning costs, Becker writes, "Every American president since Nixon has engaged in a war on illegal drugs: cocaine, heroin, hashish, and the like. And every president without exception has lost this war."[6] An exclamation point should be put behind the word "lost." Far from being successful in keeping drugs out of the United States, a study by Glenn Greenwald based on the World Health Organization's Composite International Diagnostic Interview shows the opposite result: "A survey of seventeen countries has found that despite its punitive drug policies, the United States has the highest levels of illegal cocaine and cannabis use."[7] The authors found that 16.2 percent of people in the United States had used cocaine in their lifetime, a level much higher than that of any other country surveyed. The second highest level of cocaine use—4.3 percent—was in New Zealand. Cannabis use was highest in the United States (42.4 percent) followed by New Zealand (41.9 percent).

How to tackle this thorny problem? Begin by recognizing the importance of persuading people not to take addictive drugs and then doing everything possible to deal effectively with the harmful effects of drug abuse. Let me illustrate a promising approach with a story about the construction business, an industry in which I worked for many years. If you say to me, a construction guy, "Build me a bridge across the Potomac River," I will do the soils tests, order the steel, sink the supports, and construct a bridge that you can drive a truck over. I can then say, "Problem

5. Gary Becker, "The American War on Drugs is Not Only an American Disaster," *The Becker-Posner Blog,* December 12, 2010.

6. Ibid.

7. Glenn Greenwald, *Drug Decriminalization in Portugal: Lessons for Creating Fair and Successful Drug Policies,* Cato Institute, April 2, 2009.

solved. Done with that." But if you say to me, "Build that bridge in such a way that there are no lost-time accidents during construction," and I react by putting up guardrails and other safety devices and think I've solved the problem, I will have lost. The problem is inherently insolvable. It is about attitudes—about building a culture of safety in the workplace. So if I work at it persistently, creatively, professionally, and relentlessly, I just might get the bridge built without a lost-time accident.

The use of drugs has been with mankind for centuries, but dealing with this issue is similar to the problem of building a bridge without a lost-time accident. You have to work at it constantly, creatively, and professionally. In the United States today, we tackle the problem with prosecution, incarceration, and other efforts to try to get control of it. This war-on-drugs approach has failed. A shift away from aggressive law enforcement that criminalizes every drug-related activity and everybody involved in illegal drug use and a move toward decriminalization of small-scale possession and use could have many positive effects: reduced drug use, fewer people in jail, a lower rate of diseases such as HIV/AIDS, less profit for drug lords, and a decline in violence.

A vigorous campaign against illegal drug use is essential and can have an impact, as illustrated by the positive results achieved in the campaign waged in the United States against cigarettes. Major investments in treatment centers will be critically important. Currently, drug users risk arrest if they admit their addiction and seek treatment. With decriminalization, they will be able to ask for help without fear of punitive measures. Early results from the program used in Portugal suggest that this shift will have a positive impact, particularly on young people who are not yet fully addicted.

Above all, this decriminalization and treatment approach establishes a better foundation from which to work at the problem. While maintaining the illegality of drug dealing so that heat can be kept on pushers, users can be identified and offered help, so the size of the prison population, along with its high monetary and human costs, will decline. And, as profitability of the illegal drug business plummets, so too will the violence that now undermines governance in many Central and South American countries. Meanwhile, drug dealers will still be dealt with as criminals, and the aura of censure created by illegality, buttressed by an advertising campaign, will remain in place.

Portugal has been utilizing this approach since 2001. Drugs are not condoned, but their use and small-scale possession are decriminalized. Treatment centers are established and used, since people do not have to brand themselves as criminals by admitting to drug use. This program encourages the treatment of addiction, which, along with other efforts, represents a different, less costly, and—from all the evidence—more effective way of confronting the problem, especially among young people. With this approach, you cannot walk away and say, "Problem solved," but you can say, "We are working on the problem in a constructive way."

In view of the immense costs—human as well as material—of the war on drugs and its complete failure to achieve its objectives, why haven't we done something about it?

The stark contrast between the war on drugs and Prohibition is instructive. Prohibition, which was put into effect in 1920 after the Eighteenth Amendment was ratified in 1919, produced results similar to those of the war on drugs. Thirteen years later, Prohibition was ended by the difficult process of ratifying another constitutional amendment (the Twenty-first Amendment). We came to our senses on Prohibition in thirteen years. Why can't we admit—even after forty years—that the war on drugs has failed?

Alcohol use has been generally accepted in our society, even during Prohibition. There's the Hook-'n-Eye example. In the 1920s and '30s, the Cypress Point Club in Pebble Beach, California, held a golf tournament in which half the players were members and half were guests, mainly from the East Coast. The East Coast guests came to California and said, "Who can I get a drink from?" That question morphed into "hook 'n eye," which became the name of the tournament that is still held annually.

Of course, there was serious violence during the years of Prohibition. Think of Chicago, Al Capone, and the St. Valentine's Day Massacre. My hypothesis is that the big difference between our reactions to the drug and alcohol problems is that, in the drug case, the violence occurs elsewhere. But during Prohibition, the violence took place in the United

States, where Americans could see and feel its effects. They could also see that Prohibition was not achieving its presumed objective.

Mexico and Guatemala now bear the burden of drug-related violence. Mexico is our next-door neighbor and our third-largest trading partner. With huge numbers of commuters, the US-Mexico border has the most legal crossings of any border in the world. Our culture, particularly in states like California, is heavily influenced by Mexico. Think of the missions, the city names (San Francisco, San Diego, Los Angeles), and the street names (El Camino Real, which stretches from San Diego to Sonoma, or El Escarpado, a street on which my family and I once lived). But somehow, even though violence in Mexico is starting to creep north into the United States, we still allow ourselves to think that it is Mexico's problem. We should be alarmed, let alone ashamed, that we don't recognize this as our problem, too.

What can be done? Becker suggests coupling legalization with a high tax so the price of drugs will not fall. I agree, but I also think we should consider two additional ways to influence the demand curve: decriminalization of use and small-scale possession, and a vigorous campaign against use.

After all, drug dealers want to develop their market, so they get people—particularly young people—hooked. What will the effect be of removing this incentive? The demand for drugs, as Becker points out, "is generally quite inelastic,"[8] but it may be possible to move the demand curve to the left.

Special attention should be paid to younger age groups. The Greenwald study of the Portuguese experience points out that for two critical youth groups (thirteen to fifteen years and sixteen to eighteen years), use rates for nearly every substance have declined since decriminalization. There is evidence of dramatic reductions in the use of cannabis, cocaine, "ecstasy" (MDMA), amphetamines, heroin, and hallucinatory mushrooms. The Greenwald study concludes, "In almost every category of drug, and for drug usage overall, the lifetime prevalence rates in the pre-decriminalization era of the 1990s were higher than the post-decriminalization rates."[9]

8. Gary Becker, "The Failure of the War on Drugs," *The Becker-Posner Blog,* March 20, 2005.
9. Greenwald, "Drug Decriminalization," 14.

There is an additional advantage to this decriminalization approach because drug use is related to numerous diseases. The Greenwald study notes, "The number of newly reported cases of HIV and AIDS among drug addicts has declined substantially every year since 2001."[10]

When Mary Anastasia O'Grady of the *Wall Street Journal* interviewed me in 2009, I had US foreign policy on my mind. I said, "It's gotten to the point that . . . you've got to be worried about what's happening to Mexico, and you've got to realize that the money that's financing all that comes from the United States in terms of the profits from the illegal drugs. It's not healthy for us, let alone Mexico, to have this violence taking place." But I recognized that discussion of these issues is difficult. "Right now if you are in politics you can't discuss the problem. It's just poison. The result is that we have this giant problem that is tearing Mexico apart . . . and we have plenty of problems here too and we're really not having a debate about it."[11]

In 2011, I had an opportunity to weigh in on the drug issue at a symposium in Chicago in honor of Gary Becker's eightieth birthday. My remarks there show that my attitude has become considerably more insistent about the importance of treating drug abuse as a health problem and of studying carefully the experiences other countries have had with decriminalization, as distinct from simple legalization, of drugs.

My conviction that drugs are harmful for individuals and for society continues to grow stronger. In order to tackle this critical issue effectively, we must insist that the subject gets out into the open where it can become the focus of informed discussion.

My deep concern about the effect of the war on drugs on US foreign policy, particularly with respect to our neighbors to the south, prompted me to become the honorary chairman of the Global Commission on Drug Policy, led by the former presidents of Mexico, Brazil, and Colombia. The commission has benefited greatly from the support of Ethan Nadelmann and the research and advocacy of the Drug Policy Alliance, which he founded and directs. Joining me on the commission

10. Ibid., 15.
11. George P. Shultz, quoted in Mary Anastasia O'Grady, "George Shultz on the Drug War," *TheWall Street Journal*, October 11, 2009.

is former Federal Reserve Board chairman Paul Volcker, with whom I coauthored a *Wall Street Journal* op-ed urging the United States to "break the taboo on debate and reform."[12]

As I recall the groundswell of response to my extemporaneous remarks about drug policy made almost a quarter century ago, and as I consider where the issue stands today, I see hopeful signs that, while the taboo on honest debate still exists, perhaps it is slowly beginning to lift. It's about time.

12. George P. Shultz and Paul A. Volcker, "A Real Debate About Drug Policy," *The Wall Street Journal*, June 11, 2011.

CHAPTER SIX

Effective Diplomacy Applied to Issues of Foreign Policy

Sometimes small events have a major impact on your thinking. I remember the day my Marine Corps boot camp drill sergeant handed me my rifle. He said, "This is your best friend. Take good care of it and remember: never point this rifle at anybody unless you're willing to pull the trigger." The lesson—no empty threats—was one that I have never forgotten, and its relevance to the conduct of diplomacy is obvious, yet often ignored. If you say that something is unacceptable but you are unwilling to impose consequences when it happens, your words will lose their meaning and you will lose credibility.

I also recall a time during the war when my Marine unit had taken a little island in the Pacific. We knew that natives on a nearby island made grass skirts, log canoes, and other souvenirs that we liked to send home. Occasionally, Marines were allowed to go to the island for two hours, so they wanted to make deals quickly. But I observed that the natives enjoyed the process of bargaining so they wanted to keep the process alive. Guess what happened to the prices of those souvenirs? The negotiator who knows that you are desperate for a deal will have the advantage.

I kept this lesson in mind during my years of government service as I dealt with the Soviet Union and a number of other countries. Testifying before a committee of Congress, I was occasionally asked if I was concerned that the United States had not made a major deal with the Soviets. I always replied that we were only interested in good deals, and good deals were not struck when the other party knew you were in a hurry. One of my colleagues, CIA Director Bill Casey, gave me similar advice when he cautioned, "Don't be a Pilgrim." When I asked what he meant, he replied, "Don't be an early settler!"

These are just a few examples of lessons gleaned from early experiences that have been useful throughout my career. They hint at how important it is for leaders to think carefully about their approach to negotiations and foreign policy.

Ideas for Action

Early in my tenure as secretary of state, I addressed the UN General Assembly on four basic principles for action in US foreign policy. I could make the same speech today but, unfortunately, I would have to adjust some of the wording.

1. *Start from realism.*

   If we are to change the world we must first understand it. We must face reality—with all its anguish and all its opportunities.

   Much of present day reality is unpleasant. To describe conditions as we see them is not to seek confrontation. Far from it. Our purpose is to avoid misunderstanding and to create the necessary preconditions for change. And so, when we see aggression, we will call it aggression. When we see subversion, we will call it subversion. When we see repression, we will call it repression. When we see opportunity, we will work hard to turn that opening into constructive reality.

2. *Act from strength.*

   [Today, we are allowing our strength to slip away. But then, with the buildup of our capability in the Reagan years, I could speak with confidence.] The bulwark of America's strength is military power for peace. The American people have never accepted weakness, nor hesitancy, nor abdication. We will not put our destiny into the hands of the ruthless. Americans today are emphatically united on the necessity of a strong defense. This year's defense budget will ensure that the United States will help its friends and allies defend themselves—to make sure that peace is seen clearly by all to be the only feasible course in world affairs. [I wish I could be so confident today.]

   The engine of America's strength is a sound economy. The United States, with its vast human and scientific resources, can survive an era of economic strife and decay. But our moral commitment and our self-interest require us to use our technological and productive abilities to build lasting prosperity at home and to contribute to a sound economic situation abroad.

President Reagan has instituted a bold program to get the American economy moving. Our rate of inflation is down markedly, and we will keep it down. This will add stability to the value of the dollar and give greater confidence to international financial markets.

The bedrock of our strength is our moral and spiritual character. The sources of true strength lie deeper than economic or military power—they lie in the dedication of a free people which knows its responsibility. America's institutions are those of freedom accessible to every person and of government as the accountable servant of the people. We must not step away from this commitment.

3. *Fair engagement*

The world has work to do for the realists, the pragmatists, and the free. With a clear understanding of the troubled circumstances of the hour and with a strengthened ability to act, we need, as well, the vision to see beyond the immediate present.

All of us here represent nations which must understand and accept the imperative of fair engagement on the issues before us and, beyond that, of common effort toward shared goals. Whether we are seeking to bring peace to regional conflict or a resolution of commercial differences, the time of imposed solutions has passed. Conquest, pressure, and acquiescence under duress were common in decades not long past, but not today. Not everybody who wants his concerns addressed will find us automatically receptive. But when negotiations are in order, America is prepared to go to work on the global agenda and to do so in a way that all may emerge better off and more secure than before.

4. *Conduct negotiations on the basis of the US agenda and with a belief that progress is possible.*

We manage our problems more intelligently, and with greater mutual understanding, when we can bring ourselves to recognize them as expressions of mankind's basic dilemma. We are seldom confronted with simple issues of right and wrong, between good and evil. Only those who do not bear the direct burden of responsibility for decision and action can indulge themselves in the denial of that reality. The task of statesmanship is to mediate between two—or several—causes, each of which often has a legitimate claim, and to identify where the United States interacts, and where and how to advance the US agenda.

It is on this foundation that the United States stands ready to try to solve the problems of our time—to overcome chaos, deprivation, and the heightened dangers of an era in which ideas and cultures too often tend to clash and technologies threaten to outpace our institutions of control.[1]

The Freedom Agenda

Freedom and the struggle to achieve it—the motivating ideas behind US foreign policy—were the subjects of an address I gave before the Commonwealth Club of Northern California in San Francisco on February 22, 1985. The yearning of individuals for freedom to live, congregate, and express themselves as they choose was at the core of many of the most contentious and difficult problems we faced then. The struggle continues today and requires an ongoing effort. As I said,

Any victory of communism was held to be irreversible. This was the infamous Brezhnev doctrine, first proclaimed at the time of the invasion of Czechoslovakia in 1968. Its meaning is simple and chilling: once you're in the so-called socialist camp, you're not allowed to leave. Thus the Soviets say to the rest of the world: "What's mine is mine. What's yours is up for grabs."

In recent years, Soviet activities and pretensions have run head-on into the democratic revolution. People are insisting on their right to independence, on their right to choose their government free of outside control. Where once the Soviets may have thought that all discontent was ripe for turning into communist insurgencies, today we see a new and different kind of struggle: people around the world risking their lives against com-

1. George P. Shultz, "US Foreign Policy: Realism and Progress," speech at the 37th UN General Assembly, New York, September 30, 1982.

munist despotism. We see brave men and women fighting to challenge the Brezhnev doctrine.

A revolution is sweeping the world today—a democratic revolution. This should not be a surprise. Yet it is noteworthy because many people in the West lost faith, for a time, in the relevance of the idea of democracy. It was fashionable in some quarters to argue that democracy was culture bound; that it was a luxury only industrial societies could afford; that other institutional structures were needed to meet the challenges of development; that to try to encourage others to adopt our system was ethnocentric and arrogant.

In fact, what began in the United States of America over two centuries ago as a bold new experiment in representative government has today captured the imagination and the passions of peoples on every continent.

Civilizations decline when they stop believing in themselves; ours has thrived because we have never lost our conviction that our values are worth defending.

But America also has a moral responsibility. The lesson of the postwar era is that America must be the leader of the free world; there is no one else to take our place. The nature and extent of our support—whether moral support or something more—necessarily varies from case to case. But there should be no doubt about where our sympathies lie.

It is more than mere coincidence that the last four years have been a time of both renewed American strength and leadership and a resurgence of democracy and freedom. As we are the strongest democratic nation on earth, the actions we take—or do not take—have both a direct and an indirect impact on those who share our ideals and hopes all around the globe. If we shrink from leadership, we create a vacuum into which our adversaries can move. Our national security suffers, our global interests suffer, and, yes, the worldwide struggle for democracy suffers.

When the United States supports those resisting totalitarianism, therefore, we do so not only out of our historical sympathy for democracy and freedom but also, in many cases, in the interests of national security. As President Reagan said in his second inaugural address: "America must remain freedom's staunchest friend, for freedom is our best ally and it is the world's only hope to conquer poverty and preserve peace."[2]

All these ideas underline the importance of strategic thinking—of continuously reminding ourselves of our broad objectives and of what we want to achieve in the long run. But strategic thinking requires taking time out from the unending immediate issues of the day and reflecting more widely on what is going on in the world. When I was in office, I benefited from a practice of pausing to reflect on the big picture a few times a week. I would say, "Hold all phone calls unless it's my wife or the president." I stayed away from my perpetually full in-box and settled into a comfortable chair, armed with paper and pencil. I would say to myself, "Now, what are we trying to achieve? Leaving aside the immediate issues of the day, where do we want to go and how can we get there?" These regular personal sessions helped me maintain my focus on strategy.

Global Thinking and Means of Implementation

Another set of experiences provided me with a wealth of information and a deepened realization of how interactive global developments can be despite the distinctive characteristics of each area of the world. The annual meeting of the UN General Assembly is held each September and is attended by most of the world's foreign ministers and many heads of government. When I was secretary of state, I made a practice of staying in New York for two full weeks of the meeting, using a suite at the UN Plaza Hotel across the street from the United Nations Building. I hosted numerous luncheons and dinners, often held in venues showcasing distinctive parts of New York City's history. Meeting people from around the globe was a rich educational experience in cultural diversity that reinforced my awareness of the wide repercussions that important events anywhere in the world can often have. It is essential to think internationally, and the US government, principally through the State Department, must conduct a global diplomacy.

2. George P. Shultz, "America and the Struggle for Freedom," address to the Commonwealth Club of California, San Francisco, February 22, 1985.

In a unique way, the importance of global thinking is underscored by the nature of the US population. To a degree unlike that in any other country, the United States is home to people claiming ancestry in almost every country on the globe. As a result, for every noteworthy event that occurs anywhere in the world, there is a constituency in the United States that expects the government to understand it and respond to it.

As every secretary of state quickly learns, global diplomacy is possible because the United States has developed a strong foreign service populated by dedicated individuals who spend their lives learning and thinking about the world. I consulted heavily with foreign service officers who worked diligently, skillfully, and professionally to carry out US policies.

I also worked with career people in government from the beginning of my time in the cabinet and I developed great respect for them. When I became secretary of labor in 1969, I was warned that a Republican would have an impossible job at the Department of Labor, which some described as a wholly owned subsidiary of the AFL-CIO. On the contrary, I learned that, with professional and energetic leadership, career people would give you their best work. I also found that I, a Republican, could become good friends with George Meany, then head of the AFL-CIO. I had similar experiences working with career people as director of the Office of Management and Budget and as secretary of the treasury. So when I became secretary of state, I found it natural to identify good career people who would work tirelessly with me.

Dedicated to leaving the Department of State a better place than it was when I entered it, I paid a great deal of attention to its management. That meant being aware of the career opportunities of the people I worked with and giving them the training and experience that would help advance their careers. I am proud that a foreign service training facility, now called the George P. Shultz National Foreign Affairs Training Center, was created during my tenure.

In the chapter on governance, I underlined the importance of working on a constitutionally established organizational line rather than managing through many layers of staff. As secretary of state, I decided to have only one executive assistant, a senior and well-respected foreign service officer. I announced to the line organization—the assistant secretaries who stood for confirmation in the Senate—that they would serve as my staff. I met with these individuals frequently and, in the process, their ability to execute in the field was strengthened.

The Importance of Records

The conduct of diplomacy requires a clear understanding of what is taking place in the world and an ability to make an accurate record of it and report it honestly and in depth. While these criteria may seem obvious and simple, they are not. Good diplomacy requires exceptional intellectual skill, character, and discipline. As former Senator Daniel Patrick Moynihan said, "The true diplomatist [is] aware of how much subsequently depends on what clearly can be established to have taken place. If it seems simple in the archives, try it in the maelstrom."[3]

Fast-moving media coverage, impressive though it may be, almost inevitably focuses on sensational news. US diplomacy, conducted on a global scale, is dependent on careful reporting of events from posts around the world and interpretations by people on the ground who speak the language and understand cultural nuances. Of course, results of discussions must be recorded in writing immediately because memories can often be faulty or self-serving.

We need to encourage careful record-keeping and teach and nurture that skill in the foreign service. This is no mere technical matter; in these times, issues of national security may be at stake and courage is needed. Even during my years as secretary of state, if a cable from an ambassador contained a highly critical or sensitive set of observations about the country in which he or she was stationed, the existence of that cable would often become the subject of rumor, and relentless demands to see it would almost inevitably follow. I fought those pressures because the release of such a cable would mean, of course, that the ambassador's role would be diminished, if not ended. Nonetheless, the constant pulling and hauling had an impact: candor in the cables inevitably suffered. There was increased reliance on telephone diplomacy with all its imprecision,

3. Daniel Patrick Moynihan and Suzanne Weaver, *A Dangerous Place* (Boston: Little, Brown, 1978), vii.

vulnerability to misunderstanding, and resultant loss to the vital diplomatic record.

This phenomenon is now evident more broadly in our society, whether in business or government, in the widespread and conscious reluctance to create records and the disposition to destroy those that exist. I am concerned that our ability to conduct affairs with precision and to portray history accurately will suffer if such records are not at hand and statesmen and diplomats must rely instead on their own memories, which invariably are flawed in significant ways. A living history requires tools of remembrance, so much of what we do today depends upon our understanding of the past. Each generation creates a record for succeeding generations. If we lose that past, we will also lose an important key to the future, so it is vital that members of the foreign service keep accurate records.

Foreign service careers have inherent risks. On opposite walls of the entry hall in the main Department of State building are the names of foreign service officers killed in the line of duty between 1780 and 2002. During that time we lost 209 officers: 83 in the first 187 years of our history and 126 in the next 35 years. The losses per year are now almost nine times as great as those in earlier times. All too many of these casualties were the result of acts of terror, a reality that confronts us today more urgently and in greater magnitude than ever before.

We received a vivid and tragic reminder of this brutal reality with the murder of Ambassador Christopher Stevens and three of his colleagues in Benghazi, Libya, in September 2012. They are remembered with great respect and a deep sense of loss.

The Problem of Terrorism

When I was secretary of state, the problem of terrorism as a deadly force emerged. I was a hawk on this issue and I advocated that we should adopt more than a simple law-enforcement approach toward terrorism. I recommended that we beef up our intelligence and be ready to stop potential terrorist attacks before they happened. My speech at the Park Avenue Synagogue in New York in 1984, reproduced in the appendix, sets out my views. As I said,

We must reach a consensus in this country that our responses should go beyond passive defense to consider means of active prevention, preemption, and retaliation. Our goal must be to prevent and deter future terrorist acts, and experience has taught us over the years that one of the best deterrents to terrorism is the certainty that swift and sure measures will be taken against those who engage in it. We should take steps toward carrying out such measures. There should be no moral confusion on this issue. Our aim is not to seek revenge but to put an end to violent attacks against innocent people, to make the world a safer place to live for all of us. Clearly, the democracies have a moral right, indeed a duty, to defend themselves.

If we are going to respond or preempt effectively, our policies will have to have an element of unpredictability and surprise. And the prerequisite for such a policy must be a broad public consensus on the moral and strategic necessity of action. We will need the capability to act on a moment's notice. There will not be time for a renewed national debate after every terrorist attack. We may never have the kind of evidence that can stand up in an American court of law. But we cannot allow ourselves to become the Hamlet of nations, worrying endlessly over whether and how to respond. A great nation with global responsibilities cannot afford to be hamstrung by confusion and indecisiveness. Fighting terrorism will not be a clean or pleasant contest, but we have no choice but to play it.[4]

This idea of preemption, controversial at the time, now seems to be more widely accepted, though difficult to carry out. The attacks of 9/11 awakened the United States to the essential realization that a radical force stemming from an extreme strain of Islam is trying to change the world in ways deeply antithetical to our interests. The tactic of terror attacks is a means toward that end.

This is a war, not a matter of law enforcement, and states that support terror are as guilty as the terrorists and must be held accountable. They are in the crosshairs, and the principle of state accountability is being established. These are big, far-reaching ideas that must be kept front

4. George P. Shultz, "Terrorism and the Modern World," address at the Park Avenue Synagogue, New York City, October 25, 1984.

and center. We are calling on states to step up to their internal responsibilities to end any terrorist presence, while also saying that, within the framework of our right to self-defense, we reserve the right to preempt terrorist threats within a state's borders. Our primary goal is not to punish and retaliate but to prevent acts of terror through intelligence that enables us to preempt them and ultimately to eliminate their sources. The juxtaposition of these weighty, wide-ranging ideas calls for accurate intelligence, sophisticated diplomacy, and the will to act with the courage of our convictions.

Terrorism and the Problems of Asymmetries

Dealing with terrorism has become more complicated in this age of asymmetries. Asymmetries are being used to turn our values—and the institutions, regulations, and understandings that have evolved from them—into weapons against us. The United States and our allies are currently facing this problem as we work on rules of engagement in Afghanistan. Members of the Taliban inflict, invite, and exploit collateral damage by placing their fighters in the midst of civilians while firing at our forces. As we struggle to win the hearts and minds of civilian populations, our adversaries are attempting to transform our constructive efforts into a shield to prevent us from using our firepower to defeat them.

This dilemma has developed from a long-standing effort to set rules for the use of force in war and to develop new protections for civilians, combatants, and prisoners of war. The United States has taken the lead in this movement. In the military field, it has worked to minimize harm to civilians; in the political field, it has fostered human rights; in the economic field, it has provided development assistance; and in the legal arena, it has promoted the military justice system to ensure that those who violate the laws of war are treated as war criminals, not as ordinary defendants. These efforts have gradually established standards that have been adopted by the international state system. We must hold on to these standards steadily and firmly.

Now, however, the legal and moral restrictions that we have established are being used strategically against us. Enemies of the international state system and, by extension, of civilized behavior have found advantages in the existence of asymmetry. They use the ungoverned spaces of the world to gather, plan, and train for acts of violence against legitimate states and their populations, and they do so in the service of a religiously inspired ideology aimed at destroying and replacing the established international state system.

Deliberately violating the laws of war, these enemies do not wear uniforms, carry their arms openly, engage in traditional combat, or operate under a recognized state's professional chain of command. They take the lives of civilians for their offensive, defensive, and political purposes. Embedding their weapons in public locations such as schools and hospitals, they cause great harm to innocent civilians. Such asymmetrical tactics are employed ceaselessly and as a means of stringing out conflict by making it difficult for the United States to use its comparative advantages in firepower and general military capability. The view of our enemies is that they do not need to win the war; they simply must prolong it until we grow impatient and politically dispirited, and set timelines for withdrawal—precisely what is happening now in the war in Afghanistan.

Ominously, the word "lawfare" has recently entered the vocabulary of war. Hoping to fend off legal challenges arising from asymmetries, the United States has deployed lawyers to advise our combat units on when, how, and at whom they may shoot. But this protective tactic does not address the fundamental phenomenon of asymmetry.

Legally, it has been increasingly clear since 2001 that the protections provided by the several layers of the Geneva Conventions did not envision the kind of enemy combatants we face in this asymmetrical age. Former Attorney General Michael Mukasey has noted that the civilized world tried over the course of several hundred years to establish rules of warfare so that soldiers of a professional army are treated as prisoners of war when captured. Those who follow none of the rules are to be treated as war criminals who are not entitled to the far more robust protection afforded ordinary defendants accused of ordinary crimes.

The humanitarian impetus that propelled the reforms in warfare over the past few decades has reversed the moral paradigm. Now, when illegal combatants entrench themselves and their weapons in the midst of civilian population centers, condemnation falls not on them but on the professional soldiers who cannot defend against their attacks without harming civilian life and property.

Iran, which insists on the privileges and immunities of legitimate statehood even as it works against the world order in an omnidirectional way as a rogue state, has long used asymmetrical diplomacy to its advantage. It toys with the efforts of the United States, Europe, and the International Atomic Energy Agency to use concessions and/or sanctions to persuade Iran to halt its drive for nuclear weapons. Iran knows that the UN Security Council, presumably the apex of the state system, can be routinely ignored and exploited. Whenever Iran professes a desire for a negotiated solution, world opinion gives it the benefit of the doubt and allows it more time during which it can continue its nuclear weapons program. There are ominous signs that Iran's weapons program has not been turned back and that collective security, which has no teeth, is failing. The self-imposed protocols and limitations of accepted international diplomatic practice have been used by Iran to neuter this primary means of preserving international peace and security.

The legitimacy of UN Security Council resolutions was further undermined by the UN peacekeeping operation in Lebanon. It had become the cover for a massive arms buildup from Iran through Syria to Hezbollah, in direct contravention of a UN Security Council resolution, until it was interrupted by rebellion in Syria. Once again, we see a demonstration of the need for a UN process with the authority to follow through.

Israel has released, no doubt somewhat compromising its intelligence capabilities, highly detailed maps and photographs depicting exactly where Hezbollah has placed its ever-growing numbers of missiles, command centers, and arms caches near schools and hospitals in southern Lebanese villages. Without doubt, this remarkable release of classified intelligence will not protect Israel from the world's outrage if war breaks out because the moral paradigm has shifted. We must move that moral paradigm back where it belongs, and the affected civilian populations need to reject the weapons placed in their midst.

We witnessed this problem once again in late 2012, when Hamas launched rocket attacks on Israel from installations in the Gaza Strip. The attacks were deliberately placed beside hospitals, schools, and other centers of civilian activity. When Israel retaliated, the general reaction to the resultant collateral damage was castigation of Israel rather than of Hamas.

The most horrendous asymmetrical threat of all comes from the potential use of a nuclear weapon by an extremist group that has no known address and is therefore unreachable by strategies of deterrence. The relative success of asymmetrical methods by such ideologically driven terrorists can only tempt states that are adversarial to other states, or to world order in general, to devise methods of transferring nuclear weapons to non-state groups in ways that can be disavowed or so attenuated that a nuclear attack could not be traced to the nuclear state in question.

Our first objective should be to acknowledge the reality of asymmetries and, in doing so, to help explain the difficult situation in which we find ourselves today. Recognizing the depth and severity of the problem, we can develop ways to deal with the exploitation of asymmetries by the enemies of world order.

America must continue to uphold its values. It cannot retreat by declaring that it will practice these values only at home or by reasoning that American values are no more worthy than those of the world's many cultures.

At the same time, we must recognize the inherent limitations of the strategy known as counterinsurgency, in which we seek to win the hearts and minds of local populations. There is a risk of setting ourselves up for a form of blackmail and also for exploitation of asymmetries by our adversaries. We need a strategy of preemption that hits hard against the threat of terrorism and puts severe limits on the length of time our troops remain deployed.

Lessons from the Cold War Experience

Of course, US-Soviet relations and Cold War issues played a central role in my activities as secretary of state. I testified about our policies many times before Congress. On one particular occasion in 1983, I described our approach in considerable detail. It is an approach worth examining because it is applicable to many of today's difficult situations. I began the hearing by saying that I had reviewed my testimony with

President Reagan and he had approved every word of it. In other words, I was speaking directly for the president. In this testimony, I set out a general point of view:

> Our policy is not based on trust or on a Soviet change of heart. It is based on the expectation that, faced with demonstration of the West's renewed determination to strengthen its defenses, enhance its political and economic cohesion, and oppose adventurism, the Soviet Union will see restraint as its most attractive, or only, option. Perhaps, over time, this restraint will become an ingrained habit; perhaps not. Either way, our responsibility to be vigilant is the same.[5]

Then I developed our four-point agenda:

1. We would talk about arms control.
2. We would also insist on discussing regional issues where great tensions arose and where the Soviets were often troublemakers.
3. We would discuss bilateral issues.
4. We would also insist on talking about human rights. The Soviets, particularly in the Gromyko days, refused to discuss human rights, claiming that it was their internal business, but even Andrei Gromyko accepted lists of people we were worried about.

In the end, by insisting on this four-point agenda, we derived important dividends with significant breakthroughs in the field of human rights.

To put the matter more generally, a key to success in negotiations is working from your own agenda, not the agenda of some other country. It is a concept that is as relevant today as it was in the 1980s. The Cold War experience shows the importance of getting the ideas—the guiding strategy—right and then relentlessly pursuing our own interests.

Relations with the Soviet Union during the Cold War were guided by two important ideas. Under the strategy of containment, the West under-

5. George P. Shultz, "US-Soviet Relations in the Context of US Foreign Policy," statement before the Senate Foreign Relations Committee, Washington, DC, June 15, 1983.

took to resist any expansion of the Soviet empire with the expectation that, sooner or later, internal contradictions would cause it to look inward and, in the end, to change. As time went on, this guiding idea shifted into the concept of détente: We're here, you're there, and that's life, so the name of the game is peaceful coexistence. Détente was clearly better than war, especially nuclear war, but Ronald Reagan and I preferred the earlier interpretation of the idea of containment. He denounced détente and stood by his belief that the Soviet Union would change.

A second idea, the concept of linkage, characterized the pre-Reagan approach to our relationship with the Soviet Union. When the Soviets invaded Afghanistan, President Carter was surprised, distressed, and angered. In reaction, he shut down everything from participation by US athletes in the Moscow Olympics to negotiations on arms control and even Foreign Minister Gromyko's annual visit to Washington before the opening of the UN General Assembly.

As I took office, my friend Helmut Schmidt, the West German chancellor, counseled me: "George, the situation is dangerous; there is no human contact." In other words, linkage had been carried to an extreme, with negative repercussions. President Reagan understood that linkage could work against the right outcome by encouraging the Soviets to behave badly just so they could agree to give up that behavior in order to get something else they wanted. And if the Soviets behaved well, linkage could put pressure on the United States to go along with something else they were doing wrong. Above all, Ronald Reagan and I were determined to pursue freedom and human rights and make an effort to reduce nuclear armaments no matter what else was going on.

We were severely tested when the Soviets shot down a Korean 747 airliner in September 1983. Outraged, we led the charge to condemn them and promote corrective action. At the same time, I proceeded with an earlier scheduled meeting with Foreign Minister Gromyko and we sent our arms control negotiators back to Geneva to continue their work toward agreements. Gromyko heard a forceful denunciation of the Soviets' action, and our return to negotiations helped convince people in Western Europe that we were serious in our negotiations, thereby contributing to our ability to deploy nuclear weapons in Europe to counter earlier Soviet deployments. In the end, both of these conceptual adjustments—a belief that change is possible and a rejection of linkage—helped us push for the dramatic shift that eventually took place.

These ideas were behind President Reagan's famous "Tear Down This Wall" speech, and I developed them in an address I gave at the American Academy in Berlin in 2007 on the twentieth anniversary of President Reagan's original address. I said, "One of the most important reasons for success: we in the West had a strategy that we were able to sustain for almost half a century. The basic architecture was put in place and solidified in the Truman and Eisenhower years and that architecture, particularly the NATO alliance, served us well throughout the Cold War period." I noted, "He [President Reagan] made some people nervous with his views and his rhetoric, but the idea that change is possible turned out to be an energizing and motivating stimulant, true to the original concept of containment." Furthermore, I said, "It is not evidence of weakness that you meet with your counterpart. The important point is what you say." I continued, "I believe the vital turning point in the Cold War was the deployment of Pershing missiles in Germany in late 1983. . . . If that deployment had not gone forward, our strength and our willpower could have been shattered and the outcome of the Cold War might well have been different."[6]

Today, Russia, with all the swagger and authoritarianism of the Putin regime, is a wounded bear. It has a demographic catastrophe on its hands, a long border with China with millions of Chinese on one side and hardly any Russians on the other, a virtually open rebellion in the Caucasus, and an economy heavily dependent on the price of oil and gas.

The following ideas that guided US diplomacy during the Reagan administration are as useful today as they were several decades ago.

- Start from realism (no wishful thinking) and sustainability.
- Act from strength (military capability and economic self-confidence).
- Use strength in tandem with diplomacy.

6. George P. Shultz, "'Tear Down This Wall,' Twenty Years Later," speech at the American Academy in Berlin, June 5, 2007.

- Engage to build agreements based on our agenda. A deep and continuing consultative process among like-minded people creates the understanding necessary to make hard choices.
- Conduct diplomacy with the belief that progress—change toward freedom and openness—is possible.
- Remember that economic development goes hand in hand with political openness.

The Middle East

A transformation is occurring in the Middle East today. The rebellion in Syria, the latest upheaval ignited by the Arab Awakening, is another sign that a major change is under way. Close attention to this development is necessary, for its outcome will affect the world order.

Considering the seriousness of the dramatic upheaval in the Middle East, we must decide what we want to achieve. In the past decade, the United States engaged in wars in Iraq and Afghanistan only to find itself embroiled in a national debate about how quickly and unconditionally it could withdraw. This strategy is unsustainable. We must not get involved in another war on such terms, but we can use our influence for regional stability under legitimate and responsive governance. In the Middle East, we can take a firm stand on the side of open political participation across the spectrum by responsible sects and parties, including women, in all levels of government. We can try to be helpful in many of these countries that face historic tensions between Sunnis and Shiites. We cannot expect the old regimes of the region to continue as before, so we should work constructively to help them face the reality that change is necessary.

At the same time, the United States and other countries must recognize the threat that protests sometimes lead not to freedom but to chaos. Care must be taken so that chaos is not permitted to masquerade as freedom and democracy and, in the process, lead to a takeover by radical forces.

I well remember a saying from my days working in the field of union-management relations: There is only one thing worse than a wildcat strike, and that is a successful wildcat strike. The point is that protests cannot be allowed to become a primary form of influence on governance. A strong effort is needed by those who would lead these embattled countries to bring about the stability of responsible government that can exercise sovereign authority for the common good of its citizens.

Contrary to the chaotic conditions in some areas and the pessimistic predictions by many, there are positive aspects to the recent turmoil in the Middle East. Above all, perhaps, are the new, younger voices of the Arab Awakening. However suppressed or sidelined they now may be, they have altered the temper of the times in ways that cannot be erased.

An overall strategy is needed that recognizes the interconnectedness of these events in the Middle East and the divisiveness of the rivalry between Sunnis and Shiites. The king of Morocco is leaning toward a more responsive regime, a move the United States should quietly support. We can also be helpful to Tunisia, which is struggling to put together a workable government. Remember that the spark that set off the Arab Awakening was a single frustrated entrepreneur—a vendor of fruits and vegetables—who simply wanted to earn a living. Stability will only come to this region when its populations have work to do because it is work that attaches people to reality and gives them the dignity of earning their own way. We can help these societies build better economies.

In Libya, the election had a more positive outcome than many expected. While tensions and complications persist, we can work to strengthen the rule of law there. The responsible way in which the Libyan government reacted to the tragic deaths of US Ambassador Christopher Stevens and three other US diplomats in September 2012 is an indication that the country has undergone positive change.

In Egypt, a de facto coalition of the military and the Muslim Brotherhood forms a precariously uneasy governing structure. We will want to keep that structure in place as a basis for stability and as an insurance policy against a swing to Islamic radicalism. This will buy the time needed for the younger, more secular voices of the rebellion to organize and gain adequate representation. In the meantime, a little of Ronald Reagan's "trust but verify" is in order in the treatment of women and of the Copts, a decent respect for civil liberties, and adherence to the peace with Israel. As Tom Friedman put the key point,

Yes, democracy matters. But the ruling Muslim Brotherhood needs to understand that democracy is so much more than just winning an election. It is nurturing a culture of inclusion, and of peaceful dialogue, where respect for leaders is earned by surprising opponents with compromises rather than dictates. The Nobel Prize-winning Indian economist Amartya Sen has long argued that it was India's civilizational history of dialogue and argumentation that disposed it well to the formal institutions of democracy. More than anything, Egypt now needs to develop that kind of culture of dialogue, of peaceful and respectful arguing. . . . Elections without that culture are like a computer without software. It just doesn't work.[7]

In Saudi Arabia, which has concerns about its Eastern Province and the situation in Bahrain, we can play a moderating, yet effective, role. In Bahrain, repression alone will not work. A social contract is needed between the ruling Sunni dynasty and the majority Shia population. In Saudi Arabia, young Saudis need work. The practice of having people brought in from other countries to do the real work needs modification. Generational succession is inevitable but needs clarity and can create an atmosphere for political reform in which the process of government is opened up, however gradually.

Syria's protracted and bloody struggle produces the potential for radicalism but also reveals huge numbers of people with immense courage in the face of unbridled autocracy. We can work unconventionally to back responsible successors to Bashar Assad while refraining from the misguided United Nations-led diplomatic mission that has prolonged the fighting while buying time for the regime. Syria's fate is connected to the fates of Iran and Hezbollah; the end of Assad's dictatorship would be a severe blow to these two enemies of world order. But where will Syria go? Will that country pull apart? More than being a mere spectator and commentator, the United States should be helpful to constructive forces.

Turkey has been, and can continue to be, a force for bringing a transformed Middle East into good relations with the non-Muslim world. The

7. Tom Friedman, "Egypt: The Next India or the Next Pakistan?" *The New York Times*, December 16, 2012.

United States should rebuild its ties with Turkey, offering assistance as that country copes with Syrian refugees and with the spillover of violence from Syria.

Iran is the chief danger to regional and international order. Uniquely, the Iranian Revolution of 1979 brought a radically ideological Islamist movement into control of a state that was inside the international system. For more than three decades, the ayatollahs have worked it both ways, pretending that Iran is a legitimate state when that serves their interests but suppressing dissent in their own country and working violently, deceitfully, and illegally against world order at the same time. The world now has a great deal of leverage on Iran: sanctions, cyber-operations, subversion, the diplomatic track, the military option, and the upheaval in Syria. But lacking US leadership, these various pressures are not being coordinated to maximum effect; one part or another always undercuts the opportunity to shape a larger strategy.

The Israeli-Palestinian situation continues to fester but the conflict is not intractable. Here are six principles that should guide continuing work on this issue:

- The existence, security, and well-being of Israel are the first principles of any settlement. Israel has the right to exist, and it has the right to exist in security. The reality is that Israel cannot find a peaceful and stable outcome from negotiating with Palestinian leaders who clearly seek the destruction of Israel.
- Real security results from resolving political differences that continue to fuel conflict. The location of borders is important, but more important is what crosses those borders: ideas, goods, and people instead of armies and weapons. Borders need to be recognized and secure, but political differences between neighbors need to be resolved through compromise.
- Palestinian political rights must also be recognized and addressed. Palestinians want more than the basic necessities of life. They want, and they are entitled to, political participation and influence over political and economic decisions that affect their lives.

- The history, security, and destiny of Israelis, Jordanians, Palestinians, and Egyptians are inextricably bound together. Jordan is a vibrant and heterogeneous society with a strong national identity of its own. It is not a Palestinian state. An enduring settlement must reflect the reality that eventually there must be strong, open relations among the Israeli, Palestinian, Jordanian, and Egyptian peoples.

- Peace between Israel and its neighbors will take time and growing mutual good will to succeed. All sides need to deal with one another gradually in the light of a freely negotiated agreement. Palestinians need to achieve control over political and economic decisions that affect their lives. Israelis need time to adjust to a new situation in which Palestinians—not Israeli military government officials—administer the West Bank and Gaza.

- Direct negotiations are at the heart of this process. No party should be expected to trust its vital national security interests to any mechanism except direct talks. How better to engage an adversary, take his measure, assess intentions, and probe for openings than to square off across the table? Direct talks work.

I am convinced that a constructive approach will put less emphasis on a settlement that presumes to solve the problems from above and more emphasis on constant work toward effective governance and improved quality of life on the West Bank. With quiet but genuine cooperation by Israel, this work progressed well in recent years but may now be flagging. We should continue to support this constructive effort.

In each of the major issues in the Middle East today, including an Israeli-Palestinian two-state solution, the United States must once again assume its leadership role.

Concluding Comments

As I reflect on my years in office and think about what gave me the greatest sense of purpose, the answer always has a human face. There were major achievements: working closely with our neighbors, Canada, Mexico, the countries of Central and South America, and the Caribbean; helping to bring an end to the Cold War; forging a constructive relationship with Japan, China, India, and Pakistan; and encouraging the movement toward democracy in the Philippines, Chile, South Korea, and elsewhere. But these achievements, though momentous, tend to be abstract. For me, the most rewarding work of diplomacy always involved individuals and their personal stories.

I remember as if it were yesterday a telephone call that came into my office on October 15, 1987. I had worked hard on the case of Soviet *refuse- nik* Ida Nudel, meeting her when I was negotiating with the Soviets and putting her name on a special list I had given to my Soviet counterpart, Eduard Shevardnadze. When I answered the phone that fall afternoon, the voice on the other end said, "This is Ida Nudel. I'm in Jerusalem. I'm home." I am still moved when I think of that moment.

The importance of global diplomacy weighed heavily on my mind as I testified before the Senate Committee on Foreign Relations on January 31, 1985. President Reagan had just been reelected by a landslide and I had recently returned from successful negotiations with Minister of Foreign Affairs Gromyko for the resumption of serious talks on the reduction of nuclear weapons. I said:

> Change is constant. America has recovered its strength and self-confidence. Power continues to be dispersed and the structure of political relations more complex, even as the interdependence of states increases. And as we head toward the twenty-first century, is a stable new pattern of international relations emerging? Einstein's observation takes on new relevance: our ways of thinking must adapt to new realities; we must grasp the new trends and understand their implications.
>
> But we are not just observers; we are participants, and we are engaged. America is again in a position to have a major influence over the trend of events—and America's traditional goals and values have *not* changed. Our duty must be to help shape the evolving trends in accordance with our ideals and interests, to help build a new structure of international stability that will ensure peace, prosperity, and freedom for coming generations. This is the real challenge of our foreign policy over the coming years.

I concluded my survey of the world, titled "The Future of American Foreign Policy: New Realities and New Ways of Thinking," with special emphasis on the basic theme—as valid today as it was then: "History is on freedom's side."[8]

So, as I have often repeated, America has the winning hand. Let's play that hand with confidence, patience, and persistence.

8. George P. Shultz, "The Future of American Foreign Policy: New Realities and New Ways of Thinking," statement before the US Senate Committee on Foreign Relations, Washington, DC, January 31, 1985.

CHAPTER SEVEN

Toward a World Without Nuclear Weapons

My exposure to nuclear weapons began in an obscure but dramatic way. After two and a half years fighting in the Pacific during World War II, I had just boarded a ship full of Marines headed back to the States, where we were to be formed into the fighting units that would storm the Japanese homelands. Every Marine on the ship had made at least one landing, so we knew full well that fierce battles lay ahead.

We were hardly out of port when we heard that something called an atomic bomb had been dropped on Hiroshima. None of us had any idea of what an atomic bomb was but we assumed it was important because it was so prominently reported. The ship lumbered on and we received the news that a second bomb had been dropped on Nagasaki. By the time we made port in San Diego, the war was over. However obscure the nature of the atom bomb was to us, we all assumed that it had saved many of our lives.

Back home, where I had started work on my PhD at the Massachusetts Institute of Technology, I remember being appalled when I saw the first photos of the devastation of Hiroshima and Nagasaki. Then we all saw pictures of nuclear tests in the atmosphere, later widely condemned and recognized as dangerous because of long-lasting radiation from fallout. When I served in Washington during the Eisenhower administration in the mid-1950s, we had periodic drills on what to do in case of an alert, moving to underground command centers well outside of Washington. The nuclear cloud had become an ongoing reality.

My first cabinet positions in the Nixon administration focused on domestic and international economic matters, so I had no direct connection with nuclear issues, but in those days no one could escape their presence. My involvement changed dramatically, however, when I became secretary of state.

The Cold War in the early eighties was as cold as it could get. During the UN General Assembly in New York in September 1982, I had two meetings scheduled with Soviet Foreign Minister Andrei Gromyko. After considerable internal debate, I was authorized to suggest in our first meeting that we select a few topics on which we might work collaboratively. I nominated the issues of southern Africa and nuclear nonproliferation, and at our second meeting Gromyko expressed complete agreement that we should work on nonproliferation. It was an early indication of Soviet concern about the potential spread of nuclear weapons. This modest effort was also the first real break from President Carter's post-Afghanistan freeze on working with the Soviets.

I laid out my own thinking on nonproliferation in a 1984 speech at the United Nations, the full text of which is included in the appendix. Striking an optimistic note, I said that early forecasts of extensive proliferation of nuclear weapons had been proven wrong, due in part to strong diplomatic work. But I went on to identify problems:

> Those of us who deal with this issue have long been acutely aware . . . that as long as international tension and conflict exist, there will be insecure or irresponsible leaders who seek to shift the balance of regional power dramatically by acquiring a "secret weapon."

And, in a statement relevant to today's problems with Iran, I said:

> Nevertheless, as long as that sense of insecurity exists, the threat of sanctions, although an important deterrent, may not always suffice to discourage countries with the potential to build weapons from trying to do so. . . . In the fall of 1982, Foreign Minister Gromyko and I agreed to initiate bilateral consultations on nonproliferation. Since then, three rounds of useful discussions have taken place, with both sides finding more areas of agreement than disagreement. We expect to confer again on this subject later this month. It is clear that both countries consider the horizontal spread of nuclear explosives to be in no one's interest.

I concluded:

> It is no exaggeration to say that controlling the spread of nuclear weapons is critical to world peace and, indeed, to human survival. It is a cause that deserves and receives a top priority in our foreign policy.[1]

As I delved further into the subject of nonproliferation, and as my personal relationship with President Reagan deepened, I came to realize how strongly he believed that nuclear weapons, while a deterrent, were immoral and a threat to the very existence of the United States. Early in his presidency, he had asked the Joint Chiefs, his military advisers, to estimate the casualties that would result from an all-out Soviet nuclear attack on the United States. Their answer: initial casualties of around 150 million people, with a large number of follow-on casualties because there would be no infrastructure left. Would Reagan retaliate? Yes, but I heard him say on many occasions, "What's so good about keeping the peace by having the ability to wipe each other out?" He had proposed deep cuts in US and Soviet arsenals and had announced in public speeches, "We seek to rid the world of nuclear weapons." I shared his view, but most members of the defense and intelligence communities did not.

I recently ran across a report of a chilling incident. Colonel General Viktor Ivanovich Yesin, former head of the General Staff of the Russian Strategic Rocket Forces, tells of a visit to the United States:

> I was riding around San Francisco with the Americans on a bus. Everybody was talking, laughing. And then we drove past a beacon. I looked at it and said, "I know this beacon." The Americans [said]: "How could you know it if you are in San Francisco for the first time?" And [I] responded, "You have forgotten that I used to work in nuclear planning. And this beacon here—it was a targeting point." After that, we drove in silence to the designated place.[2]

1. George P. Shultz, "Preventing the Proliferation of Nuclear Weapons," address before the UN General Assembly, New York City, November 1, 1984.

2. Excerpt from an undated article in *Komsomolskaya Pravada* contained in an e-mail message to author, January 11, 2012.

Especially disturbing is the fact that the targeting point—San Francisco—is a heavily populated city. Within the doctrine of Mutual Assured Destruction (MAD) was the potential for large-scale destruction of major population centers.

Reading the monumental biography *Eisenhower in War and Peace* by Jean Edward Smith, I recently came upon the following passage regarding the Potsdam conference of July 15, 1945, which was attended by the triumphant civilians and military leaders who had defeated Hitler:

> It was while the Potsdam conference was taking place that Eisenhower first learned of the atomic bomb. During a long talk at Ike's Frankfurt headquarters, Secretary Stimson, who was the cabinet officer responsible for the bomb's development, informed Eisenhower of the successful test in New Mexico and said the government was preparing to drop the bomb on Japan unless the Japanese surrendered quickly. This was Ike's first introduction to atomic weapons, and he was appalled. As Secretary Stimson laid out the facts, Eisenhower recalled that he was overcome by depression.
>
> > "So I voiced to him my grave misgivings, first on the basis of my belief that Japan was already defeated and that dropping the bomb was completely unnecessary, and secondly because I thought that our country should avoid shocking world opinion by the use of a weapon whose employment was no longer mandatory as a measure to save American lives. . . . I disliked seeing the United States take the lead in introducing into war something as horrible and destructive as this new weapon was described to be."
>
> Eisenhower was the only one at Potsdam who opposed using the bomb. And when Ike expressed his misgivings, Stimson became highly agitated, "almost angrily refuting the reasons I gave for my quick conclusions" . . . . Alone among those present at Potsdam, Eisenhower recognized that once the genie was out of the bottle it could not be put back in. The bomb would increase world tension, just when it seemed possible that it might be controlled.

As president, Eisenhower would twice be presented with recommendations from his National Security Council and the Joint Chiefs of Staff that the bomb be used; first, in Vietnam to protect the French at Dien Bien Phu, then against China at the time of the Formosa Strait crisis. Both times Eisenhower rejected the recommendations. As a former supreme commander, Eisenhower had the confidence to do so, where other presidents might not have. And by rejecting the use of the bomb, there is no question that Eisenhower raised the threshold at which atomic weaponry could be employed—a legacy we continue to enjoy.[3]

I must add that, as president, Ike used the idea of massive retaliation as a deterrent to war and, shrewd poker player that he was, he used calculated ambiguity as a hole card. His role in the nuclear arena is discussed in detail by Evan Thomas in his biography, *Ike's Bluff*, the very title of which makes the essential point.

I accompanied President Reagan to his first meeting with General Secretary Mikhail Gorbachev in October 1985 in Geneva, where they agreed that "a nuclear war cannot be won and must never be fought."[4] This initial encounter was the prelude to the dramatic meeting between the two leaders in Reykjavik in October 1986. I sat beside President Reagan in a small room in Hofdi House, where he and Gorbachev agreed to sharp reductions in nuclear weaponry and discussed the prospect of the ultimate elimination of nuclear weapons and the ballistic missiles that carried many of them.

The dramatic ideas espoused by Reagan and Gorbachev at Reykjavik elicited deeply hostile reactions. Prime Minister Margaret Thatcher arrived in Washington and taught me the meaning of the phrase "to be handbagged" with one of her trademark purses of sturdy leather. She castigated me, saying, "George, how can you sit there and allow the president to agree to abolish nuclear weapons?" "But Margaret," I responded, "he's the president." "Yes, but you're supposed to be the one with his feet on the ground," she chided. "Margaret, I agree with him," I explained.

In an effort to consolidate the historic ground we had covered at Reykjavik, I delivered what I regarded as an important speech at the

3. Jean Edward Smith, *Eisenhower in War and Peace* (New York: Random House, 2012), 449–451.

4. Ronald Reagan and Mikhail Gorbachev, Joint Statement, Geneva Summit, November 21, 1985.

University of Chicago in 1986. I recounted the history of efforts to control nuclear weapons and, while retaining the vision of their eventual elimination, emphasized the importance of the reductions in intermediate-range and strategic nuclear weapons that had been explicitly identified at Reykjavik. In the speech "Nuclear Weapons, Arms Control, and the Future of Deterrence," which is in the appendix. I pointed out:

> A defense strategy that rests on the threat of escalation to a strategic nuclear conflict is, at best, an unwelcome solution to ensuring our national security. . . . [Such a strategy] may appear a bargain—but a dangerous one. [Nuclear weapons] make the outbreak of a Soviet-American war most unlikely; but they also ensure that should deterrence fail, the resulting conflict would be vastly more destructive, not just for our two countries but for mankind as a whole.

And I concluded:

> Just as what happened forty-four years ago in the squash court under old Stagg Field opened up both new horizons and new dangers, so we now see new possibilities for protecting our security, as well as new risks if we don't manage them well. So it is up to us—working together with both allies and adversaries—to ensure that we use these new opportunities to achieve a more stable and secure peace.[5]

Significant progress was made after the Reykjavik meeting. In 1987, the United States and the Soviet Union signed a treaty on intermediate-range nuclear forces (INF) that eliminated this category of nuclear weapons from their arsenals. It was the first time such a sweeping action had been taken. The verification provisions in the treaty, including agreement for on-site inspections, led the way to similar arrangements in subsequent agreements and can be a useful precedent as work progresses

---

5. George P. Shultz, "Nuclear Weapons, Arms Control, and the Future of Deterrence," address before the International House of Chicago and the *Chicago Sun-Times* Forum at the University of Chicago, November 17, 1986.

on the reduction of nuclear arsenals by other countries and on a global basis. As Ronald Reagan often cautioned, "Trust but verify." A treaty on strategic-range weapons providing for 50 percent reductions in nuclear weapons followed, and the envelope for future negotiations was significantly enlarged.

I returned to Stanford University's Hoover Institution at the end of the Reagan presidency. In 1996, the tenth anniversary of the Reykjavik meeting, I convened a conference on "The Future of Nuclear Deterrence" that was attended by several European and Asian leaders from my days as secretary of state. At that time, the prevailing attitude toward ridding the world of nuclear weapons was still one of skepticism.

At Stanford, I developed a close friendship with Sid Drell, a prominent physicist, and in 2006, along with former Secretary of Defense William Perry, we planned another conference at the Hoover Institution to discuss the implications of what had taken place at Reykjavik. By this time—twenty years after the Reykjavik summit—nuclear arsenals were approximately one-third of the size they had been in 1986, so we felt entitled to believe that real progress is possible.

One of the important results of that 2006 conference and subsequent conferences was a series of *Wall Street Journal* op-eds that I coauthored with Bill Perry, former Secretary of State Henry Kissinger, and former Senator Sam Nunn. Two-thirds of the living former secretaries of state, secretaries of defense, and national security advisers endorsed the vision expressed in our 2007 op-ed. It was a view that President Reagan espoused in a speech before the Japanese Diet in 1983: "I know I speak for people everywhere when I say our dream is to see the day when nuclear weapons will be banished from the face of the earth." Our op-eds stirred up global interest in nuclear issues and stimulated widespread support for work to eliminate nuclear weapons. Op-eds on the vision of a world free of nuclear weapons, the steps to achieve that vision, and the doctrine of nuclear deterrence are reprinted in the appendix. As we said in 2007,

> Reassertion of the vision of a world free of nuclear weapons and practical measures toward achieving that goal would be, and would be perceived as, a bold initiative consistent with America's moral heritage. The effort

could have a profoundly positive impact on the security of future generations. Without the bold vision, the actions will not be perceived as fair or
urgent. Without the actions, the vision will not be perceived as realistic
or possible.[6]

An indication of the worldwide interest generated by these op-eds
was a February 2008 conference in Oslo sponsored by the government of
Norway. Representatives from twenty-nine nations attended the meeting,
the agenda of which was based explicitly on the work that had been done
at the Hoover Institution and by Sam Nunn's organization, the Nuclear
Threat Initiative (NTI). Following the Oslo conference, our team stopped
in London to continue the discussion on the elimination of nuclear weapons, first with British parliamentarians and then with a group of global
leaders including representatives from the United States, Russia, Britain,
France, Germany, Norway, Canada, Sweden, and the United Nations.

Stimulated by this work, the governments of the United Kingdom and
Norway carried out a joint exercise on verification issues, and further
worldwide developments ensued. In 2010, the Australian and Japanese
governments reaffirmed a Joint Package of Practical Nuclear Disarmament and Non-Proliferation Measures on their shared commitment to
the goal of a world free of nuclear weapons. Their action followed the
release of a report on a project that studied our ideas and made recommendations. That report basically supported the program we had put
forward in our op-eds. Another conference inspired by our work was
held in Rome in 2009. Mikhail Gorbachev and I cochaired the meeting,
which was attended by representatives of eighteen countries.

With some encouragement on our part, both candidates in the 2008 US
presidential election, Senator John McCain and Senator Barack Obama,
endorsed our vision, thus giving the issue the nonpartisan character that
we have striven to preserve. After the election, President Obama moved
forward with an explicit call for a world free of nuclear weapons and
Senator McCain made a strong supporting speech on the Senate floor.

6. George P. Shultz, William Perry, Henry Kissinger, and Sam Nunn, "Toward a
Nuclear-Free World," *The Wall Street Journal*, January 4, 2007.

On April 13, 2010, President Obama convened a meeting of forty heads of state in Washington, DC, to discuss the vital issue of securing fissile material, one of the essential steps we had identified in our op-eds. The meeting was followed two years later by a conference in South Korea that served to move the subject forward.

A formal meeting of the UN Security Council on September 24, 2009, chaired by President Obama, considered a resolution "to create the conditions for a world free of nuclear weapons." All the heads of government present voted in favor of the resolution and each made a statement explaining his or her country's vote. The Gang of Four—Bill Perry, Henry Kissinger, Sam Nunn, and I—attended the meeting, where several heads of state explicitly referred to our work in their comments.

I summarized these developments in a speech at the Global Zero Summit in Paris in February 2010 and added:

My first point: these statements show that the idea of a world free of nuclear weapons has extraordinary staying power.

Why the staying power? The answers are that we know all too well that these weapons are unique in their immense and inhumane destructive power, that the consequences of their use would be devastating, and that access to nuclear materials is in the process of proliferating.

UN Security Council Resolution 1887 shows something else, particularly juxtaposed to many recent statements by leaders in many countries of their support for this goal. So my second point: this idea not only has staying power but we are also entitled to hope and believe that this is an idea whose time has come.

I continued:

So where do we go from here, and how?

I believe we must go carefully, remembering that we are talking about the national security of each country and all of us collectively.

I say we must go carefully, but care does not mean an attitude that time is irrelevant. Time is not on our side, so the key phrase must be "careful urgency."

We know that the ability to verify that agreements are kept is essential. And then there are the issues of enforcement. What to do when some country or group steps out of line?[7]

The full text of this speech is included in the appendix along with an essay on the nuclear enterprise that I coauthored with Sid Drell.

In a sense, weapons are one side of a coin. On the other side is deterrence, the doctrine governing their use, which was the focus of another conference at the Hoover Institution. A subsequent op-ed written by our Gang of Four stated:

As long as there has been war, there have been efforts to deter actions a nation considers threatening. Until fairly recently, this meant building a military establishment capable of intimidating the adversary, defeating him, or making his victory more costly than the projected gains. This, with conventional weapons, took time. Deterrence and war strategy were identical.

The advent of the nuclear weapon introduced entirely new factors. It was possible, for the first time, to inflict at the beginning of a war the maximum casualties. The doctrine of mutual assured destruction represented this reality. Deterrence based on nuclear weapons, therefore, has three elements:

- It is importantly psychological, depending on calculations for which there is no historical experience. It is therefore precarious.
- It is devastating. An unrestrained nuclear exchange between superpowers could destroy civilized life as we know it in days.
- Mutual assured destruction raises enormous inhibitions against employing the weapons.

Moving from mutual assured destruction toward a new and more stable form of deterrence with decreasing nuclear risks and an increasing measure of assured security for all nations could prevent our worst nightmare

---

7. George P. Shultz, "A World Free of Nuclear Weapons, An Idea Whose Time Has Come: Where We Are and Where We Need to Go," address at the Global Zero World Summit, Paris, February 2, 2010.

from becoming a reality, and it could have a profoundly positive impact on the security of future generations.[8]

The late Max Kampelman, a close friend and a colleague when I was secretary of state, spoke eloquently of the importance of the movement from what *is* in our present day to the *ought* to which we aspire, and how that movement has made the United States the democratic country we cherish today. Our Declaration of Independence and our Constitution contain numerous *oughts,* but it has taken us many years to end slavery, to grant voting rights to all our citizens, and to guarantee civil rights, to give a few examples. We're proud that our Declaration of Independence contains the phrase "all men are created equal" because that is the *ought.* As Max said, that *ought* has wielded huge power. Calling attention to the aspiration has helped move the *is* closer to the *ought.* And Max argued that we should add another *ought* to our list: the abolition of nuclear weapons.

Today, the critical importance of coming to grips with the nuclear threat is greater than ever. We are in danger of stalling out in the effort to diminish and, in the end, eliminate the nuclear threat. We live in an era in which terrorist groups would not shrink from using a nuclear weapon of the size used at Hiroshima if they could get their hands on one. The threat of proliferation, illustrated by the nuclear ambitions of Iran and North Korea, is all too real, as are the explosive possibilities emanating from the tensions between nuclear-armed Pakistan and India.

So the threats of proliferation and use of nuclear weapons are great, and greatly disturbing. If North Korea succeeds in the development of a long-range missile, the scope of its threat is enhanced. North Korea is also a clandestine supplier of nuclear material to other countries. If Iran succeeds in its effort to create a nuclear weapon capability, other states in its neighborhood will follow. More ominously, Iran continually expresses its determination to wipe out Israel. We are at a difficult tipping point. Negotiations with Iran appear to be a sham, and we are close—and

---

8. George P. Shultz, William Perry, Henry Kissinger, and Sam Nunn, "Deterrence in the Age of Nuclear Proliferation," *The Wall Street Journal,* March 7, 2011.

moving closer day by day—to the point where major military action may be the only option.

But we should remember that major action is not the only approach. In his book *Taking on Iran* (2012), my colleague Abe Sofaer calls attention to the fact that Iran has attacked and continues to attack Americans and our allies without any response from the United States. For example, Iran has supplied arms to fighters in Iraq and Afghanistan that enable the killing of Americans, and it was behind the attempted assassination of the Saudi ambassador to the United States on US soil. On November 1, 2012, Iran fired at an unarmed US drone over international waters, with no real reaction. Limited but effective responses on targets removed from population centers would make it clear to Iran's leaders that we know what they are doing and we are ready to act in defense of our interests. Such exercises of strength would increase the prospect of successful negotiations and a peaceful outcome.

India and Pakistan present completely different issues. The urgent need is to diminish tensions between them and thereby lessen the need for nuclear weapons and reduce the possibility of their use. Work is under way on this subject and some progress has been made, particularly in encouraging greater flows of trade and other economic engagements between the two countries. Clearly, the way ahead will be long, difficult, and dangerous. This problem is complicated by tensions between India and China, with its impressive and somewhat obscure nuclear-weapons program.

Where do we go from here beyond working at the tough issues just discussed? We need to stay on the offensive, continuing to expand positive efforts to move the world in the direction of reduced reliance on nuclear weapons with the goal of eliminating them entirely. One obvious line of work stems from the connection of the vision of a world free of nuclear weapons with the important steps needed to get to that goal. We need to move beyond the expectation of further reductions in US and Russian arsenals, which are clearly needed. The steps call for work on a global scale with the many countries that have an interest and a stake in this area. We must create what might be called a Joint Nuclear Enterprise—a way of enlisting all the relevant nations to work toward taking the steps that will lead to a world free of nuclear weapons.

The unanimous vote in the UN Security Council on September 24, 2009, was an important marker. Periodic meetings of the 189 nations that are signatories of the Non-Proliferation Treaty are also cause for optimism. In addition, with strong leadership by the United States, two meetings of some forty heads of government have been held to discuss ways to gain better control of fissile material. This model could be expanded to include other key steps, recognizing that each one, individually, will make the world safer while accelerating movement toward the ultimate goal of the total elimination of nuclear weapons. My three colleagues and I expand on this idea in an op-ed that appears as the last entry in the appendix to this chapter.

Difficult work and real dangers lie ahead. We must move forward with firm resolve, remembering an existential fact. The devastation that might result from the use of even one thermonuclear weapon, infinitely more powerful than the one that hit Hiroshima, underlines the vital importance for all humanity of this effort to rid the world of nuclear weapons.

CHAPTER EIGHT

Final Reflections

What can be done to recapture the sense of relative stability in the world that emerged from the creative efforts of statesmen after the end of World War II? The preceding chapters contain some recommendations for action on six critical issues: how to govern better, reignite our economy, take advantage of new energy opportunities, deal more effectively with the problems posed by addictive drugs, conduct a stronger diplomacy, and get control of the existential threat posed by nuclear weapons. Where do we go from here?

Freedom and American Exceptionalism

As described in chapter 1, the past century has seen war, economic distress, social upheaval, and terror. It has also been an era of positive transformation in the human condition that has been more dramatic than at any time in history. These hopeful changes have been shaped by America's exceptional engagement with the world and its emphasis on political and economic freedom.

Freedom is the topic now in front of us as the Arab Awakening once again demonstrates the universal drive for liberation. Individual freedom is the essence of what it means to be human. Historically, however, freedom and democracy, its political form, have been elusive. The reality is that the majority of people throughout history have lived under autocratic or dictatorial regimes.

In view of the current fragmented and politically oriented debate in Washington and elsewhere on the appropriate relative roles of governmental authority and the private marketplace, it is essential to look at the broader picture in order to understand what is at stake. It is also encouraging to recognize that progress is possible, as the record shows. Each year, Freedom House, an outstanding organization, surveys the world and places countries into three categories: free, partly free, and not free.

In the decade 1980–1989, the number of free countries increased from 51 to 61. With the end of the Cold War and the breakup of the Soviet Union in the next decade (1990–1999), the number of free countries expanded to 88. So far in the twenty-first century, that picture has remained relatively unchanged.

American exceptionalism is defined by freedom. The founders' brilliant achievement was to design a democracy capable of thriving on a continental scale. They created a country in which everyone should have the opportunity to reap the rewards of their own hard work, ingenuity, or willingness to take risks. Over time, and often with great difficulty, including the devastating Civil War, the power of *ought*—the recognition that "all men are created equal"—closed in on reality. Millions of people eventually came to America and migrated across a great continent to enjoy the benefits of freedom. Alexis de Tocqueville recognized that democracy, if it were to succeed as what he sensed was a force of history, would depend on what Americans made of their freedom. The world took careful note as it watched America wage its monumental Civil War to end slavery and then amend the Constitution to guarantee in law the freedoms won in battle.

The rise of wealth and military might tempted the United States to become one of the imperial powers that dominated the world in the early twentieth century. It soon turned away from overseas territorial control and entered World War I as a force for freedom. As that war was ending, President Wilson made imperial Germany's call for an armistice conditional on the kaiser's abdication and the establishment of republican government.

In the 1920s and 1930s, the United States stepped away from world politics only to find itself indispensable in dealing with the growing aggressions of imperial Japan and the Third Reich. During World War II, the United States assumed an expanded role as leader of the free world against regimes bent on destroying world order. In the postwar years, the United States helped Germany and Japan become democracies, pillars of responsible government, and market-based economies along with other countries in Europe and Asia. Then, through the long decades of the Cold War, fraught with anxiety, the United States upheld the cause of freedom against a Marxist-Leninist ideology utterly opposed to every element of the established international system, including the state, diplomacy, international law, human rights, open trade, and market economics.

From the very outset of the Cold War, the United States uniquely set and supported a global agenda that laid the foundation for world progress ever since. And that progress has centered on freedom: a market-based open-trading global economy; freedom of expression, which naturally called forth democratization; and adherence to an international system that included the juridical doctrine of the equality of states. Just as individuals could be citizens of a state, so states could be citizens of a world order with democratic freedoms, as we Americans urged. The United States also promoted collective security as the preferred way to contain or turn back aggression. When collective security proved unattainable, the United States had the courage, and weathered the political criticism, when necessary, to act unilaterally in defending world order.

In recent years, the idea has emerged that the world should not expect the United States to continue the constructive leading role it has taken in the past. It is imperative to recognize that abandoning that role would result in a world that in no way resembles the one we have known for three-quarters of a century.

Strategic decisions are now required in every major category of national interest and international security. Americans must decide what kind of nation the United States will be, whether to follow the European social model or revitalize the unique American way. Only the latter is capable of getting the economy on track with sustainable, strong growth without inflation. Reviving the American approach also will allow continuing military strength from which the United States can meet new versions of old challenges, maintaining the freedom of the seas through a strong navy and a ratified Law of the Sea Treaty and confronting the unprecedented problems of cyberspace.

Research and development are at peak levels on the critical issues of energy, climate change, and health; breakthrough possibilities are in sight. But if these efforts falter, not only will there be a slowdown in progress but adversarial trends will worsen. America has been a leader in R&D in many areas, including medical science and pharmaceutical breakthroughs for the betterment of the world. Failure to control the huge costs of growing entitlement programs will prevent the development of life-enhancing innovations. More fundamentally, investment in R&D and its accompanying entrepreneurship is indispensable to propelling a growth economy upon which everything else depends.

Greater investment in R&D and entrepreneurship will allow us to play from a strong hand, conducting a more effective diplomacy for the balanced management of big power relations and employing international organizations as responsible mechanisms for peace, progress, and democratization. The United States must once again carry the torch of freedom.

The Urgent Need for a Strong United States

As we have seen, the world at this moment is awash in change. The reemergence of the United States as a strong, respected player on the global stage is the key to a more coherent future. As in the Reagan era, we Americans need to stand tall, proud of our heritage.

The United States could lead at the end of World War II because it was the only country left standing. As we found our own way to a vibrant and successful economy and as we continued to flourish as an open and democratic country, the United States became an example to the world. In many ways, our nation was justifiably regarded as a shining city on a hill.

The United States must get its economic house in order and once again produce a healthy and expanding economy without inflation. Today, our economy is lackluster at best and our democratic friends in Europe are in the midst of a financial crisis. Our first step, therefore, should be to take the actions necessary to get our economy on track. These actions, discussed in chapter 3, are briefly summarized here:

- Put into place economic policies consistent with prosperity without inflation and leave them there. Emphasize permanent rather than temporary measures. This will entail sharp reform in the personal and corporate tax systems, stripping out preferences—largely used by the wealthy—and lowering rates for everyone.

- Reform the Social Security system by changing the indexing of benefits from wages to prices, and design a health-care system that provides universal access and in which consumers are more involved in the process. Greater consumer involvement will help get costs under control, especially as more information on prices and outcomes becomes available and as markets grow more competitive.
- Point spending toward the level of revenue that would be generated at high employment by the emerging tax system.
- Establish a simple-to-understand regulatory framework.
- Create the foundation for rules-based policies (as distinct from discretionary and unpredictable policies) by the Federal Reserve as the system works its way out of excessive support for the debt of the US Treasury.

As the committee I chaired in 1980 counseled President-elect Reagan on general principles, sharp change in present economic policy is an absolute necessity. Though our problems are severe, they are not intractable. Having been produced by government policy, they can be redressed by a change in policy. Here are the key points:

- The essence of good policy is good strategy. The need for a long-term point of view is essential to allow for the time, the coherence, and the predictability so necessary for success.
- Consistency in policy is critical to effectiveness. Individuals and business enterprises plan on a long-range basis. They require an environment in which they can conduct their affairs with confidence.
- The success of economic policy will be a direct reflection of our ability to maintain a steady course. Rough times will come and crises of one kind or another—some small, some of great moment—will arise. Sustained effort through these testing times requires a public that understands and supports the policies that are in place. Of equal and related importance is an informed and supportive Congress.

The United States can regain its leadership on the world's stage on the basis of economic and military strength and confidence in the freedoms we advocate and demonstrate. Now is the time for America to take a leading role in the creation of a new global economic and security commons, the advantages of which will benefit countries around the world, including the United States.

America has arrived at a fundamental turning point in its history. We must raise our sights, realizing that what is at stake is nothing less than the strength and security of this great nation for generations to come.

The United States and its allies have difficult work ahead. The need is clear, the path is well marked, and the stakes are monumental. Let us maintain a sense of urgency as we take the bold actions required to secure our future.

Epilogue

As I was completing work on this book, two great occasions in my life underlined the importance of recent history and of personal relationships.

On May 24, 2012, I was awarded the Kissinger Prize at an event sponsored by the American Academy in Berlin. The large audience included Germany's foreign minister and finance minister. Two friends of long standing with whom I served at critical times offered tributes containing important bits of history. Helmut Schmidt was finance minister (and, subsequently, chancellor) of West Germany when I was secretary of the treasury. We worked together diligently on vital issues and developed a deep friendship, and Helmut's advice and counsel were available and essential to me in subsequent posts. Henry Kissinger, whom I have known for four decades, was a cabinet colleague at pivotal times and remains a close friend and wise counselor to this day. His patriotism and grasp of world events have always inspired and educated me.

Two weeks after the event in Berlin, I traveled to the magnificent Ronald Reagan Presidential Foundation and Library in Simi Valley, California. There, on June 5, 2012, I was taken by surprise as I was ushered into a special ceremony officially dedicating the Global Issues and Reagan-Gorbachev Summit Galleries in my honor. A photograph of the plaque that hangs in the exhibition space and a gracious letter from Nancy Reagan, my friend of many years, are found in the photo section.

These momentous events reminded me of the occasion on January 19, 1989, when, along with former Senate majority leader and US ambassador to Japan Mike Mansfield, I received the Presidential Medal of Freedom. The remarks that President Reagan, Mike, and I made on the crucial importance of freedom are reprinted here. This book concludes with my tribute to Ronald Reagan, delivered on June 9, 2004, as he lay in state in the Capitol Rotunda in Washington, DC.

Comments by Helmut Schmidt
2012 Henry A. Kissinger Award Ceremony
Berlin, Germany
May 24, 2012

Ladies and gentlemen,

The American Academy in Berlin gave me an unexpected pleasure this spring in asking me to deliver a citation honoring George Shultz.

You will know or at least guess, George, that I was only too happy to undertake this duty. I am glad to have this very official opportunity, at the end of my life, to express to you in very personal terms my confidence in your steadiness, my trust in the constancy of your fundamental ethical convictions, and my confidence in your fairness to each and every one of your interlocutors and negotiating partners.

In awarding you the Henry A. Kissinger Prize here on German soil today, the board undoubtedly wishes to express its appreciation of your entire life's work. George P. Shultz, American citizen, has served his country in many different ways: as a soldier in the Marine Corps in East Asia during the Second World War, as professor and dean in Chicago, as an adviser and secretary in various departments in Washington, DC, as a businessman heading the Bechtel Group on the West Coast, as secretary of state for over six years, and finally as a professor once more.

Today you are a professor-at-large, responsible for the major, decisive questions facing the world—and especially for the necessary steps towards a nuclear-weapon-free world. As a politician you are a man of your party, but your supreme loyalty has always been to the welfare of your country. This prize recognizes your life as an American patriot.

With just a few exceptions, I have been able to follow my friend's career only from a great distance. During Hitler's World War we stood on opposite sides. I had to become a soldier in 1937. Because of my father's illegitimacy and my Jewish grandfather, I had not become a

Nazi. With a lot of good luck and a large measure of fear, my family succeeded in keeping this secret right up until my father's death. This notwithstanding, it was only in the fall of 1944 that I realized the Nazis were criminals.

But I had known since 1941 that Germany was going to lose the war. And I also knew that what we were fighting for was bad. George was fighting for the right thing, a good thing.

The end of Hitler's world war was inevitable. But in the wake of the ensuing chaos in Germany and the division of my country into four zones of occupation, the Americans introduced monetary reform in the three Western zones in 1948, and this, in combination with the Marshall Plan, was a success. Above all, under American aegis, the three Western zones became the Bonn Republic in 1949.

From that point on, things gradually got better in Germany. In 1990, it was once again the energetic leadership of an American president that made unification with the GDR possible. Germany owes the alliance with the United States far more than the US owes the Germans.

It is now 40 years since we first met when we were our countries' finance ministers. Back then, your predecessor, John Connally, told the Europeans: "The dollar is our currency, but it is your problem." At the time, the United States was in the process of gradually but then rapidly abandoning the Bretton Woods system of fixed but adjustable exchange rates by devaluing the dollar. It felt that its public sector borrowing was more important than maintaining a fixed dollar exchange rate. George Shultz shared this opinion.

But at the same time George understood the resistance on the part of the Europeans and Japanese and invited their leading finance ministers to a joint discussion of the situation. This was the Library Group (so called because it met in the library of the White House in Washington). Within this group there developed a fundamental trust between George Shultz on the one hand and Takeo Fukuda, Valéry Giscard d'Estaing, Tony Barber, and myself on the other. In the fall of 1975 this developed into what was to become the annual G7 Summit, Italy and Canada soon having joined in.

Over a year earlier, in March 1974, George had called to tell me he was going to resign that day because of Watergate. His sense of morals transcended party loyalty. In the summer of 1975, when President Gerald Ford asked me in Helsinki whom he should appoint as sherpa for the meeting, I said: "Why don't you take George Shultz as sherpa?" which he then did.

Seven years later, in June 1982—Ronald Reagan had been in office for a year and a half and had already had one secretary of state—George told me the president wanted him to take up the post. I shared neither Reagan's Star Wars illusion nor George Shultz's preference for his conservative president. But I knew Shultz and so I placed my trust in his doggedness. So all I said in response was: "In the long run you will prevail because President Reagan cannot afford a third mistake."

The proof of the pudding came a few years later in Reykjavik 1986. The Reykjavik Summit between Presidents Reagan and Gorbachev plus their foreign secretaries was generally considered a failure. But in fact it became the watershed in the Cold War.

The two world powers had come closer than ever before and George Shultz diligently brought his president to understand that Gorbachev was a trustworthy man. And only a little later, this mutually shared feeling led to the INF treaty, which was the very first real disarmament treaty between the then two world powers. It paved the way, as much as did Solidarnosc in Poland and Charta 77 in Czechoslovakia, for the great change that was to happen in Europe in 1990.

In 1988, with the end of the Reagan administration, George Shultz became a private citizen again. But he continued to serve his country in manifold ways. For instance, as a professor at Stanford, he again established an international group, which included the Chinese. And he particularly included Lee Kuan Yew as an outstandingly successful and at the same time knowledgeable critical observer of China on its way to regaining the status of a world power.

Today everybody knows that Russia, as a successor state of the Soviet Union, is still a world power militarily. But China has become an economic and financial world power and is on its way to developing once again into a world power in general. Nobody has expressed the need to understand this fact of life better than Henry Kissinger. In his recent book, *On China,* he stresses the need to respect the more than 4,000 years of Chinese civilization, as well as the necessity of cooperation—while at the same time remaining technological and economic competitors.

I have tried to describe the career of my friend George Shultz from a German point of view and from a very personal point of view as well.

For a long time I have agreed with Henry, who once wrote: "If I have to name an American to whom I would entrust the nation in a crisis, it would be George Shultz."

Let me in conclusion quote another friend of mine, now long deceased, Herbert Weichmann. Being a Jew, Weichmann had to flee Germany and he became an American citizen. In 1946 he returned to his original home country and in the end became the mayor of my home city, Hamburg. In June 1982—almost exactly 30 years ago—he addressed the German Bundestag. And in his speech, one of the wisdoms of his life was: "Die Weisheit der Demokratie ist schließlich die Weisheit des Kompromisses" ("In the end the wisdom of democracy lies in the wisdom of compromise"). That could have been said by George Shultz. But George might have added: It needs a personal relationship and it needs trust in your adversaries' veraciousness (Wahrheitsliebe).

The Declaration of Independence and the foundation of the United States of America, its Constitution and the Bill of Rights—all these globally important events took place more than 200 years ago. George Shultz was born only in 1920. So far he has lived for over 91 years—but what a life! He could not meet George Washington or Thomas Jefferson, nor did he meet Abraham Lincoln. Instead he became a contemporary of Franklin Roosevelt, of Harry Truman, of George Kennan, of George Marshall, of Eisenhower, and of Kennedy. Since then he has served as a colleague and as a successor of Henry Kissinger. He has served the continuity of American grand strategy.

George, you are also one of those American leaders who established friendship with the Germans—after two world wars in which we Germans had been your enemies. And for that I will ever remain your thankful friend.

Comments by Henry A. Kissinger
2012 Henry A. Kissinger Award Ceremony
Berlin, Germany
May 24, 2012

It is a moving occasion to share this platform with two men who have been an inspiration to me for most of my political life. I went with George and Helmut through the Cold War; I admired their actions in the formation of the European Union and the strengthening of the Atlantic Alliance, and their reaction to the redistribution of the center of gravity of the world's power centers towards formerly colonial regions. It has been an honor to be their contemporary.

Never before has an international order included all the continents. Nor, until now, was it possible to view events across the world in real time. Modern weapons make war between major powers—especially nuclear powers—all but unthinkable. But at the same time, they have created possibilities for disturbances of international order by non-state groups whose primary purpose is the propagation of chaos.

Such times call for guides to lead us through their complexities. What qualities are required for such leadership? They are, above all, character and courage. Character, because the turmoil of our period presents itself in ambiguous form. With the pros and cons of major decisions very close—often "51–49"—it requires strength of character to make the choice, and courage to help lead a society, in the face of opposition from those wedded to the more familiar, from where it is to where it has never been.

In my memoirs, I wrote that there was no position in government for which George Shultz would not be my first choice. No other public figure has held so many positions of trust: secretary of labor, director of the Office of Management and Budget, secretary of the treasury, secretary of state. His resolve steadied the nation in challenging times. His optimism and vision gave our society the confidence to face the tasks ahead of it.

George Shultz served as secretary of state when the security policy of deterrence was based on the doctrine of mutual assured destruction. Its basic tenet was that the total vulnerability of a country's own population represented the ultimate deterrent. But a mutual suicide pact could not be sustained as the permanent principle of international order, even less so in a time when nuclear weapons spread to ever more countries. George Shultz was one of the first leaders to articulate this as a matter of American policy. At Reykjavik, he and President Reagan put forward a sweeping plan to overcome the existential threat to civilization posed by nuclear weapons. Ahead of its time then, its basic objectives have given impetus to governmental and private initiatives ever since, several of them under George Shultz's leadership.

Beyond the weapons field, George Shultz applied his questing mind to other important issues. In 1984, he made the first major American governmental speech on political terrorism at a time when leading political figures were dealing with it largely as a criminal matter. In 1986, he delivered the first major assessment of the Information Age, providing meaning for this new phenomenon long before the spread of the Internet.

George Shultz's dogged determination to advance the cause of peace in the Middle East gave Israel the confidence to adopt an open economic approach, put in place a "quality of life" program for Palestinians, and finally gained acceptance of principles enabling both parties to negotiate. When George Shultz was secretary of the treasury, the globalized world was given an institutional forum in the evolution of the European Union and the elaboration of the Atlantic partnership as parts of a global design. The friendship between George Shultz and Helmut Schmidt was a principal driving force of this effort.

George's reach did not end when he left office. He speaks and writes and briefs political leaders in the US and abroad on energy, nuclear disarmament, drug policy, diplomacy, and, perhaps most consequentially for long-term global trends, demography. He has an exceptional ability to create study groups on these subjects, using his prestige to assemble the most thoughtful participants and his open-mindedness and commitment to encourage their purposes.

How has George Shultz been able to make such vital contributions to such a range of issues? Perhaps, most of all, because he embodies an essential American characteristic. Most societies mourn a golden age conceived to have existed in a distant past. America's golden age has always been derived from faith in the limitless possibilities of the future. George has approached every problem with this spirit of optimism and pragmatic determination. His first principle, which I have heard him invoke often, is that in a discussion or negotiation, neither side should allow itself to be tempted to overlook a problem for fear of spoiling a good relationship. It is, in George's view, their obligation to raise it, take off the sharp edges by respect for the other point of view, and thereby move to a better world.

As secretary of labor, George served as head of a task force on energy. George laid down principles which enabled the Nixon administration to work with its allies to overcome the energy crisis of the 1970s. In the effort to devise a common program for the consuming nations most affected by the Arab oil embargo, George—who, at this point, held no formal government position—was enlisted as an indispensable troubleshooter. The formation of the International Energy Agency, in which Helmut Schmidt played such a seminal role, owed a great deal to the behind-the-scenes advice of George Shultz.

As treasury secretary, he—and Helmut Schmidt—took the lead in creating a new and highly productive set of personal relationships among the finance ministers of the leading economic nations. They began with a meeting in the White House Library. This "Library Group" was instrumental in the historic revision of the Bretton Woods system.

As a private citizen during the Ford administration, George continued to lend his considerable talents to forging economic cooperation among the Western democracies. He did so in a manner emblematic of the confidence he inspired. President Ford selected George as his personal point of contact with the heads of major Western economies. These consultations laid the foundation for the Rambouillet Summit of the then-G5 in November 1975. That summit, an exceptionally effective meeting of heads of state, was the forerunner of what would become the G7, the G8, and, eventually, today's G20.

As secretary of state, George emphasized the importance of close personal relationships with his counterparts, starting with a backyard barbecue at his Washington home for the foreign minister of Japan. A comparable bond with the leaders of Canada and Mexico brought about an unprecedented North American three-country bond—the forerunner of NAFTA. These investments in personal relationships reflected his conviction that—whatever their political or ideological differences—he and his counterparts were engaged in a common enterprise: building a shared world order that would both fulfill the imperatives of peace and give increased scope to human ingenuity and the desire for progress.

In the same spirit, George conducted an active diplomacy with the Soviet Union against the bitter opposition of leading members of the Reagan administration (but not the president himself). At the same time, he worked closely with Western European counterparts, many of whom faced significant domestic opposition for their commitment to transatlantic principles of defense. George navigated this passage with skill, perspicacity, and no little courage. This brought about the successful INF Treaty, which resulted in a significant reduction of nuclear deployments in Europe, and the global elimination of an entire class of nuclear weapons—a signal contribution to ending the Cold War.

Let me conclude with a personal word. No colleague has ever matched the scope and impact on me of George Shultz. And there was no individual I felt more confident turning to for steady wisdom in a crisis than George. Throughout my government service, I always involved George Shultz in key decisions, even when they were not strictly in his sphere of responsibility. The most notable example occurred when, at the beginning of Watergate, President Nixon dismissed his senior White House staff. George Shultz, Arthur Burns, and I reviewed matters addressed to the president during the weeks until a new chief of staff was appointed.

The reason for George Shultz's impact is his towering integrity. Some moments stand out: his refusal to use his authority as treasury secretary to carry out a plan to use Internal Revenue Service tax audits as a political weapon; or to accept directives to require State Department officers to undergo regular lie-detector tests. George's core belief was that "trust is the coin of the realm," and if you want your people to be trustworthy, you have to start by trusting them. Ralph Waldo Emerson said an institution is the lengthened shadow of a man. This has been the impact of George Shultz on the many institutions in which he has been involved in America and around the world. As we meet the challenges of an era of rapid and unprecedented change in international order, we are fortunate to work in George's "shadow"—with his influence and example extending to so many areas of human endeavor. Thanks to George, we have an Atlantic alliance that is improved; a world economy and international financial system characterized by greater cooperation among the major industrial powers; an academic literature that is richer and more varied; and a community of statesmen, scholars, scientists, and activists newly dedicated to bringing about a world in which nuclear weapons are reduced, never used, and eventually eliminated.

It is my great honor to participate in an occasion that involves two men seminal in my life and in the cause of freedom. It is in this spirit that I would now ask George to come forward and accept the American Academy in Berlin 2012 Kissinger Prize.

Remarks by President Reagan, George P. Shultz, and Mike Mansfield

Medal of Freedom Award Ceremony
Washington, DC
January 19, 1989

The President. Truly, one of the privileges of this office which I've found the greatest joy in exercising has been the opportunity to present our nation's highest civilian honor, the Medal of Freedom. To stand, as I have had the honor of doing, with the recipients of this award has been to stand with the flesh and blood and spirit that is the greatness of America, men and women who have so greatly served our nation and helped keep her free. The contribution of each recipient has been unique and noteworthy, and today is no exception, as we honor two remarkable Americans: Mike Mansfield and George Shultz.

Mike Mansfield has dedicated the entirety of a very long and productive lifetime to public service. He served in both Houses of Congress, spanning seven presidents, and held the post of Senate majority leader longer than any other person. A former professor of Far Eastern history, he played an important part in shaping America's Asian policy, serving on both the House Foreign Affairs Committee and the Senate Foreign Relations Committee and then as our ambassador to Japan. For a sizable portion of America's history as a nation, Mike Mansfield has been in service to his country.

George Shultz—why did my voice crack just as I got to you— [laughter]—George Shultz has been a marine, an academic, a businessman, and a public servant. He has held four Cabinet-level posts, distinguishing himself as a secretary of labor, director of the Office of Management and Budget, treasury secretary, and finally as one of America's great secretaries of state. Over the last six and a half years, in managing our foreign policy, he has served wisely and met great challenges and great opportunities. George Shultz has helped to make the world a freer and more peaceful place.

And there's nothing so precious and irreplaceable as America's freedom. In a speech I gave 25 years ago, I told a story that I think bears repeating. Two friends of mine were talking to a refugee from Communist Cuba. He had escaped from Castro, and as he told the story of his horrible experiences, one of my friends turned to the other and said, "We don't know how lucky we are." And the Cuban stopped and said, "How lucky you are? I had someplace to escape to."

Well, no, America's freedom does not belong to just one nation. We're custodians of freedom for the world. In Philadelphia, two centuries ago, James Allen wrote in his diary that "If we fail, liberty no longer continues an inhabitant of this globe." Well, we didn't fail. And still, we must not fail. For freedom is not the property of one generation; it's the obligation of this and every generation. It's our duty to protect it and expand it and pass it undiminished to those still unborn.

Now, tomorrow is a special day for me. I'm going to receive my gold watch. And since this is the last speech that I will give as president, I think it's fitting to leave one final thought, an observation about a country which I love. It was stated best in a letter I received not long ago. A man wrote me and said: "You can go to live in France, but you cannot become a Frenchman. You can go to live in Germany or Turkey or Japan, but you cannot become a German, a Turk, or a Japanese. But anyone, from any corner of the Earth, can come to live in America and become an American."

Yes, the torch of Lady Liberty symbolizes our freedom and represents our heritage, the compact with our parents, our grandparents, and our ancestors. It is that lady who gives us our great and special place in the world. For it's the great life force of each generation of new Americans that guarantees that America's triumph shall continue unsurpassed into the next century and beyond. Other countries may seek to compete with us; but in one vital area, as a beacon of freedom and opportunity that draws the people of the world, no country on Earth comes close.

This, I believe, is one of the most important sources of America's greatness. We lead the world because, unique among nations, we draw our people—our strength—from every country and every corner of the world. And by doing so we continuously renew and enrich our nation. While other countries cling to the stale past, here in America we breathe life into dreams. We create the future, and the world follows us into tomorrow. Thanks to each wave of new arrivals to this land of opportunity, we're a nation forever young, forever bursting with energy and new ideas, and always on the cutting edge, always leading the world to the next frontier. This quality is vital to our future as a nation. If we ever closed the door to new Americans, our leadership in the world would soon be lost.

A number of years ago, an American student traveling in Europe took an East German ship across the Baltic Sea. One of the ship's crewmembers from East Germany, a man in his sixties, struck up a conversation with the American student. After a while the student asked the man how he had learned such good English. And the man explained that he had once lived in America. He said that for over a year he had worked as a farmer in Oklahoma and California, that he had planted tomatoes and picked ripe melons. It was, the man said, the happiest time of his life. Well, the student, who had seen the awful conditions behind the Iron Curtain, blurted out the question, "Well, why did you ever leave?" "I had to," he said, "the war ended." The man had been in America as a German prisoner of war.

Now, I don't tell this story to make the case for former POWs. Instead, I tell this story just to remind you of the magical, intoxicating power of America. We may sometimes forget it, but others do not. Even a man from a country at war with the United States, while held here as a prisoner, could fall in love with us. Those who become American citizens love this country even more. And that's why the Statue of Liberty lifts her lamp to welcome them to the golden door.

It is bold men and women, yearning for freedom and opportunity, who leave their homelands and come to a new country to start their lives over. They believe in the American dream. And over and over, they make it come true for themselves, for their children, and for others. They give more than they receive. They labor and succeed. And often they are entrepreneurs. But their greatest contribution is more than economic, because they understand in a special way how glorious it is to be an American. They renew our pride and gratitude in the United States of America, the greatest, freest nation in the world—the last, best hope of man on Earth.

The Medal of Freedom represents the reverence the American people have for liberty, and it honors the men and women who through their lives do greatest honor to that freedom. The lives of the two men we honor here today tell a story about freedom and all its possibilities and responsibilities, and, well, those that inhere in each free man and woman and those that fall upon a great and free nation. Our honorees have dedicated their lives to preserving and protecting America's freedom. They have engaged themselves in the larger cause, that of humanity and of the world, to help extend freedom to people of other lands. There is no task more fitting for Americans than that.

So, I will now read the citations for our two very distinguished award recipients and present to them their medals. Perhaps I should mention that our first recipient today—the one who calls me kid—[laughter]—is the son of immigrants, from a country called Ireland.

And now, if Michael Mansfield and George Shultz would please come forward.

"During World War I, Mike Mansfield, not yet 15, enlisted in the United States Navy, crossing the Atlantic seven times before he was discharged. His service to country would span seven decades and would help shape America's destiny as a Pacific power. Through 34 years in Congress—including 16 as Senate majority leader—and with more than a decade as US Ambassador to Japan, Mike Mansfield has set his indelible mark upon American foreign policy and distinguished himself as a dedicated public servant and loyal American."

Ambassador Mansfield. Mr. President, First Lady, Mr. Secretary of State and Mrs. Shultz, Ambassador Matsunaga and Mrs. Matsunaga, my former colleagues from both the House and the Senate, our distinguished guests, ladies and gentlemen, I can't begin to express in words, Mr. President, my deep appreciation for what you've said about me and the encouragement which you've given me in my post as your ambassador, your personal representative, our country's ambassador to Japan.

However, I think that much of the credit should go to Maureen, my wife, who down through the years has been such a wonderful helpmate; whose advice, counsel, and understanding I appreciated; who worked harder at any job I've had and received little credit in the process. So, I want to say how much I owe to her, how much I'm indebted to her; how much I appreciate what the president has said—who has laid out a sound policy for our future in the Pacific and East Asia. I appreciate the advice and counsel that George Shultz has given to me from time to time. And I appreciate the fact that, for the first time in memory, that we have both a president of the United States and a secretary of state who are actively interested in the Pacific, in Japan, and in East Asia. I anticipate that the policies these men have laid down will be continued.

In conclusion, we may recall that Robert Sandburg [Frost], one of our poets, said on a certain occasion, there are things to do, miles to go, and promises to keep before we sleep. Well, Maureen and I have traveled many miles. We have had and still have things to do. And we still have the promises we made over half a century ago when we were joined together. So, to her I want to give special thanks for all that she has been able to do with me. And to the President and Nancy, my thanks, my appreciation for their thoughtfulness and consideration. Thank you very much.

The President. "Unyieldingly dedicated to the protection of the American national interest, the advancement of freedom and human rights, the battle against tyranny, and reductions in nuclear arms, George P. Shultz has presided over the Department of State during one of the most critical periods in the history of this nation's foreign policy. For years of public service and his vital part in inaugurating a new era of hope in foreign policy, his countrymen honor him."

Secretary Shultz. Mr. President, you know, O'Bie [Helena Shultz] has been traveling a million miles around the world with me. So, it's been a great partnership. But, Mr. President, I feel very special about receiving this award from you, and let me explain why. There's a phrase that's catching on—"the Reagan years." There's a ring to it. And, Mr. President, it is the ring of freedom. You have advocated it, fought for it. You have known that the price of freedom is eternal vigilance. You have known this is a matter of principle on which you don't compromise. You have known that there are times when it requires action—sometimes, at least initially, not necessarily popular action—but you have to do it.

You have also known—and I've heard you say many times—that the strength comes from "We the People," that we get our legitimacy and you get your legitimacy as president from the people. And you've never been in any doubt, and none of us have, about who we came here to serve: the American people.

And I see you there with your arm around Nancy. I had the privilege of going with Nancy a couple of months ago to the United Nations where she spoke about drugs. And she had the courage to say that one of the root causes of this worldwide problem is use of drugs in the United States. And we have to say no. So Nancy, too, has been a fighter for freedom—freedom from drugs. And we love you for it and revere you for it, Nancy.

So, all of these things make me especially proud to have served with you, to have been your secretary of state. And to receive a medal from you called the Medal of Freedom has a significance for my life and O'Bie's life and my children that we will never forget.

Thank you, Mr. President.

Tribute to Ronald Reagan
George P. Shultz
June 9, 2004

We have lost Ronald Reagan, but his ideas remain with us, as vital as ever. We can remember the gifts he gave us—his advocacy of freedom, his contributions to our security, his belief in America, and his restoration of our belief in ourselves.

When he took office as governor of California, Ronald Reagan took responsibility for a state that was in rocky shape; when he left office, California was golden again. When Ronald Reagan took office as the president of the United States, the country was adrift, inflation was out of control, the economy was in the doldrums, and the Cold War was as cold as it had ever been. When he left office, inflation was under control, the economy was expanding, the Cold War was all over but the shouting, and America once again stood tall.

Ronald Reagan brought so much to this country. He started with carefully thought-out ideas and he put them to work effectively. He had a strong and constructive agenda, much of it labeled impossible and unattainable in the early years of his presidency. He challenged the conventional wisdom: on arms control, on the possibility of movement toward freedom in the Communist-dominated world, on the need to stand up to Iran in the Persian Gulf, on the superiority of market- and enterprise-based economies. The world learned when Ronald Reagan faced down the air-traffic controllers in 1981 that he could dig in and fight to win. The world learned in Grenada that he would use military force if needed. He did not accept that extensive political opposition doomed an attractive idea. He would fight resolutely for an idea, believing that, if it was valid, he could persuade the American people to support it. He changed the national and international agenda on issue after issue. He was an optimist; he spoke the vocabulary of opportunity. He had a vision of what he stood for and what we aspire to as a nation.

Ronald Reagan had and could express a clear and simple view of a complex world. Every Sunday he brought acorns down from Camp David to feed the squirrels outside the Oval Office. The squirrels at the White House hadn't had it so good since Ike cleared the area to put in a putting green. His most endearing aspect was his fundamental decency. He appealed to people's best hopes, not their fears; to their confidence rather than their doubts.

Ronald Reagan was a doer, a pragmatist, a man who enjoyed hard physical tasks, as in the ranch work he loved to do. But that brush clearing and fence fixing was a symbol, too; he wanted to be doing it himself because from the land came not only strength and clarity, but a vision—the vision of the West and the endless horizon. The American people liked Ronald Reagan and reelected him in one of the biggest landslides in history because he trusted them and he conveyed to them that they need not be bound, tied down by class, or race, or childhood misfortune, or poverty, or bureaucracy. They, the people, could make something of themselves; indeed, they could remake themselves, endlessly.

But beneath this pragmatic attitude lay a bedrock of principle and purpose with which I was proud to be associated. He believed in being strong enough to defend our interests, but he viewed that strength as a means, not an end in itself. Ronald Reagan had confidence in himself and in his ideas and was ready to negotiate from the strength so evident by the mid-1980s.

He was a fervent anti-Communist who could comprehend and believe that people everywhere would choose to throw off the Communist system if they ever had the chance. And he worked hard to give them that chance. He favored open trade because he had confidence in the ability of Americans to compete, and he had confidence that an integrated world economy would benefit America. He stuck to his agenda.

The points he made, however consummate the delivery, were unmistakably real in his mind and heart, an American creed: defend your country, value your family, make something of yourself, tell the government to get off your back, tell the tyrants to watch their step. Ronald Reagan conveyed simple truths that were especially welcome because "nowadays everything seems so complicated." What he said ran deep and wide among the people.

Reagan as president was a Republican, a conservative, a man of the right. But these labels will mislead historians who do not see beyond them, for Americans could see some of Ronald Reagan in themselves. You couldn't figure him out like a fact because to Reagan the main fact was a vision. He came from the heartland of the country, where people could be down-to-earth yet feel that the sky is the limit—not ashamed of, or cynical about, the American dream. Not far from Ronald Reagan's small town of Dixon, Illinois, is Jane Addams's small town of Cedarville; not far from Cedarville is Ulysses Grant's small town of Galena. And not far from Galena is Carl Sandburg's Galesburg. Reagan had something of them all: his heart going out to the people; his will ready to fight for the country; his voice able to move the nation. And, as Carl Sandburg wrote,

> The republic is a dream.
> Nothing happens unless first a dream.

Photographs appear in the order of their relevance to the text.

I present the Department of State's Distinguished Service Award to my friend Paul Nitze, July 28, 1988.

A New Year's golf game with Lee Trevino, President Reagan, Tom Watson, and our referee, Walter Annenberg, at Sunnylands, Rancho Mirage, December 31, 1988.

Burning Tree Club

WASHINGTON, D. C.

	1	2	3	4	5	6	7	8	9	TOTAL	← HOLE →	10	11	12	13	14	15	16	17	18	TOTAL	GRAND TOTAL
	396	449	136	397	359	396	391	174	455	3153	← FRONT TEE →	383	174	300	366	147	372	482	394	404	3022	6175
	424	489	165	434	385	428	413	198	481	3417	← BACK TEE →	411	196	340	396	161	404	496	423	418	3245	6662
	4	5	3	4	4	4	4	3	5	36	← PAR →	4	3	4	4	3	4	5	4	4	35	71
Arnold Palmer	5	4	3	3	4	4	4	3	4	34		4	3	3	3	4	4	6	4	4	35	69
George Smith	6	5	3	4	5	4	4	3	5	39		5	2	3	4	4	5	5	4	5	36	75
← HANDICAP STROKES →	5	11	17	1	13	3	9	15	7	OUT		6	16	14	10	18	2	8	12	4	IN	

AGGREGATE

← LOW BALL →

U.S.G.A. RULES

DATE 4/27/71

SCORER George P. Smith

ATTEST Arnold Palmer

Golfing with Arnold Palmer, I almost made it on the back nine, April 27, 1971.

(*Above*) I set one up for
Boris Becker, April 7, 1986.

(*Left*) Suited up for
Princeton football, 1941.

(*Above*) Under Secretary of
Labor James Hodgson and
I share comments about my
official Labor Department
portrait by C. J. Fox.

(*Left*) I argue against wage
and price controls during
a press conference in San
Francisco on May 28, 1970.

Senator Hugh Scott gave me his tally sheet after the vote to strike the Philadelphia Plan Rider to the Supplemental Appropriations Bill, September 18, 1969.

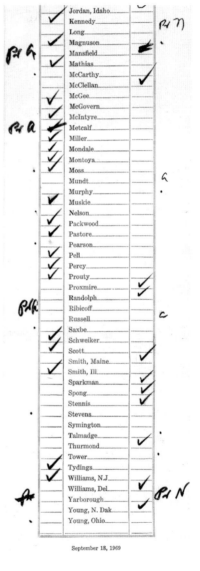

(*Above*) Discussing the state of the economy with Roy Ash, director of the Office of Management and Budget, President Nixon, and Herb Stein, chairman of the Council of Economic Advisers, September 6, 1973.

(*Left*) I am presented with an award from members of the United States Senate shortly before leaving the State Department, January 18, 1989. Beneath the photo, Kennedy wrote, "To Secretary Shultz, a tiger who burned bright in the eyes of Congress and the World. With respect, Ted Kennedy."

Pope Paul VI was generous with his time and counsel.

I'm listening, George - I'm listening!
love Nancy

Nancy Reagan and I confer after her speech on illegal drugs at the United Nations on October 25, 1988.

(*Left*) After a battle in one of the Palau Islands, ca. 1944.

(*Below*) Speaking to a Stanford alumni group in Paris, ca. 1990.

George Meany, who became a good friend during my Labor Department days, and I had constructive talks with President Nixon, ca. 1970.

Reporting to the president in Ireland, June 1984.

With two of my favorite Britishers: Lord Peter Carrington, who was Secretary-General of NATO, and Lord Geoffrey Howe, British Foreign Secretary, London, December 1985.

My Chinese counterpart, Wu Xuegian, and I accomplished a lot together, March 7, 1988.

An informal moment with King Hussein in the back yard of our home in Washington, DC, June 9, 1986.

WELL, AT LEAST THEY AGREE ON SOMETHING!

"The Shultz Plan" for Arab-Israeli peace, 1988. "Well, at least they agree on something."

With Yasuhiro Nakasone, former prime minister of Japan, a real leader in US-Japan relations, 1983.

With Shimon Peres and Yitzhak Shamir, former prime ministers of Israel, at Yad Vashem, the Holocaust Memorial, Jerusalem, May 10, 1985.

With Eduard Shevardnadze, Soviet Foreign Minister. We accomplished a lot together and developed a genuine friendship, September 25, 1985.

(*Left*) Still a smile despite tension on key issues. With Mikhail Gorbachev in Moscow, October 23, 1987.

(*Below*) All eyes on British Prime Minister Margaret Thatcher, London, June 2, 1988.

After the signing ceremony, cheers. President Reagan, Mikhail Gorbachev, and Eduard Shevardnadze, Soviet-US Summit, Moscow, May 29–June 2, 1988.

(*Above*) With my colleagues Sam Nunn, Henry Kissinger, and Bill Perry, working toward a world free of nuclear weapons, Hoover Institution, January 14, 2013.

(*Left*) With my colleague and fellow Princetonian, Sid Drell.

Reuniting with old friends, Helmut Schmidt and Henry Kissinger, in Berlin, where I received the American Academy in Berlin's Kissinger Prize on May 24, 2012.

★

The Global Issues and
Reagan-Gorbachev Summits Galleries
are dedicated in honor of

THE HONORABLE GEORGE P. SHULTZ
U.S. SECRETARY OF STATE
(1982-1989)
For his determination and courage
in pursuit of
President Ronald Reagan's commitment to
Peace through Strength.

Made possible by the generosity of
The S. D. Bechtel, Jr. Foundation

The Global Issues and Reagan-Gorbachev Summits Galleries at the Ronald Reagan Presidential Foundation in Simi Valley, CA, were dedicated in my honor on June 5, 2012.

June 7, 2012

Dear George,

I just wanted to drop you a note to let you know how pleased
I am to know that the Peace Through Strength Gallery at
Ronnie's Library has been dedicated to you. I'm told it was a
complete surprise (Charlotte is a great keeper of secrets!) and
that your family came to celebrate with you. I'm sure it was a
wonderful day for all of you.

Congratulations, George. I am thrilled to know that your work to
end the Cold War, as well as your invaluable support of Ronnie,
will always be remembered in this important part of the Reagan
Library museum. Please give my love to Charlotte, and I hope to
see you both before too long.

Fondly,

Nancy

The Honorable George Shultz
Hoover Institution
434 Galvez Mall
Stanford, CA 94305

A letter from my friend Nancy Reagan, June 7, 2012.

Conferring with the president in the Oval Office, February 24, 1988.

I receive the Medal of Freedom from President Reagan, January 19, 1989.

APPENDIX ONE

Our Challenges

Representation: A Lesson from My Days with Nixon
George P. Shultz
1993

I had no high expectations for the PLO before or after they met our conditions. Their capacity for change and accommodation was, by their past performance, a question mark at best. Nevertheless, in my discussions with the Israelis, I repeatedly emphasized the importance of having as opposite numbers in negotiations Palestinians who were not involved in terrorism but who were legitimate, who truly represented their constituencies. At some point, sooner or later, Israel would have to face up to that truth. Over an informal and private dinner at his official residence, I discussed my views with Prime Minister Yitzhak Shamir on April 15, 1988. "You need strong representation on the other side of any bargaining table," I said. To deliver on any deal, the deal makers must have the full confidence of their constituencies. To underscore my point, I told Shamir a long story about my involvement in the desegregation of the schools in the American South, an account meant to dramatize for him the importance of credible and legitimate representation if the outcome of a negotiation is to get support. He listened patiently as I recounted my own personal story from a page of US history.

As late as 1970, I told him, the schools in seven of our Southern states were still segregated by law. The *Brown v. Topeka Board of Education* decision by the Supreme Court in 1954 had declared such segregation unconstitutional. Time passed. Tension mounted. The whole subject was intensely controversial, with great arguments over the problems of busing in areas where the schools were segregated.

In March 1970, President Nixon had declared the *Brown v. Board of Education* decision to be "right in both constitutional and human terms" and expressed his intention to enforce the law. He decided to form a cabinet committee to work on this process in a direct, managerial way. Vice President Spiro Agnew was made chairman, and I was the vice chairman. Our problem was how to manage the transition to desegregated schools in the seven affected states: Alabama, Arkansas, Georgia, Louisiana, Mississippi, North Carolina, and South Carolina.

Agnew wanted no part of this problem and basically declined to participate in the committee's deliberations. So I wound up as de facto chairman. I had strong help from Presidential Counselor Pat Moynihan, Special Counsel Len Garment, and Ed Morgan, a savvy former advance man for the president. I first formed biracial committees in each of the seven states. We determined, with the president's agreement, that politics should have nothing to do with the selection of the people for these committees. We wanted people in equal numbers of black and white who were truly representative of their constituencies. And so, with great care, we picked strong, respected leaders from each of these states.

This was a key point. I told Shamir, "We didn't pick people who agreed with us or with each other. We picked people who were respected by those they would represent."

The first group invited to Washington in the late spring of 1970 came from Mississippi. I took them into the Roosevelt Room of the White House, right opposite the president's Oval Office, and started in. The discussion was civil, but the deep divisions were evident. The blacks argued that desegregation of the schools would be good for education and that it was absolutely essential. The whites were resistant. Both sides were tough but truly representative. I let them argue and get it out of their systems. There came a point in the meeting, after about two hours— and this happened with regularity as groups from the other states came in—when I felt that it was time to shift gears. By prearrangement, I had John Mitchell standing by. He was known throughout the South as the tough guy, and on the whole was regarded by the whites as "their man." I asked Mitchell, as attorney general, what he planned to do insofar as the schools were concerned. "I am attorney general, and I will enforce the law," he growled in his gruff, pipe-smoking way. He offered no value judgments and did not take part in the debate about whether this was good, bad, or indifferent. "I will enforce the law." Then he left. No nonsense. Both the blacks and the whites were impressed.

This message from the attorney general, I explained to Shamir, allowed me to move our discussion forward from "whether" to "how," to managerial and administrative topics. The fact was, desegregation *was going to happen.* The only question for these outstanding community leaders was, *how would it work?* Would there be violence? How would the educational system in their communities be affected? What would be the effect on their local economies? They had a great stake in seeing that this effort was managed in a reasonable way, whether they liked it or not, I told them.

The same was true on the West Bank and Gaza, I told Shamir. "The status quo is not stable. Change will come. The questions are, how and to what."

When lunchtime arrived, back then in the spring of 1970, I took the whole group over to the diplomatic reception rooms in the State Department where we were surrounded by the artifacts of colonial America. I pointed out the desk designed by Jefferson on which he wrote portions of the Declaration of Independence: "dedicated to the proposition that all men are created equal." I sat with the two strong men I wanted to cochair the Mississippi advisory committee.[1] I argued that if they would accept, the committee would immediately have great credibility with whites and blacks; their acceptance would thereby enhance the ability of the committee to attain its goal: a desegregated school system with the least possible disruption and the greatest chance to enhance the quality of education for their children.

I saw that I was making headway, so I left them alone for a bit, much to the consternation of an observer from the Justice Department. "I learned long ago that when parties get that close to agreement, it is best to let them complete their agreement by themselves," I told the perplexed

1. Warren Hood, the president of the Mississippi Manufacturers' Association, and Gilbert Mason, president of the Biloxi chapter of the NAACP.

observer. "That way, the agreement belongs to them—it's theirs—and they will try hard to make it work." As lunch ended, these two tough, respected leaders shook hands on their own deal. We were in business in what many regarded as the most problematic state.

Gradually, after we returned to the White House, the whole group came around, and individuals started to make suggestions about how to handle this or that potential problem. A small kitty out of HEW flexible funds had been set aside, so I was able to say to the committee members that if they judged that funds were needed for minor expenditures, I could provide them on a fast-track basis. That seemed to help.

When I felt the time was right, again by prearrangement, I let President Nixon know that we were ready for him. We then walked across the hall and into the Oval Office, where he met each of them and sat them down. President Nixon spoke to them with a great sense of conviction and with considerable emotion. Looking around the room, he said, in essence, "Here we are in the Oval Office of the White House. Think of the decisions that have been made here and that have affected the health and the security of our country. But remember, too, that we live in a great democracy where authority and responsibility are shared. Just as decisions are made here in this office, decisions are made throughout the states and communities of our country. You are leaders in those communities, and this is a time when we all have to step up to our responsibilities. I will make my decisions, and I count on you to make yours. We must make this work."

By the time he got through and people were ready to leave, they were charged up to get their backs into making the school openings and subsequent operations of the schools go forward as smoothly and constructively as possible.

The group went home to Mississippi, and they were able to provide real leadership. They were strong people, and they were accepted as legitimate and valid representatives within their communities of the true feelings that people had. We went through the same process with representatives of five other states before the school year was to start. The last state to go was Louisiana. I suggested to the president that we hold this meeting in New Orleans. We would go to the South, where the action would take place. I would do my part in the morning. He could fly down from Washington and do his part with the Louisianans at the end of the morning meeting. Then, in the afternoon, we would invite the cochairmen from each of the seven states to join the president and me for an overall discussion of the school openings.

I remembered well a meeting in the Oval Office to discuss this possible set of events, I recounted to Shamir. Vice President Agnew strongly warned the president not to go. He said: There you will be in that room, Mr. President, half the people there will be black, half will be white. The schools will be opening, beginning the following week. There will be blood running throughout the streets of the South, and if you go, this will be blood on your hands. This is not your issue. This is the issue of the liberals who have pushed for desegregation. Let them have it. Stay away.

President Nixon looked at me, the nonpolitician in the crowd. I thought he had already decided to go and didn't need arguments from me. But I told him what I thought: "Well, Mr. President, I can't predict what will happen. The vice president may very well be right about violence in the streets, but this is your country. You are the president of all the people, and it seems to me that we have seen some very reasonable and strong people come up here. You've met with them and have had a big impact on them. We should do everything we can to see that the schools open and operate peacefully and well."

The president decided to go ahead with our plan. Down we all went to New Orleans, except for Vice President Agnew, who stayed home.

I left the night before the president and started in the morning with the biracial Louisiana group. The going was tough, much more so than with any other state. As I struggled, I thought, maybe my problem was the closeness of the school opening, maybe the more restricted amount of time, maybe we just missed the ambience of the White House. President Nixon was due to arrive about noon to put on his final touch. As noon arrived, I had not achieved the degree of agreement that I usually had by the time the president met with the group. We took a recess. I went out to meet with the president. "Mr. President," I told him, "I'm sorry to tell you that I haven't got this group to the point you usually find when you meet with them. They're still arguing. I'm afraid this time you're going to have to do the job yourself."

Nixon came in. He listened. He talked. He raised the sights of everyone. He stepped up to the problem, did a wonderful job, and brought them all on board.

That afternoon we had our meeting with the cochairmen from the seven states. The meeting was highly publicized throughout the South. President Nixon talked eloquently about the importance of what was going to happen and the stake that everyone had in seeing it go smoothly. There were strong pledges of cooperation from whites and blacks alike. A sense of determination in a joint, compelling enterprise filled the room.

Riding home on *Air Force One,* we gathered around to discuss the day's activities—Pat Moynihan, Len Garment, Bryce Harlow, the president, and I. We felt very good about the day's activities. Bryce Harlow, who was from Oklahoma and the only real Southerner in the crowd, said that he thought things would go pretty well in the South. But, he said, wait until this process of desegregation comes to the North. The lawyers from Boston have been coming South preaching all these years. But wait until they have to face desegregation in their own communities.

The president said, "How do you figure that, Bryce?"

He said, "Well, Mr. President, people in the South have been living with the Negro for all these years, side by side. In the South, we love the Negro as a human being, but we hate the Negro as a race. In the North, it's just the opposite. There is no experience of living together as human beings, so Northerners love the Negro as a race, but they hate the Negro as an individual. Therefore, and since this all comes down in the end to individual human relationships, it will go better in the South than in the North."

As the schools opened, we worried about how this would be covered on television. Len Garment went around to the leading networks and told them that they should report the facts as they were. He said to them, "Suppose a hundred schools open, and there is violence at one of them.

What is the story? I think the story is that the schools opened 99 percent peacefully." The schools opened, and all went well. The openings were peaceful, much to the amazement of almost everyone. The leaders in their communities had done a fine job. They stood up to their responsibilities.

After having told this long, involved story, I looked at Shamir. "There are two big lessons in this story as I see it," I told him. "The first is that if you are to give legitimacy to an effort, involve people who truly represent their own constituencies, not people who think the way you do and are easy for you to talk to. The other big lesson has to do with the human relationships involved. Jews and Palestinians have been living side by side throughout the region for centuries. I have traveled around in the Middle East a fair amount, and I have heard many expressions of admiration, respect, and affection for human beings across ethnic lines. Just as in our South, there are personal relationships of long standing. Although deep and abiding hatreds exist—and the intifada and Israel's harsh reaction are intensifying those hatreds—there is also personal rapport and respect to be nurtured.

I hoped also that Shamir would gain inspiration from the example of President Nixon, who had courageously stepped up to this historic and difficult problem and had given the leadership needed at a critical moment. "The moment must come," I said, "when strong Arabs and Israelis step up to their possibilities as well as their problems, when 'whether' turns to 'how,' and when the job of creating better and more stable conditions of life begins."

That was my exit from the peace process. I left with ideas on the table that I hoped could be taken up anew by new players. I remembered my first visit to Jerusalem in 1969 and the words of Mayor Teddy Kollek: "Jerusalem is like a beautiful mosaic. The colors don't run into each other, but if you put them together in the right way, they can make a beautiful picture." I also remembered Shamir's statement to me that "somehow we will find a way to live together peacefully."

Somehow, but how?

Tough decisions on all sides were needed, made with a foresight that eluded the Middle Eastern scene. Otherwise, the drift would continue toward spiraling violence and positions that become more and more irreconcilable. The United States had, and has, a unique ability to bring together all the parties and to help them overcome hatreds and forge solutions to their deep-seated problems. But those who reside in the Middle East, and those who lead them or aspire to, must in the end bear the burden of responsibility for conditions where they live.

Better Governance

The Constitution Doesn't Mention Czars

George P. Shultz

April 11, 2011

Unaccountable White House aides are a product of a broken cabinet-nomination process. This is not the form of government the Founders intended.

A pattern of governance has emerged in Washington that departs substantially from that envisaged in our Constitution. Under our basic concept of governance: (1) a president and vice president are elected; and (2) the departments of government are staffed by constitutional officers including secretaries, undersecretaries, assistant secretaries and others who are nominated by the president and confirmed for service by the consent of the Senate. They are publicly accountable and may be called to testify under oath about their activities.

Over time, this form of governance has changed. Presidents sometimes assume that the bureaucracy will try to capture a secretary and his or her immediate staff so that they will develop a departmental, rather than a White House, point of view. So presidents will name someone in the White House to oversee the department and keep a tight rein on its activities.

In national security and foreign policy, the National Security Council (NSC) was established after World War II by the National Security Act of 1947. As late as 1961, under President Dwight Eisenhower, the NSC was supported by a small staff headed by an executive secretary with a "passion for anonymity" and limited to a coordinating role. In subsequent administrations, that passion disappeared and staff members took on operational duties that formerly were the responsibility of constitutionally confirmed cabinet officials. This aggrandizement of the staff function then spread into fields far beyond national security.

More recently, the situation has been worsened by the difficulty of getting presidential nominees to cabinet and subcabinet positions approved and in place. The White House vetting process has become exhaustive, with potential appointees required to fill out extensive questionnaires on such things as foreign travel and personal acquaintances, let alone financial matters. Mistakes are potentially subject to criminal penalties. The result is a drawn-out and often disagreeable process from the time a person agrees to a job to the actual nomination.

Formal nominations do not necessarily receive quick consideration by Senate committees, which routinely request additional information. Sometimes a nomination, voted legitimately out of the committee, can be put on hold indefinitely as one member of the Senate uses the hold as a bargaining chip to get some matter, often unrelated, settled to his or her satisfaction.

These long delays make for great difficulty in assembling an administration, particularly in its crucial first year. The result has been appointment of people to the White House staff with de facto decision-making power over all the major areas of government. This practice also extends to foreign affairs, as a variety of special envoys and "special representatives" are appointed, often with ambiguity about whether they report directly to the president or to the secretary of state.

The practice of appointing White House "czars" to rule over various issues or regions is not a new invention. But centralized management by the White House staff has been greatly increased in recent years.

Beyond constitutional questions, such White House advisers, counselors, staffers and czars are not accountable. They cannot be called to testify under oath, and when Congress asks them to come, they typically plead executive privilege.

The consequences, apart from the matter of legitimate governance, are all too often bad for the formation and execution of policy. The departments, not the White House, have the capacity to carry out policies and they are full of people, whether political appointees or career governmental employees, who have vast experience and much to contribute to the making of policy. When White House staffers try to formulate or execute policy, they can easily get off track in a way that would not happen in a regular department.

As secretary of state under President Ronald Reagan, I experienced this with great pain when White House people developed and ran an off-the-books program of arms sales to Iran. It erupted in the Iran-Contra scandal involving the unconstitutional transfer of funds not appropriated by Congress to the Contras, and with close to devastating consequences for the president.

Iran-Contra is a dramatic example, but the more general problem is the inability to take full advantage of available skills and expertise in policy making, and the difficulty in carrying out the functions of government nationally and internationally.

What must be done?

To return to a more effective and constitutionally sound use of cabinet members and their departments in helping the president formulate policy, cabinet secretaries could be grouped into important functional categories—national security and foreign policy, economics, natural resources, human resources, the rule of law, education, health and others. All of these subjects involve more than one department. Sometimes the natural convener is obvious; in other instances the leading role might simply rotate.

With the help of staff coordinators in the White House, cabinet members might convene by themselves and then with the president. This would involve the departments and, at the same time, ensure that a presidential, rather than a departmental, point of view would prevail. Policy execution would be improved, as would support for legislative initiatives.

The main goal is to assure that a cabinet member—not a White House aide—is always in charge. The result would be not so much cabinet government as presidential government with the heavy involvement of accountable officials in the administration.

Then, and foremost, the appointment process must be moved back to what it was even as recently as the Reagan administration. The assumption is that honorable people want to serve honorably. Reasonable vetting, such as a review of Internal Revenue Service and Federal Bureau of Investigation records, can be done quickly. A bad apple will surely be discovered and can be discarded.

I remember a passage in the late great American statesman Paul Nitze's autobiography. A friend in the FDR administration called and asked him to work in government—he would receive no pay, only an extra desk and an assistant. In this wholly illegitimate way, he began his career in the federal government.

Nitze's record of public service is legendary. I was lucky to serve with such a great and honorable man. I am not recommending that today's vetting process be like his, but I worry: Could we attract a Paul Nitze to the government today?

Today's problems are daunting and of critical importance. We need today's Paul Nitzes involved in the process of governance. It's imperative that we get back to a constitutional and accountable form of government before confidence in our capacity to govern further erodes.

The Shape, Scope, and Consequences
of the Age of Information
Paris, France
March 21, 1986

Following is an address by Secretary Shultz before the Stanford University Alumni Association's first International Conference, Paris, March 21, 1986.

I'm always pleased to be in Paris. And I'm especially pleased to be here when the centennial celebration of the Statue of Liberty is only a few months away. That engineering marvel of the 19th century is an apt symbol of my theme tonight—the relationship between the advance of technology and the advance of liberty. For 100 years, that statue has been a beacon to mankind and a testimony to the unbreakable bond between our nations. On behalf of Americans everywhere, I extend our appreciation and deepest affection to France.

I'm also pleased to be speaking as the Secretary of State from Washington to an audience of ex-Californians, Parisians, and other Europeans at a meeting organized by Stanford University. Tonight's gathering is an appropriate setting for my subject: the shape, scope, and consequences of the age of information. Geography and borders have always constrained everyday life. Today, the information revolution is undermining their ancient dictates. It is shifting the balance of wealth and strength among nations, challenging established institutions and values, and redefining the agenda of political discourse.

The information revolution promises to change the routine of our planet as decisively as did the industrial revolution of the past century. The industrial age is now ending. In some places, it has already passed.

United States Department of State, Bureau of Public Affairs, Washington, DC.

The United States and most of the free nations in the developed world are already seeing how the age of information is transforming our economies. A century ago, we moved from an agricultural to an industrial phase in our development. Today, we remain agriculturally and industrially productive; but the basis of our economy is shifting rapidly from industrial production to information-based goods and services. Our economic indices—such as productivity and the structure of employment—are being decisively altered by our entry into the new age.

Yet these changes have been so pervasive, and their pace so rapid, that we have been unable to comprehend them in their full scope. We are very much like the leaders of the early 19th century as they tried to grasp the unfolding consequences of industrialization. No one has taken the full measure of our own new age. But if we are to seize the opportunities and understand the problems that this new phase of technological transformation will bring, we must try to grasp both its particulars and its broad outlines.

Dimensions of the New Age

What is the information age? The answers to that question are as numerous as the age itself is pervasive. There is, most obviously, a scientific dimension. Our thinking about our physical environment is changing with unprecedented speed. That change has been reflected most dramatically in our technological prowess—particularly in the development, storage, processing, and transfer of information. While the industrial age found its proper symbol in the factory, the symbol of the information age might be the computer, which can hold all the information contained in the Library of Congress in a machine the size of a refrigerator. Or its proper symbol may be a robot, a machine capable of supplementing age-old manual labor and liberating human beings from the most arduous and repetitive of tasks. Or perhaps its symbol is the direct broadcast satellite, which can send television programs directly into homes around the globe.

This list does not begin to capture the variety or capacity of these new technologies. Indeed, these are only the beginnings of what will be far-reaching and profound technical developments. Two decades from now, our computers will be 1,000 times more powerful than they are today. In a few short years, the most advanced technology of 1985 will seem as obsolete to us as the transistor—which made its debut some 40 years ago—seems today. Our scientific advances are affecting everything from the biological sciences to national defense. The President's Strategic Defense Initiative (SDI), with its promise of making deterrence more stable by reducing reliance on offensive nuclear weapons, is one dramatic example of the impact of intellectual and scientific change on our ways of dealing with the world. SDI can well be described, in fact, as a gigantic information processing system.

The economic dimension of this new age is just as revolutionary as its scientific and technological counterparts. Information, as Walter Wriston observed years ago, is our new international standard. Fortunes rise and fall according to its dissemination. With the advent of "real time" transfers of information, an announcement made in the Rose Garden can be reflected two minutes later in the stock market in Singapore. The information age is bringing a new conception of economic efficiency not just to entrepreneurs, and not just to corporations, but to the entire global market.

These and other economic consequences of the new age are transforming the way nations trade with one another. They are bringing new uncertainties to the marketplace and to the politics of regulation. Across the globe, the foreign policy agenda reflects new economic disputes as developing and advanced nations alike struggle to come to grips with transborder data flows, technology transfers, satellite transmissions, and the crowding of the radio spectrum. Some of these disputes are between governments. Others are between governments and private corporations. US computer manufacturers, for example, are now disputing with several European governments over the issue of transborder data transfers. The US companies believe that they should be allowed to compile data and have market access rights, while some governments believe that the data should be centrally controlled. Like the technologies themselves, the disputes created by the permeability of geographical borders to information flows are growing at a rapid rate.

Yet, these economic disputes are only one example of the effects of information technologies on international relations. The proliferation of information has also sparked new concerns over national security. Information is intrinsically neutral. It can be used for multiple purposes, good and bad. Governments everywhere are finding it harder to control the flow of sensitive information in the critical areas of intelligence and national defense. In free countries, where openness is valued in its own right, we must be careful not to underestimate the ability of others to manipulate new technologies for repressive purposes. In the TWA hijacking and in other such incidents, for instance, terrorists exploited our open system of mass communication to create a global forum for their brutal acts.

The social dimension of the information age may seem more intangible, but it is equally profound. More than 6 million American homes now have personal computers. By 1990, according to some estimates, half of all our households—and an untold number of our schools, offices, and factories—will be computerized. The impact of that change on our young people is already extraordinary. Their attachment to now commonplace video games and to video cassettes is a symbol of adaptation to the new age. Whole generations are now growing up with the computer, taking it for granted, understanding its languages, and using it with ease. What does their nonchalance imply? I was thinking of this recently as I watched my granddaughter play with a computerized toy. To her generation, the technologies of tomorrow will be as integral to her lifestyle as the telephone is to ours.

Nor is the social revolution limited to the most developed countries. Television, for example, lets people see how others live in distant countries and invites comparison. The information revolution is raising expectations not only in advanced nations but in corners of the world that have little experience of high technology itself.

These various dimensions—technological, economic, political, and social—are only a few ways of describing what the information revolution is about. Today, in the middle of the 1980s, the outlines of some broader implications are also becoming clear. I would like to reflect on some of the deeper economic and political challenges that the new age is bringing to us and then say a few words about America's response to them.

The Challenge to Individuals

First of all, any nation that wants to profit from the information revolution must understand where innovation comes from. In this era of rapid technological change, the pace of obsolescence is accelerating as never before. Innovation—and risk-taking—are more than ever the engines of progress and success. This is true both in the economic marketplace and in the marketplace of ideas. So the challenge of economic success in this new age is, in large part, a challenge to the individual entrepreneur.

For obvious reasons, the free nations of the world are best positioned to meet this challenge. By their very nature, they guarantee the individual freedom that is necessary to the entrepreneurial spirit. And they have the confidence in their citizenry to encourage, rather than stifle, technological development.

In the United States, inventors, innovators, and entrepreneurs are symbols of our pioneering tradition. Our nation grew because there were enterprising Americans willing to take economic risks. A few statistics from our recent economic recovery tell the story. Last year over 666,000 new corporations were established in the United States—nearly 100,000 more than in 1981. Of these, some 50,000 failed—a dramatic measure of entrepreneurial spirit and the willingness to take risks.

We have also generated over 9 million new jobs in the past five years, reflecting the commercialization of new technologies. Our tax system encourages the economic risks that lead to innovation. In 1983 alone, we committed over $2.8 billion in venture capital to start-up costs. Public and private institutions alike encourage us to try the untried, to adapt ourselves to the unaccustomed.

And Americans as consumers are familiar and comfortable with technological innovation. Our fascination with gadgets and new products is legendary. From the days of the first automobile, Americans have been willing and eager for the novel, the improved, the latest model.

So we are disposed, as a people, to encourage entrepreneurship and to accept innovative technologies.

We have our qualms, of course. Like all other peoples, we have been sensitive to the impact of technological advance on the workplace—to the dislocations that follow from the replacement of manual labor. But, more than most nations, we tend to have confidence in our ability to resolve the social dilemmas that changing technologies present. Silicon Valley is only one symbol of our dedication to risk and reward. To us, the information age represents a new avenue to economic growth, an opportunity to do what we do best: to explore, to innovate, and, ultimately, to succeed.

The United States is far from alone, of course, in the development of new information technologies. France has pioneered the remarkable MINITEL system—a keyboard and TV screen linked to the phone system that now gives nearly 3 million subscribers instantaneous access to more than 1,200 different data bases, banking and financial services, press hookups, and educational and cultural channels. Such information technology gives the individual enormous personal outreach, expanding to global limits his access to information, ideas, and personal services.

Free Trade: The Challenge to the Free World

Success in the information age depends on more than our own innovation and entrepreneurship. The new age also presents us all with a global challenge. New technologies circumvent the borders and geographical barriers that have always divided one people from another. Thus, the market for these technologies depends to a great extent on the openness of *other* countries to the free flow of information.

Open markets allow comparative advantage to express itself. The United States, as a country that seeks to explore and trade in technological services, has always opposed international attempts to stifle the workings of the information revolution. In our view, every country willing to open itself to the free flow of information stands to benefit.

Some critics have charged us with simple self-interest. The United States, they say, urges open trade because it is so well positioned to profit from it. They point out that American research, development, and marketing can compete favorably with those of other countries.

The interesting thing about this charge is that it captures a truth, but it expresses that truth exactly backwards. The United States does not advocate free trade because we are adept at pioneering technologies; we are adept at them *because* the dedication to freedom is intrinsic to our political culture. By maintaining that dedication throughout our history, we have been the pioneers of change both at home and abroad—in the agricultural phase of our development, in our industrial phase, and now, in the age of information.

Opposition to open trade is sometimes linked to a charge of cultural imperialism. The more international markets are open, it is said, the more smaller countries will be flooded with American movies and American television and radio programs—resulting in a kind of "cultural imperialism." I find this view ironic. If any nation would seem to be vulnerable to the widespread import of information and news from other cultures, it is the United States itself. As a nation of immigrants, we are the most international society on earth. Our cultural heritage—not to mention our cuisine—has been shaped by Asians, Europeans, Africans, and Latin Americans; by Christianity, Judaism, Islam, Buddhism, Hinduism; by almost every religious and ethnic influence imaginable. We urge would-be cultural imperialists to take note: the United States, with our international heritage, represents the largest market in the world for information from other cultures.

That international heritage is already encouraging foreign entrepreneurs. The Spanish International Network, for example, which is programmed *outside* the United States, now has over 200 broadcast and cable outlets in our country. The United States does not fear an influx of information from other countries. On the contrary, we welcome it. And our reasons for welcoming it go beyond any simple adherence to the free flow of ideas and to open markets, beyond even the economic benefits that open trade would surely bring us. Those reasons go to the heart of the broad philosophical and political questions that the age of information has raised anew for all of us.

Fundamental Freedoms

The information age poses profound *political* challenges to nations everywhere. As any economist knows—or, for that matter, any alumnus of the Stanford Business School—the laws of economics do not exist in a vacuum. Even the most commonplace decisions—such as where to open a plant and when—must take into account social and political realities as well as economic considerations. Likewise, the freedom that makes America's economic success possible does not stand on its own; it is an integral part of our political system. So is the intellectual freedom that makes innovation and entrepreneurship possible.

The relationship between individual rights and economic dynamism is fundamental. The United States has seen that truth at work in our early agricultural age, in our age of industry, and in today's era of information. The Model T, the Wright brothers' plane, the telephone, the movie reel, the transistor radio, the VCR [video cassette recorder], the personal computer—these and other innovations have shaped and revolutionized our society. They have spread prosperity not just to an elite but to everyone. Thus, they mark the success of our democracy and the progress of our freedom. They are the material symbols of our dedication to individual choice, free enterprise, open markets, free scientific inquiry— indeed, to the very idea that the freedom of the individual, not the power of the state, is the proper foundation of society.

The same is true of free governments everywhere. The technological and economic successes of the entire free world are direct consequences and incontrovertible proof of the benefits that flow from self-government. The more the West dedicates itself to its freedoms, the stronger it becomes—both politically, as an attractive and viable alternative to statism, and economically, as a dynamic and expanding system of material productivity that brings benefits on a mass scale. In an era of technological revolution, our rededication to the liberty that makes innovation possible is imperative.

That rededication has strategic importance as well. The information revolution is already shifting the economic balance between East and West. The leaders of closed societies fear this shifting economic base, and for good reason. First, they are afraid that information technologies will undermine the state's control over its people—what they read, watch, hear, and aspire to. In most of these countries, familiar means of communication like the mimeograph machine and photocopier are already kept under lock and key. The specter of direct broadcast satellites alarms their leaders even more. In Moscow, they're paying up to 300 rubles—that's $450—for black market videotapes smuggled in from the West.

East-bloc leaders also fear that they will be unable to compete with the research, development, and marketing of information age technologies. Here, too, they are right to be worried. The incentive to improve information technology is unlikely to come from countries in which the pen is regarded as an instrument of subversion. The science and technology of the future will be directly tied to access to information, for the important scientific ideas will come from the accumulation and manipulation of data bases.

So these regimes face an agonizing choice: they can either open their societies to the freedoms necessary for the pursuit of technological advance, or they can risk falling even farther behind the West. But, in reality, they may not have a choice. The experience of the Chinese communists, who are now trying to release the talents of a billion people, will continue to be a fascinating test of whether a once-closed society can be opened.

That is why the promise of information technology is so profound. Its development not only strengthens the economic and political position of democracies: it provides a glimmer of hope that the suppressed millions of the unfree world will find their leaders forced to expand their liberties. But that is not all. If totalitarian leaders do loosen their grip in order to compete with the free countries, they may find themselves, in that process, contributing dramatically to an improvement in relations between East and West. That easing of tensions would benefit not only the Soviet Union and the United States but the nations across the globe whose destinies are linked to the East-West conflict.

The developing world, too, stands to benefit from an expanded flow of information. Some of these nations are already seizing their opportunities. I notice that Barbados, for instance, advertises to potential investors by emphasizing that it has a sophisticated telecommunications system. Other countries are using information technologies to enhance their agricultural or industrial capacities. With the aid of modern communications, Colombia now markets fresh-cut flowers in New York City. Developing countries that profited from the "green revolution" know that information modernization offers the vast promise of integration into the world economy.

Nations throughout the developing world must decide how to view these new international markets. If they fear outside influences and seek to restrain technological trade, they will only fall farther behind the developed world and increase the gulf between us. If, on the other hand, they remain open, they will find themselves rewarded with rare opportunities for developing their material and human resources and for accelerating their movement toward modernization.

In the industrially advanced world, the information revolution is already transforming the multinational corporation. Today, sophisticated communications enable people from across the oceans to work together with the same efficiency of those who work across town. In the coming years, we can expect to see new supranational corporate entities whose employees are drawn from all corners of the world. That's one possible consequence of the shrinking importance of geography. Another is that the developing nations will have access as never before to data and communications in the advanced nations—access that could only increase the efficiency with which developing nations use their resources.

A Test of Principle

Because of the information revolution, all nations—free and unfree, developing and developed—must confront a key challenge that I have already mentioned: the way nations trade with one another. None of the opportunities before us will bear fruit unless the free nations can agree to open rather than restrictive trade in these revolutionary products and services.

This same challenge is also affecting our diplomacy. Technologies are being transformed even as we negotiate over their transfer abroad. The United States has pressed strongly for a new round of multilateral trade negotiations in the GATT [General Agreement on Tariffs and Trade] to ensure that key issues relating to the trade in these emerging technologies are taken up. Meanwhile, we are keeping open the possibility of increasing bilateral free trade arrangements, as we are pursuing now with Israel and Canada. Our overall purpose remains the same: to maximize the development of and trade in these information age products and services, especially those that increase the free flow of data and ideas.

To do otherwise would betray the vast promise that the information age holds out to us.

That betrayal would be a great misfortune for the free world—yes, because of the economic opportunities that would be lost but, more, because of the implications for the idea of freedom. We are proud of our freedom, and we are right to be proud. But today's disputes over the technologies that cut across our borders put our dedication and commitment to a new test. Are we secure enough in our principles to act in ways that promote, rather than discourage, the technologies that leap across borders?

The United States is confident in its own answer. We welcome these technologies as we have welcomed, in times past, other advances whose implications were uncertain. In fact, we invite other nations to practice a little "cultural imperialism" of their own on us. We weren't shaken when Mr. Gorbachev appeared live via satellite on our televisions. And it doesn't bother us to hear that engineers from the Soviet Union have been known to amuse themselves by intercepting Hollywood movies from American satellite transmissions. We just hope they enjoyed *Rambo*.

Approaching Horizons

This cultural dimension leads me to my final point. The greatest minds of the past century bent their powers toward understanding the significance of the industrial revolution. Theorists and intellectuals, novelists and poets alike devoted themselves to examining the dimensions of their new age. Today, with the passing of the industrial era, a new consciousness is developing. Its impact on our art and literature and music is already apparent; its impact on our social behavior is already under way. In the long run, the most exciting challenge posed by the new age is not to nations or corporations or societies but to the individual human imagination.

Meanwhile, those of us who must grapple with the daily realities of the information revolution face formidable challenges of our own. We can learn a practical lesson from a wise and thoughtful banker. Fifteen years ago, when even pocket calculators were a novelty, Walter Wriston foresaw the implications of this new age for the field of finance. His vision helped to revolutionize the entire financial industry and turned his company, Citicorp, into a giant of imagination and profit.

Wriston succeeded because he was able to grasp both the particular details of his chosen sector and the daunting conceptual outlines of the information revolution at large. By never losing sight of either, he contributed to both. Those of us who confront other practical dimensions of our new age—in my own case, the political dimension—can benefit from his example.

So, as we face the many challenges that the new age presents, we must never lose sight of our most fundamental principles. We are reminded with every advance that in this age of revolution our commitment to freedom is our single greatest asset. With all the information we have amassed, with all the discoveries at the frontiers of all the sciences, we still find that answers bring with them new questions. Our policies must always be based on the fundamental process of freedom—freedom of thought, freedom of research, and the free flow of ideas. If we keep that in mind, we will benefit from our dedication to liberty even as we secure it.

Return to a Vibrant Economy

Prescription for Economic Policy:
"Steady As You Go"
Chicago, IL
April 22, 1971

Address by George P. Shultz, director of Office of Management and Budget, before the Economic Club of Chicago.

I have a simple but apparently controversial thesis to present this evening: the basic strategy of economic policy and its current tactical implementation are generally on course and economic policy can benefit from application of the old nautical phrase, "Steady as you go."

For we are *going*—forward with expansion of the economy, as the war in Vietnam continues to wind down, and as the pressures of inflation diminish in their intensity.

But also, with each passing day, the pressures mount to alter the course and to steer, not by the compass but by the wind, tossing caution to the wind in the process. I can assure you that these counsels meet strong resistance from the President.

Of course, there are problems. There are uncertainties to be monitored and adjusted for in the tactics of economic policy as new data become available. There are changes in the structure of demand and supply in the marketplace which must be taken into account. Unemployment is too high and there are pockets of unemployment created mainly by the shift from war to peacetime production that must be treated directly.

But beyond these issues, what are the broad objectives of the President's economic policy?

One strategic purpose of this administration has been to slow a rapidly escalating inflation without inducing a downturn in economic activity.

Another has been to stop the government budget from creating instability, which it had been doing, and get the budget onto a more sustainable basis, which is what we are doing now.

A third has been and is to create the conditions for steady economic expansion in a way that nourishes the freedom and innovative spirit of management, labor, and individuals—in a way that does not involve the takeover of the economy by government.

Now, let's look at the results so far.

Inflation has begun a turn downward after a relatively mild slowing of the economy. It has taken longer than we hoped and unemployment has been higher than we wanted, but the progress is unmistakable. The Consumer Price Index, for example, has declined in its rate of increase from over 6 percent in the first half of 1970 to a little under 5 percent in the second half of 1970 to about 2.7 percent in the first quarter of 1971. This is the lowest quarterly increase since the first quarter of 1967.

A balance in the budget at full employment has been attained and held for all three Nixon years after three years of rapidly rising and ultimately tremendous deficits at full employment, thereby removing a destabilizing government influence from the economy and replacing it with a steadying influence.

And now the economy is moving forward, having registered a solid advance of 6.5 percent in real GNP in the first quarter of this year, with the upward movement clearly and substantially stronger and more broadly based toward the end of the quarter than at the beginning.

Yet there are real differences in approach to economic policy today, and we would do well to recognize the disagreements and clarify the arguments.

There is a school of thought that our economy has changed to such an extent that the free market economy will no longer work well enough. In order to achieve stability, this school says, government must do much more to manage the private sector. Some members of this school believe that more government management is needed not only temporarily to cure our current inflation, but indefinitely.

It is time to challenge the basic premise that the economy has changed drastically over the past decade. "Times have changed" is a truism that is hard to refute—but let us see what has changed and what has not.

A principal argument that has been used to justify this seeming new-ness is that corporations and labor now have a great deal more market power than they previously had.

In fact, however, there is little evidence that the power of business has grown, has become more concentrated or monopolistic in recent times. Studies of horizontal integration, which use concentration ratios and rates of return, find little evidence of a secular increase in this indicator of monopoly. Likewise, a study of vertical integration, which uses sales to value-added ratios, finds no evidence for a secular trend. Monopoly power does not appear to be on the rise.

When conglomeration was in vogue a few years ago, the spectre was raised of a dozen supercorporations dominating the business scene. But because conglomeration did not provide a magic formula for manage-ment or financial success, that threat has receded. Waves of conglomerate activity have been experienced in the US economy before. As before, the aftermath of the recent wave has been its reversal. Antitrust enforcement was a factor, but the free market itself provided the main self-cleansing force. The trend in business today is toward more competition, not less, and the successful conglomerates have often been the agents of this sharper competition.

Only in an atmosphere of false boom, of an economy superheated by government, covering up errors of business judgment, can inefficient aggregations of enterprise prosper. We have now seen what happens when government stops racing the economic engine beyond its capacity to perform: the wheeling and dealing gives way to a more fundamental, and more healthy, form of competition among business enterprises.

But what about organized labor? Has it grown in power so markedly in recent years that new regulations are needed in the labor market and in collective bargaining?

Let us look at the government sector of the economy. Here we see both rapid growth in union membership and rapid growth in employment, with the proportion rising from about 12.6 percent to about 18.2 percent of the government labor force over the years from 1956 to 1968. It is noteworthy but perhaps not surprising under the circumstances, that wage rates have risen especially rapidly in this sector of the economy. In my judgment, the problems of employer-employee relations in government will deserve and will command more and more attention in the years ahead. Certainly, we are far from a resolution of the fundamental problems involved and they are problems that will affect not only wages and costs—taxes—in the public sector but the private labor market as well. This is indeed a new factor in the picture.

In the private non-farm sector of the economy by sharp contrast, union membership grew only slightly, not nearly so fast as employment, so that its proportionate importance declined from about 38 percent to about 32 percent of this labor force. Lack of growth does not mean a lack of issues about present arrangements in the labor market; but, it seems fair to say, the issues are not newly created. It cannot be argued that the current inflation is associated with rising union strength.

Broad statistics on the increase in average hourly earnings of private non-farm workers show a level of increase that must be reduced if we are to have an extended period of price stability. At the same time, they tend to confirm the picture of no basic change in the arrangements of labor markets. The rise in wages and benefits over 12-month spans has moved largely within a narrow band between 6 and 8 percent for about five years. There are differential movements by industry, with non-union areas such as "trade" moving up more sharply when labor markets were at their tightest and reacting more quickly to the current slack. It may be noted that conditions in labor markets did not ease greatly until mid-1970. Conversely, fixed-term contracts tend to produce a slower response in union rates when the labor market tightens but to project that response, unfortunately sometimes at an unwarranted and unwise level, on into a period of changed economic circumstances. This is, however, a well-known phenomenon, identifiable throughout the post–World War II period.

Another well-known movement is also under way, one that has created great difficulty in the fight against inflation but which will now provide us some help. The top of a boom and a time of slowing economic activity are always times when the growth of output per man-hour—productivity—also slows. But, as output rises again, productivity does so as well and initially at a rate above its long-term average. A little noted but very important aspect of the first-quarter results was the appearance again of this predictable development: productivity rose at a rate better than 5 percent after three years of below-average growth. This shift will make a dramatic difference in unit costs of labor and is a hopeful factor insofar as inflation is concerned.

But that is not the main point here. The point is that events are proceeding generally in accord with what might be expected on the basis of past experience.

There are special problems. High expectations for performance of the economy create a dynamic of their own. We have already noted the area of government employment. The construction industry has long been in difficulty and may well be helped out of at least some of its problems through efforts now being made, with stimulation from the President. And there are a number of other industries, notably transportation, where high wage settlements pose difficult cost problems.

The steel industry is very much on our minds. The problem here is not one of setting an inflationary wage pattern: steel is at the end of the round, not the beginning. Nor is the industry so large and important that it can force a generally higher cost level on the economy. The problem is the reverse: the industry is weak, beset with competition from substitute materials, losing ground in world markets, and showing a rate of return that can hardly impress investors. These problems will be facing labor and management whatever the outcome of their wage bargaining and would be badly aggravated by a settlement that extends fixed, high increases into future years.

The answer to these problems is not more severe import quotas, for these will only put American steel users in a poorer and poorer competitive position at home as well as abroad.

Management and labor have a common and severe problem here. Working together with a common goal, they can make a big difference in cost per ton, even without major changes in technology. Perhaps government can help. Certainly a union that produced a Clint Golden and a Joe Scanlon can draw upon its traditions for constructive alternatives. We need leadership from the industry to produce a program that combines fair wages and competitive cost through high productivity. In this direction, there is a chance for secure jobs, important to young and older workers alike, and of adequate returns for the capital necessary to the long-run health of the industry.

Two other problem areas deserve special note.

Economic activity in 1970 was substantially disrupted by strikes, which occurred with relatively high frequency. Strikes are unfortunate. Peaceful settlements are certainly to be preferred and we may expect 1971 to be somewhat more peaceful than its predecessor. But we must also remember that strikes occur most often when an economy is shifting its gears. Last year, when the brakes were applied to inflation, profit margins narrowed, making it difficult for companies to meet the rising demands of labor, demands often reflecting the absence of any gain in real earnings during the prior contract term. The result was conflict. But the fact of this conflict is not evidence that our system is breaking down. It is evidence that the system is working—reacting, as it must, to the end of a spiraling rate of inflation.

Over the past two decades, we have engaged in more and more trade with the rest of the world. The high returns from this increase in trade have been shared by both Americans and foreigners.

In addition, competition from abroad has served to protect the consumer in the United States. The share of the economy represented by trade in goods and services has increased from about 9 percent to over 12 percent of GNP since 1950, with exports growing from about 5 percent to 6 ½ percent of the GNP and imports from a little over 4 percent to about 6 percent.

But this increased trade, especially the imports, has posed severe problems in many industries and imposed inequities in some cases. The whole area of international economic policy deserves careful, hard-nosed, and comprehensive review. That review is going forward now under the aegis of the new Council on International Economic Policy created last February by the President's Executive Order.

The President, who has travelled to 67 countries over the past 24 years, is determined that, when American business goes abroad, its interests will be strongly represented and advocated by our government.

Perhaps the most troublesome problem from the standpoint of economic policy generally is the area to which I am the closest: the Federal Budget. The upward thrust built into this gigantic flow of spending is awesome, and there is a continuous and continuing threat that outlays will develop a momentum carrying them well beyond full employment revenues. Tempting though the immediate prospect of such free spending seems to be, it is bad news for the long-run prospects of the economy. Inflation or a tax increase follow in its wake.

For Fiscal Year 1971, despite a deficit we now estimate at about $19 billion, outlays will be held just within full employment revenues; but only because of the President's willingness to veto apparently popular spending bills and of the willingness of a sufficient number of congressmen to stand with him.

Fiscal Year 1972 will not start for another ten weeks, and Congress has barely started its work on this budget. Yet actions so far on other things remaining in the President's budget already carry the deficit above $15 billion and outlays to a level well above full employment revenues.

We desperately need a steadiness, a sense of balance, and longer-term perspective in our budget policy. The years 1971 and 1972 are certainly important to this administration, but we must operate also with an eye to 1973 and beyond.

Do we have the ability—perhaps a better word is "guts"—to hold a steady course on the budget? I can assure you of a strong effort from this administration.

The President has been earning the reputation for credibility and perseverance the hard way. When he came into office, he said he would slow the increasing momentum of inflation. Others said the inflationary thrust could never be contained without a virtual takeover of economic activity or a major depression. It was, and without either.

The decisions were not easy to make. The cutbacks required to balance the full employment budget and the degree of monetary restraint necessary to slow the inflation were not popular. But now we can see a reduction of the rate of inflation.

A portion of the battle against inflation is now over; time and the guts to take the time, not additional medicine, are required for the sickness to disappear. We should now follow a noninflationary path back to full employment, assessing developments as we go and ready to provide stimulation as needed.

But the temptation is there to go overboard on excessive stimulation. These pressures exist on both the monetary and budgetary fronts. We must again provide the steadiness to resist these pressures.

The effects of balanced stimulation appear to be taking hold. Interest rates have fallen sharply and, as is usually the case, new housing starts have increased substantially.

As you all have also read recently, the increase in gross national product from the fourth to the first quarter was the largest absolute increase in history. Although we can't recover from an auto strike every quarter, we expect solid increases in output for the remainder of the year.

These facts, along with a policy of "steady as you go" have been accompanied by an unprecedented rise in the stock market. It was just about a year ago that the President suggested that it might be a good time to buy stocks. Stocks are up about 30 percent from the time he made that statement.

The facts reviewed here do not suggest a sharp departure from prior experience. Perhaps the only significant departure is the "steady as you go" policy. A colleague of mine at the University of Chicago, in a recent *Newsweek* column, said the major threat to prudent management of the economy is the "For God's sake, let's do something" philosophy. I think there is a great deal of merit in what he says.

Government does have the responsibility to remove artificial props to wages and prices when the free market system is abused. And in selective cases, in a critical industry, or in an especially flagrant situation, government should be willing to be the catalyst in achieving voluntary stabilization, and, when necessary, to help restructure the bargaining process.

But we will not be drawn into a series of steps that will lead to wage and price controls, rationing, black markets, and a loss of the effectiveness of the free economic system.

A single theme runs through everything this administration does. In foreign policy, our government will help others help themselves, where they are willing to bear the major portion of their own defense, and where it is in our national interest to help. In domestic policy, the federal government is moving to help people more, in a way that returns power and responsibility to states and localities. And in economic policy, the federal government will seek to create the climate in which a free economy can expand steadily and solidly, without domination by government.

There is a consistency to this philosophy, a balanced approach that permits the diffusion of power in the foreign, domestic, and economic areas.

Those of you familiar with sailing know what a telltale is—a strip of cloth tied to a mast to show which way the wind is blowing.

A captain has the choice of steering his ship by the telltale, following the prevailing winds, or to steer by the compass.

In a democracy, you must keep your eye on the telltale, but you must set your course by the compass. That is exactly what the President of the United States is doing. The voice from the bridge says, "Steady as you go."

Economic Strategy for the Reagan Administration
A Report to President-elect Ronald Reagan from His Coordinating Committee on Economic Policy
November 16, 1980

Sharp change in present economic policy is an absolute necessity. The problems of inflation and slow growth, of falling standards of living and declining productivity, of high government spending but an inadequate flow of funds for defense, of an almost endless litany of economic ills, large and small, are severe. But they are not intractable. Having been produced by government policy, they can be redressed by a change in policy.

The Task Force reports that you commissioned during the campaign are now available. They contain an impressive array of concrete recommendations for action. More than that, the able people who served on the Task Forces are available to provide further detail and backup information to you or your designees. We all want to help and you can count on enthusiastic and conscientious effort.

Your Coordinating Committee has reviewed the Task Force reports. With due allowance for some differences in view about particulars and relative importance, we have found that they offer a substantial base for action by you and the team you assemble. We focus here on guiding principles, on priorities and linkages among policy areas, and on the problem of getting action.

You have identified in the campaign the key issues and lines of policy necessary to restore hope and confidence in a better economic future:

- Reestablish stability in the purchasing power of the dollar.
- Achieve a widely shared prosperity through real growth in jobs, investment, and productivity.

- Devote the resources needed for a strong defense and accomplish the goal of releasing the creative forces of entrepreneurship, management, and labor by:
  - Restraining government spending.
  - Reducing the burden of taxation and regulation.
  - Conducting monetary policy in a steady manner, directed toward eliminating inflation.

This amounts to emphasis on fundamentals for the full four years as the key to a flourishing economy.

Guiding Principles

The essence of good policy is good strategy. Some strategic principles can guide your new administration as it charts its course.

- *Timing and preparation are critical aspects of strategy.*
  The fertile moment may come suddenly and evaporate as quickly. The administration that is well prepared is ready to act when the time is ripe. The transition period and the early months of the new administration are a particularly fertile period. The opportunity to set the tone for your administration must be seized by putting the fundamental policies into place immediately and decisively.
- *The need for a long-term point of view is essential to allow for the time, the coherence, and the predictability so necessary for success.*
  This long-term view is as important for day-to-day problem-solving as for the making of large policy decisions. Most decisions in government are made in the process of responding to problems of the moment. The danger is that this daily fire-fighting can lead the policy maker farther and farther from his goals. A clear sense of guiding strategy makes it possible to move in the desired direction in the unending process of contending with issues of the day. Many failures of government can be traced to an attempt to solve problems piecemeal. The resulting patchwork of ad hoc solutions often makes such fundamental goals as military strength, price stability, and economic growth more difficult to achieve.

- *Central problems that your administration must face are linked by their substance and their root causes.*

  Measures adopted to deal with one problem will inevitably have effects on others. It is as important to recognize these interrelationships as it is to recognize the individual problems themselves.

- *Consistency in policy is critical to effectiveness.*

  Individuals and business enterprises plan on a long-range basis. They need to have an environment in which they can conduct their affairs with confidence.

- *Specific policies as well as long-term strategy should be announced publicly.*

  The administration should commit itself to their achievement and should seek congressional commitment to them as well. Then the public, as well as the government, knows what to expect.

- *The administration should be candid with the public.*

  It should not over-promise, especially with respect to the speed with which the policies adopted can achieve the desired results.

Seizing the Initiative

The fundamental areas of economic strategy concern the budget, taxation, regulation, and monetary policy. Prompt action in each of these areas is essential to establish both your resolve and your capacity to achieve your goals.

Budget

Your most immediate concern upon assuming the duties of the President will be to convince the financial markets and the public at large that your anti-inflation policy is more than rhetoric. The public, and especially the financial community, is skeptical and needs a startling demonstration of resolve. Many question whether you are serious about a sizeable cut in budget outlays. Credible FY 1981 and 1982 budgets which do that clearly and unambiguously would evoke an extraordinary response in the financial markets and set the stage for a successful assault on inflation and a decline in mortgage and other interest rates.

The FY 1981 budget will be almost four months along by the time you take office and a FY 1982 budget will have been submitted for consideration by the Congress. There are now estimates of alarming increases in these swollen budgets. Prompt and strong action is necessary if these budgets are to be brought under control, as they must be. The nation can no longer afford governmental business as usual.

The formal budget alone is far from the whole story, though it is visible and important. Off-budget financing and government guarantees mount and expand programs through the use of the government's borrowing capacity, draining the nation's resources without being adequately recorded in the formal spending totals. In addition, the mandating of private expenditures for government purposes has gained momentum as the spotlight has illuminated direct spending. These mandates are also a clear call by government on the nation's resources. Efforts to control spending should be comprehensive; otherwise, good work in one area will be negated in another. And these efforts should be part of the administration's development of a long-term strategy for the detailed shape of the budget four or more years into the future.

The Weinberger Task Force has identified an extensive and promising array of areas for potential savings, but it will be up to your administration and the Congress to do the job. It takes top-notch people to do it. We recommend that:

- A Budget Director, permanent or pro tem, be chosen and set to work now.
- A small team from OMB be assembled explicitly to work with the newly designated Director.
- The Director's recommendations be a part of your discussion with Cabinet and sub-Cabinet appointees as these appointments are made.

Amendments calling for dramatic reductions in the FY 1981 budget should be submitted to the Congress within the first week of your administration. A thoroughly revised FY 1982 budget provides even greater opportunities for large further reductions, and this budget should be submitted as soon as possible.

Finally, it has become all too evident in recent years that current budget procedures are biased in an expansionary direction. The congressional budget process defined by the Budget Act of 1974 has failed to achieve its purpose of removing the "runaway" bias. We therefore recommend a presidential task force to develop new techniques which can help to rein in the growth of federal outlays. It should examine the presidential line-item veto, renewed presidential power to refrain from spending appropriated funds, and other initiatives to hold down spending. This task force should report to you within two months.

Tax Policy

Tax policy is properly the province of your Secretary of the Treasury. The making of that appointment should have a high priority so that important work can go forward. The Walker Task Force provides the materials needed to pose the issues to you in concrete form and to translate your decisions into a proposal to the Congress. This proposal should be presented early in the new administration in tandem with other key elements of your economic program. It should embody the main thrust of tax policy for the whole of your first term, not simply for the year 1981. We consider that the key ingredients should be your proposals for the Kemp-Roth cut in personal income tax rates, simplification and liberalization of business depreciation, and a cut in effective taxes on capital gains (see Innovation Task Force). Consistent with your proposals earlier this year, the effective date for these reductions should be January 1, 1981.

Other key proposals are tax incentives for the establishment of enterprise zones in the inner cities and such other items as tuition tax credits, reductions in the windfall profits tax, inheritance taxes and the taxation of Americans living abroad, and the restoration of restricted stock options.

Regulation

The current regulatory overburden must be removed from the economy. Equally important, the flood of new and extremely burdensome regulations that the agencies are now issuing or planning to issue must be drastically curtailed. The Weidenbaum Task Force sets out the needed blueprint for personnel selection, immediate administrative action, and legislation. Again, the key to action is a knowledgeable and forceful individual to develop and coordinate strategy and to form a team to carry it out. Such an appointment should be made promptly, with the expectation that the effort would carry forward through the transition for at least a year into your administration. Your appointee and his team should be located within the Executive Office of the President. Achieving regulatory reform will take informed, strong, and skillful work with the Congress as well as with those in charge of departmental and agency regulatory efforts. The person heading up this effort will require your continued, wholehearted support.

Many of our economic problems today stem from the large and increasing proportion of economic decisions being made through the political process rather than the market process. An important step to demonstrate your determination to rely on markets would be the prompt end of wage and price guidelines and elimination of the Council on Wage and Price Stability.

To advance the entire regulatory effort—both to galvanize public support and to strengthen the positions of administration appointees—we urge you to issue a message on regulatory reform in tandem with the budget and tax messages. The message should call upon state and local governments to launch similar regulatory reform efforts—as a few have already done.

Energy

The battle between government regulation and the private market is nowhere more apparent than in energy, where the market has a decisive comparative advantage. Governmental intrusion into energy production and use provides a glaring example of how regulation costs us all dearly. Alternatives to imported oil exist here in the United States. As the Halbouty Task Force emphasizes, market pricing and market incentives will accelerate the development of these alternatives just as surely as present regulations and the politicization of this field inhibit them. Its recommendations and the issues it poses for careful review cover the energy field in a comprehensive manner and deserve immediate attention.

We recommend, also, that you promptly exercise the discretion granted to the President to remove the price controls on crude oil and petroleum products rather than continue with the present calendar, which postpones complete decontrol until October 1981. This decisive action will eliminate at once the regulatory apparatus administering the entitlements program and discourage continued efforts by special interests to prevent or slow down decontrol and deregulation. Also, the Natural Gas Policy Act of 1978 should be repealed so that all natural gas prices are decontrolled. These measures are particularly urgent because the uncertainty of our critical Middle East oil supplies, dramatized by the Iran-Iraq war, makes it all the more necessary to get the earliest possible incentive effect of free market pricing.

The Synthetic Fuels Corporation is incompatible with the free market pricing of energy and should be promptly eliminated.

The Department of Energy has become a large and unmanageable institution with a variety of programs ranging from essential to useless. The essential functions should be transferred and the department eliminated. This should be the main task of your Secretary of Energy.

Monetary Policy

A steady and moderate rate of monetary growth is an essential requirement both to control inflation and to provide a healthy environment for economic growth. We have not had such a policy. The rate of monetary growth declined sharply in the early months of 1980 and rose rapidly in recent months. These wide fluctuations are adversely affecting economic conditions and may continue to do so into 1981.

The McCracken Task Force emphasizes that the attainment of a proper monetary policy deserves the very highest priority and that such a monetary policy can be achieved through effective use by the Fed of its existing powers. The Task Force also brings out the relationship of monetary policy to budgetary and other economic policies.

The Federal Reserve is an independent agency. However, independence should not mean lack of accountability for what it does. In practice, independence has not meant that the Federal Reserve is immune to presidential and congressional influence. The problem is how to assure accountability while preserving independence. We suggest that you:

- Request the Fed to state targets for monetary growth year by year for the next five years that, in its opinion, will end inflation. Influential members of relevant committees of Congress have already urged the Fed to specify such long-term targets.
- Assure the Fed that you will propose and fight for fiscal and other policies compatible with the elimination of inflation.
- Improve the procedures for coordinating Federal Reserve monetary policy with the economic policies of the administration and the Congress and support congressional efforts to monitor the Fed's performance and to recommend changes in the procedures that could improve performance.

With these fundamentals in place, the American people will respond. As the conviction grows that the policies will be sustained in a consistent manner over an extended period, the response will quicken. And a healthy US economy, as the Burns Task Force states, will restore the credibility of our dollar on world markets, contribute significantly to smoother operation of the international economy, and enhance America's strength in the world.

Organizing for Action

The activities of a wide variety of departments, agencies, and other units of government within the executive branch impinge on economic policy. But the flow of economic events does not recognize organization lines. The economy itself operates as a system in which constituent parts are linked, sometimes tightly. The combination of interwoven problems and disparate organizations means that, in the process of policy formulation and implementation, some people high in your administration must identify the central ideas and problems and devise a strategy and tactics for dealing with them. Your leadership is essential to this effort.

One arrangement that has worked well in the past is for the Secretary of the Treasury to be the chief coordinator and spokesman on economic policy, domestic and international. To carry out this mandate effectively, the Secretary should be one of your key staff members as well as a departmental head with a White House title and office. Since economic developments are often closely related to security, the Secretary should be a member of the National Security Council. For this coordinating role, an Economic Policy Board, with comprehensive membership, should be established; it should meet regularly and be the avenue through which economic issues come to your Executive of the Cabinet and to your desk. The Council of Economic Advisers might suitably provide the secretariat for this group.

Maintaining a Steady Course

Our final point is our most important one. The success of your economic policy will be a direct reflection of your ability to maintain a steady course over your full first term. Rough times will come and crises of one kind or another—some small, some of great moment—will arise. Sustained effort through these testing times means that public understanding and support are essential. Of equal and related importance is the understanding and support of the Congress.

This last task—gaining understanding and support of the Congress—is of crucial importance. As a result of the voting on November 4, the 97th Congress, we are convinced, will be more cooperative on economic and financial issues. That cooperation will be fostered if, during the transition, the Secretary of the Treasury (designate) consults intensively with key members of Congress on the design and implementation of your economic policies.

You have emphasized in your successful campaign precisely the strategy set forth in this document. In moving to implement it, you will be doing what the people voted for. Every effort must be made to maintain and broaden your base of support by improving public understanding and by close cooperation with the Congress. Cabinet officers and others in your administration can help in these tasks. Their ability to do so should be one important criterion in their selection.

At the end of the day, however, the burden of leadership falls on you: leadership to chart the course ahead; leadership to persuade that your course is the one to take; leadership to stay on course, whatever way political winds may blow. Through effective advocacy of the sharp changes so sorely needed, your leadership has brought us to this long-hoped-for opportunity at a critical moment for the nation. Your leadership can maintain this advocacy in the convincing manner necessary for a successful outcome.

"Think Long" to Solve the Crisis

George P. Shultz

January 30, 2009

The current economic crisis must be viewed as a gigantic wake-up call. We have been living beyond our means for some years now, and the message is clear: We must change our ways. We are so blessed with human talent and resources that we can meet the challenges and succeed.

How did this crisis get started? The effort to identify the sources of the problem can easily lead us into staggering complexity, but the outline is simple. In the first place, the environment included a prolonged period of Fed-provided, exceptionally easy money.

People and institutions behave more responsibly when they have some of their own equity at stake, some "skin in the game." The current financial crisis emerged after this principle became virtually inoperative. In an effort to make housing more affordable, financial wizards, with the implicit backing of the federal government, figured out how to give houses away: no down payment and few if any questions asked about ability to service loans.

When you give something away, demand rises rapidly, as do prices, so rapidly rising prices made the easy terms look reasonable and seemed to validate them. Meanwhile, financial intermediaries packaged these mortgages and traded in them, in all too many cases with very high (30 or more-to-1) leverage. Once again, there was little equity in these deals.

All this separated the originator of the mortgage (that is, the risk) from the eventual holders and, at the same time, created financial instruments that were obscure. So people had little equity in the game but made lots of money even while not knowing exactly what they were doing. As

Charles Prince, then head of Citicorp, said, "[A]s long as the music is playing, you've got to get up and dance." What a party!

And now we have the hangover: bailouts of many financial institutions by the taxpayers. The Fed and the Treasury already have exposures in the trillions of dollars.

These events are not isolated instances that sprung from the blue. Rather, they're the product of our failure to deal adequately with clear problems and to think ahead about future consequences. So now, think long.

Taken as a whole, our society has been living beyond its means for a long time now. The fact that we consume more than we produce is made possible by the ever-larger deficits in our trade balance with the rest of the world. We import more than we export. This negative balance of trade has its financial counterpart.

In recent times, we have failed to save enough to finance our own investments. This is true of Americans as individuals and families, but also of our biggest collective effort—the federal government. Deficits, acts of dis-saving, have, with the exception of a few years, become chronic. When we support our activities by financing from abroad, we are selling to others a piece of our future. So, with all due recognition of the immediate need to encourage spending, let us not forget the long-term need for a return to a pattern of higher savings.

The fact is well known and well documented that Social Security will soon reach a point where the large inflow of money generated by the payroll tax is insufficient to cover promised benefits. This prospect presents a major budget problem. We know how to fix this problem in the long run without threat to the incomes of older people and without increasing the payroll tax. This can be done by using one of several possible changes in the method of indexing benefits and, eventually, indexing retirement age to account for greater longevity, with workers 55 or older and with workers at the low end of the income scale completely protected.

We know that the costs of our health-care system are spinning out of control, and we also know that a large amount of that money is wasted. We need a system that avoids those wastes, improves quality, keeps costs under control, and is universally available. There are paths to these goals. We also know that wage and price controls, with their important, adverse consequences in the long run, are not among them.

We know that the reason for our impressive health and longevity compared with earlier years is largely attributable to a breathtaking run of basic research and its application. In some cases progress is slow, and in others it is dramatic, as in the conquest of polio with the Salk vaccine. Funding for this basic research effort and for basic science generally is an investment in our future.

We have been on an energy roller coaster for the last four decades or so. This time, more brilliant scientific minds than ever are at work, and more ideas with genuine applicability are appearing. Keep this effort going so that we can get on to a steady course of a more secure and less threatening energy future.

We are blessed with opportunities and with inventive and productive people. If we roll up our sleeves today, we will emerge stronger and with confidence in our future. A competent, sustained effort to deal effectively with long-term issues is essential to reap real benefits from any immediate stimulus to the economy.

Principles for Economic Revival

George P. Shultz, Michael J. Boskin, John F. Cogan,
Allan H. Meltzer, and John B. Taylor

September 16, 2010

Our prosperity has faded because policies have moved away from those that have proven to work. Here are the priorities that should guide policy makers as they seek to restore more rapid growth.

America's financial crisis, deep recession, and anemic recovery have largely been driven by economic policies that have deviated from proven fact-based principles. To return to prosperity we must get back to these principles.

The most fundamental starting point is that people respond to incentives and disincentives. Tax rates are a great example because the data are so clear and the results so powerful. A wealth of evidence shows that high tax rates reduce work effort, retard investment and lower productivity growth. Raise taxes, and living standards stagnate.

Nobel Prize-winning economist Edward Prescott examined international labor market data and showed that changes in tax rates on labor are associated with changes in employment and hours worked. From the 1970s to the 1990s, the effective tax rate on work increased by an average of 28 percent in Germany, France and Italy. Over that same period, work hours fell by an average of 22 percent in those three countries. When higher taxes reduce the reward for work, you get less of it.

Long-lasting economic policies based on a long-term strategy work; temporary policies don't. The difference between the effect of permanent tax rate cuts and one-time temporary tax rebates is also well documented. The former creates a sustainable increase in economic output, the latter at best only a transitory blip. Temporary policies create uncertainty that dampens economic output as market participants, unsure about whether and how policies might change, delay their decisions.

Having "skin in the game," unsurprisingly, leads to superior outcomes. As Milton Friedman famously observed: "Nobody spends somebody else's money as wisely as they spend their own." When legislators put other people's money at risk—as when Fannie Mae and Freddie Mac bought risky mortgages—crisis and economic hardship inevitably result. When minimal co-payments and low deductibles are mandated in the insurance market, wasteful health-care spending balloons.

Rules-based policies provide the foundation of a high-growth market economy. Abiding by such policies minimizes capricious discretionary actions, such as the recent ad hoc bailouts, which too often had deleterious consequences. For most of the 1980s and '90s monetary policy was conducted in a predictable rule-like manner. As a result, the economy was far more stable. We avoided lengthy economic contractions like the Great Depression of the 1930s and the rapid inflation of the 1970s.

The history of recent economic policy is one of massive deviations from these basic tenets. The result has been a crippling recession and now a weak, nearly nonexistent recovery. The deviations began with policies—like the Federal Reserve holding interest rates too low for too long—that fueled the unsustainable housing boom. Federal housing policies allowed down payments on home loans as low as zero. Banks were encouraged to make risky loans, and securitization separated lenders from their loans. Neither borrower nor lender had sufficient skin in the game. Lax enforcement of existing regulations allowed both investment and commercial banks to circumvent long-established banking rules to take on far too much leverage. Regulators, not regulations, failed.

The departures from sound principles continued when the Fed and the Treasury responded with arbitrary and unpredictable bailouts of banks, auto companies and financial institutions. They financed their actions with unprecedented money creation and massive issuance of debt. These frantic moves spooked already turbulent markets and led to the financial panic.

More deviations occurred when the government responded with ineffective temporary stimulus packages. The 2008 tax rebate and the 2009 spending stimulus bills failed to improve the economy. Cash for clunkers and the first-time home buyers tax credit merely moved purchases forward by a few months.

Then there's the recent health-care legislation, which imposes taxes on savings and investment and gives the government control over health-care decisions. Fannie Mae and Freddie Mac now sit with an estimated $400 billion cost to taxpayers and no path to resolution. Hundreds of new complex regulations lurk in the 2010 financial reform bill with most of the critical details left to regulators. So uncertainty reigns and nearly $2 trillion in cash sits in corporate coffers.

Since the onset of the financial crisis, annual federal spending has increased by an extraordinary $800 billion—more than $10,000 for every American family. This has driven the budget deficit to 10 percent of GDP, far above the previous peacetime record. The Obama administration has proposed to lock a sizable portion of that additional spending into government programs and to finance it with higher taxes and debt. The Fed recently announced it would continue buying long-term Treasury debt, adding to the risk of future inflation.

There is perhaps no better indicator of the destructive path that these policy deviations have put us on than the federal budget. The nearby chart puts the fiscal problem in perspective. It shows federal spending as a percent of GDP, which is now at 24 percent, up sharply from 18.2 percent in 2000.

Future federal spending, driven mainly by retirement and health-care promises, is likely to increase beyond 30 percent of GDP in 20 years and then keep rising, according to the Congressional Budget Office. The reckless expansions of both entitlements and discretionary programs in recent years have only added to our long-term fiscal problem.

As the chart shows, in all of US history, there has been only one period of sustained decline in federal spending relative to GDP. From 1983 to 2001, federal spending relative to GDP declined by five percentage points. Two factors dominated this remarkable period. First was strong economic growth. Second was modest spending restraint—on domestic spending in the 1980s and on defense in the 1990s.

The Cost of Washington

Federal budget outlays as a percentage of GDP

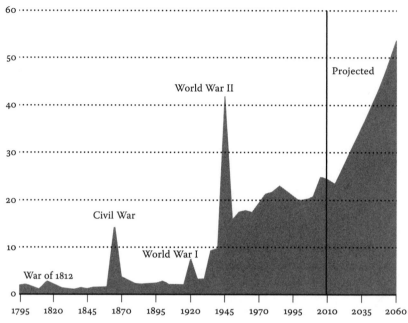

Source: Economic History Services, March 2004; Annual Report of the Secretary of the Treasury, Statistical Appendix; United States Budget, fiscal year 2011; Congressional Budget Office 2011.

The good news is that we can change these destructive policies by adopting a strategy based on proven economic principles:

- *First, take tax increases off the table.* Higher tax rates are destructive to growth and would ratify the recent spending excesses. Our complex tax code is badly in need of overhaul to make America more competitive. For example, the US corporate tax is one of the highest in the world. That's why many tax reform proposals integrate personal and corporate income taxes with fewer special tax breaks and lower tax rates.

    But in the current climate, with the very credit-worthiness of the United States at stake, our program keeps the present tax regime in place while avoiding the severe economic drag of higher tax rates.

• *Second, balance the federal budget by reducing spending.* The publicly held debt must be brought down to the pre-crisis safety zone. To do this, the excessive spending of recent years must be removed before it becomes a permanent budget fixture. The government should begin by rescinding unspent "stimulus" and TARP funds, ratcheting down domestic appropriations to their pre-binge levels, and repealing entitlement expansions, most notably the subsidies in the health-care bill.

The next step is restructuring public activities between federal and state governments. The federal government has taken on more responsibilities than it can properly manage and efficiently finance. The 1996 welfare reform, which transferred authority and financing for welfare from the federal to the state level, should serve as the model. This reform reduced welfare dependency and lowered costs, benefiting taxpayers and welfare recipients.

• *Third, modify Social Security and health-care entitlements to reduce their explosive future growth.* Social Security now promises much higher benefits to future retirees than to today's retirees. The typical 30-year-old today is scheduled to get an inflation-adjusted retirement benefit that is 50 percent higher than the benefit for a typical current retiree.

Benefits paid to future retirees should remain at the same level, in terms of purchasing power, that today's retirees receive. A combination of indexing initial benefits to prices rather than to wages and increasing the program's retirement age would achieve this goal. They should be phased in gradually so that current retirees and those nearing retirement are not affected.

Health care is far too important to the American economy to be left in its current state. In markets other than health care, the legendary American shopper, armed with money and information, has kept quality high and costs low. In health care, service providers, unaided by consumers with sufficient skin in the game, make the purchasing decisions. Third-party payers—employers, governments and insurance companies—have resorted to regulatory schemes and price controls to stem the resulting cost growth.

The key to making Medicare affordable while maintaining the quality of health care is more patient involvement, more choices among Medicare health plans, and more competition. Co-payments should be raised to make patients and their physicians more cost-conscious. Monthly premiums should be lowered to provide seniors with more disposable income to make these choices. A menu of additional Medicare plans, some with lower premiums, higher co-payments and improved catastrophic coverage, should be added to the current one-size-fits-all program to encourage competition.

Similarly for Medicaid, modest co-payments should be introduced except for preventive services. The program should be turned over entirely to the states with federal financing supplied by a "no strings attached" block grant. States should then allow Medicaid recipients to purchase a health plan of their choosing with a risk-adjusted Medicaid grant that phases out as income rises.

The 2010 health-care law undermined positive reforms under way since the late 1990s, including higher co-payments and health savings accounts. The law should be repealed before its regulations and price controls further damage availability and quality of care. It should be replaced with policies that target specific health market concerns: quality, affordability and access. Making out-of-pocket expenditures and individual purchases of health insurance tax deductible, enhancing health savings accounts, and improving access to medical information are keys to more consumer involvement. Allowing consumers to buy insurance across state lines will lower the cost of insurance.

- *Fourth, enact a moratorium on all new regulations for the next three years, with an exception for national security and public safety.* Going forward, regulations should be transparent and simple, pass rigorous cost-benefit tests, and rely to a maximum extent on market-based incentives instead of command and control. Direct and indirect cost estimates of regulations and subsidies should be published before new regulations are put into law.

Off-budget financing should end by closing Fannie Mae and Freddie Mac. The Bureau of Consumer Finance Protection and all other government agencies should be on the budget that Congress annually approves. An enhanced bankruptcy process for failing financial firms should be enacted in order to end the need for bailouts. Higher bank capital requirements that rise with the size of the bank should be phased in.

• *Fifth, monetary policy should be less discretionary and more rule-like.* The Federal Reserve should announce and follow a monetary policy rule, such as the Taylor rule, in which the short-term interest rate is determined by the supply and demand for money and is adjusted through changes in the money supply when inflation rises above or falls below the target, or when the economy goes into a recession. When monetary policy decisions follow such a rule, economic stability and growth increase.

In order to reduce the size of the Fed's bloated balance sheet without causing more market disruption, the Fed should announce and follow a clear and predictable exit rule, which describes a contingency path for bringing bank reserves back to normal levels. It should also announce and follow a lender-of-last-resort rule designed to protect the payment system and the economy—not failing banks. Such a rule would end the erratic bailout policy that leads to crises.

The United States should, along with other countries, agree to a target for inflation in order to increase expected price stability and exchange rate stability. A new accord between the Federal Reserve and Treasury should reestablish the Fed's independence and account-ability so that it is not called on to monetize the debt or engage in credit allocation. A monetary rule is a requisite for restoring the Fed's independence.

These pro-growth policies provide the surest path back to prosperity.

Time for a Budget Game-Changer
Gary S. Becker, George P. Shultz, and John B. Taylor
April 4, 2011

Assurance that current tax levels will remain in place would provide an immediate stimulus. House Republican budget planners are on the right track.

Wanted: A strategy for economic growth, full employment, and deficit reduction—all without inflation. Experience shows how to get there. Credible actions that reduce the rapid growth of federal spending and debt will raise economic growth and lower the unemployment rate. Higher private investment, not more government purchases, is the surest way to increase prosperity.

When private investment is high, unemployment is low. In 2006, investment—business fixed investment plus residential investment—as a share of GDP was high, at 17 percent, and unemployment was low, at 5 percent. By 2010 private investment as a share of GDP was down to 12 percent, and unemployment was up to more than 9 percent. In the year 2000, investment as a share of GDP was 17 percent while unemployment averaged around 4 percent. This is a regular pattern.

In contrast, higher government spending is not associated with lower unemployment. For example, when government purchases of goods and services came down as a share of GDP in the 1990s, unemployment didn't rise. In fact it fell, and the higher level of government purchases as a share of GDP since 2000 has clearly not been associated with lower unemployment.

To the extent that government spending crowds out job-creating private investment, it can actually worsen unemployment. Indeed, extensive government efforts to stimulate the economy and reduce joblessness by spending more have failed to reduce joblessness.

Above all, the federal government needs a credible and transparent budget strategy. It's time for a game-changer—a budget action that will stop the recent discretionary spending binge before it gets entrenched in government agencies.

Second, we need to lay out a path for total federal government spending growth for next year and later years that will gradually bring spending into balance with the amount of tax revenues generated in later years by the current tax system. Assurance that the current tax system will remain in place—pending genuine reform in corporate and personal income taxes—will be an immediate stimulus.

All this must be accompanied by an accurate and simple explanation of how the strategy will increase economic growth, an explanation that will counteract scare stories and also allow people outside of government to start making plans, including business plans, to invest and hire. In this respect the budget strategy should be seen in the context of a larger pro-growth, pro-employment government reform strategy.

We can see such a sensible budget strategy starting to emerge. The first step of the strategy is largely being addressed by the House budget plan for 2011, or HR1. Though voted down in its entirety by the Senate, it is now being split up into "continuing" resolutions that add up to the same spending levels.

To see how HR1 works, note that discretionary appropriations other than for defense and homeland security were $460.1 billion in 2010, a sharp 22 percent increase over the $378.4 billion a mere three years ago. HR1 reverses this bulge by bringing these appropriations to $394.5 billion, which is 4 percent higher than in 2008. Spending growth is greatly reduced under HR1, but it is still enough to cover inflation over those three years.

There is no reason why government agencies—from Treasury and Commerce to the Executive Office of the President—cannot get by with the same amount of funding they had in 2008 plus increases for inflation. Anything less than HR1 would not represent a credible first step. Changes in budget authority convert to government outlays slowly. According to

An Easy Path to Sustainable Spending

Government outlays as a percentage of GDP

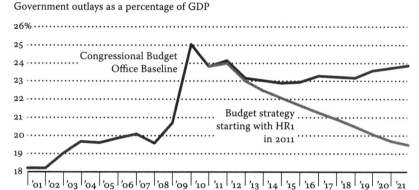

Sources: Congressional Budget Office, the authors.

the Congressional Budget Office, outlays will only be $19 billion less in 2011 with HR1, meaning it would take spending to 24 percent of GDP in 2011 from 24.1 percent today.

If HR1 is the first step of the strategy, then the second step could come in the form of the budget resolution for 2012 also coming out of the House. We do not know what this will look like, but it is likely to entail a gradual reduction in spending as a share of GDP that would, in a reasonable number of years, lead to a balanced budget without tax rate increases.

To make the path credible, the budget resolution should include instructions to the appropriations subcommittees elaborating changes in government programs that will make the spending goals a reality. These instructions must include a requirement for reforms of the Social Security and health-care systems.

Health-care reform is particularly difficult politically, although absolutely necessary to get long-term government spending under control. This is not the place to go into various ways to make the health-care delivery system cheaper and at the same time much more effective in promoting health. However, it is absolutely essential to make wholesale changes in ObamaCare, and many of its approaches to health reform.

The nearby chart shows an example of a path that brings total federal outlays relative to GDP back to the level of 2007—19.5 percent. One line shows outlays as a share of GDP under the CBO baseline released on March 18. The other shows the spending path starting with HR1 in 2011. With HR1 federal outlays grow at 2.7 percent per year from 2010 to 2021 in nominal terms, while nominal GDP is expected to grow by 4.6 percent per year.

Faster GDP growth will bring a balanced budget more quickly by increasing the growth of tax revenues. Critics will argue that such a budget plan will decrease economic growth and job creation. Some, such as economists at Goldman Sachs and Moody's, have already said that HR1 will lower economic growth by as much as 2 percent this quarter and the next and cost hundreds of thousands of jobs. But this is highly implausible given the small size of the change in outlays in 2011 under HR1, as shown in the chart. The change in spending is not abrupt, as they claim, but quite gradual.

Those who predict that a gradual and credible plan to lower spending growth will reduce job creation disregard the private investment benefits that come from reducing the threats of higher taxes, higher interest rates and a fiscal crisis. This is the same thinking used to claim that the stimulus package worked. These economic models failed in the 1970s, failed in 2008, and they are still failing.

Control of federal spending and a strategy for ending the deficit will provide assurance that tax rates will not rise—pending tax reform—and that uncontrolled deficits will not recur. This assurance must be the foundation of strategy for a healthy economy.

Education Is the Key to a Healthy Economy

George P. Shultz and Eric A. Hanushek

April 30, 2012

If we fail to reform K–12 schools, we'll have slow growth and more income inequality.

In addressing our current fiscal and economic woes, too often we neglect a key ingredient of our nation's economic future—the human capital produced by our K–12 school system. An improved education system would lead to a dramatically different future for the US, because educational outcomes strongly affect economic growth and the distribution of income.

Over the past half century, countries with higher math and science skills have grown faster than those with lower-skilled populations. In the chart nearby, we compare GDP-per-capita growth rates between 1960 and 2000 with achievement results on international math assessment tests. The countries include almost all of the Organization for Economic Cooperation and Development (OECD) countries plus a number of developing countries. What stands out is that all the countries follow a nearly straight line that slopes upward—as scores rise, so does economic growth. Peru, South Africa, and the Philippines are at the bottom; Singapore and Taiwan, the top.

The US growth rate lies above the line because—despite the more recent shortcomings of our schools— we've long benefited from our commitment to the free movement of labor and capital, strong property rights, a limited degree of government intrusion in the economy, and strong colleges and universities. But each of these advantages has eroded considerably and should not be counted on to keep us above the line in the future.

With Knowledge Comes Growth

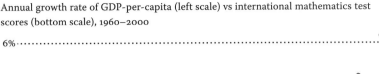

Annual growth rate of GDP-per-capita (left scale) vs international mathematics test scores (bottom scale), 1960–2000

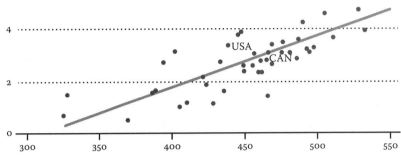

Source: Eric A. Hanushek and Ludger Woessmann, "The High Cost of Low Educational Performance" (OECD, 2012). Reprinted with permission.

Current US students—the future labor force—are no longer competitive with students across the developed world. In the OECD's Programme for International Student Assessment (PISA) rankings for 2009, the US was 31st in math—indistinguishable from Portugal or Italy. In "advanced" performance on math, 16 countries produced twice as many high achievers per capita than the US did.

If we accept this level of performance, we will surely find ourselves on a low-growth path.

This doesn't have to be our fate. Imagine a school improvement program that made us competitive with Canada in math performance (which means scoring approximately 40 points higher on PISA tests) over the next 20 years. As these Canadian-skill-level students entered the labor force, they would produce a faster-growing economy.

How much faster? The results are stunning. The improvement in GDP over the next 80 years would exceed a present value of $70 trillion. That's equivalent to an average 20 percent boost in income for every US worker each year over his or her entire career. This would generate enough revenue to solve easily the US debt problem that is the object of so much current debate.

The drag on growth is by no means the only problem produced by our lagging education system. Greater educational disparity leads to greater income-distribution disparity. If we fail to reform our K–12 education system, we'll be locking in inequality problems that will plague us for decades if not generations to come.

Take our own state of California. Once a leader in education, it is now ranked behind 40 other US states in math achievement, placing it at the level of Greece and foreshadowing a bleak future of ballooning debt and growing income disparity.

But the averages mask the truly sad story in the Latino population, soon to become California's dominant demographic group. Hispanics attending school in California perform no better than the average student in Mexico, a level comparable to the typical student in Kazakhstan. An alarming 43 percent of Hispanic students in California did not complete high school between 2005 and 2009, and only 10 percent attained a college degree.

Anyone worried about income disparity in America should be deeply disturbed. The failure of the K–12 education system for so many students means that issues associated with income distribution—including higher taxes and less freedom in labor and capital markets—will be an ever-present and distressing aspect of our future.

Examples abound of the ability to make sharp improvements in our K–12 system. By not insisting on immediate and widespread reform we are forgoing substantial growth in our standard of living. The problem is obvious. The stakes are enormous. The solutions are within our reach.

The Magnitude of the Mess We're In

George P. Shultz, Michael J. Boskin, John F. Cogan,
Allan H. Meltzer, and John B. Taylor

September 16, 2012

---

*The next Treasury secretary will confront problems so daunting that even
Alexander Hamilton would have trouble preserving the full faith and credit
of the United States.*

Sometimes a few facts tell important stories. The American economy
now is full of facts that tell stories that you really don't want, but need,
to hear.

Where are we now?

Did you know that annual spending by the federal government now
exceeds the 2007 level by about $1 trillion? With a slow economy, rev-
enues are little changed. The result is an unprecedented string of federal
budget deficits, $1.4 trillion in 2009, $1.3 trillion in 2010, $1.3 trillion in
2011, and another $1.2 trillion on the way this year. The four-year increase
in borrowing amounts to $55,000 per US household.

The amount of debt is one thing. The burden of interest payments is
another. The Treasury now has a preponderance of its debt issued in very
short-term durations, to take advantage of low short-term interest rates.
It must frequently refinance this debt which, when added to the current
deficit, means Treasury must raise $4 trillion this year alone. So the debt
burden will explode when interest rates go up.

The government has to get the money to finance its spending by taxing
or borrowing. While it might be tempting to conclude that we can just
tax upper-income people, did you know that the US income tax system

is already very progressive? The top 1 percent pay 37 percent of all income taxes and 50 percent pay none.

Did you know that, during the last fiscal year, around three-quarters of the deficit was financed by the Federal Reserve? Foreign governments accounted for most of the rest, as American citizens' and institutions' purchases and sales netted to about zero. The Fed now owns one in six dollars of the national debt, the largest percentage of GDP in history, larger than even at the end of World War II.

The Fed has effectively replaced the entire interbank money market and large segments of other markets with itself. It determines the interest rate by declaring what it will pay on reserve balances at the Fed without regard for the supply and demand of money. By replacing large decentralized markets with centralized control by a few government officials, the Fed is distorting incentives and interfering with price discovery with unintended economic consequences.

Did you know that the Federal Reserve is now giving money to banks, effectively circumventing the appropriations process? To pay for quantitative easing—the purchase of government debt, mortgage-backed securities, etc.—the Fed credits banks with electronic deposits that are reserve balances at the Federal Reserve. These reserve balances have exploded to $1.5 trillion from $8 billion in September 2008.

The Fed now pays 0.25 percent interest on reserves it holds. So the Fed is paying the banks almost $4 billion a year. If interest rates rise to 2 percent, and the Federal Reserve raises the rate it pays on reserves correspondingly, the payment rises to $30 billion a year. Would Congress appropriate that kind of money to give—not lend—to banks?

The Fed's policy of keeping interest rates so low for so long means that the real rate (after accounting for inflation) is negative, thereby cutting significantly the real income of those who have saved for retirement over their lifetime.

The Consumer Financial Protection Bureau is also being financed by the Federal Reserve rather than by appropriations, severing the checks and balances needed for good government. And the Fed's Operation Twist, buying long-term and selling short-term debt, is substituting for the Treasury's traditional debt management.

This large expansion of reserves creates two-sided risks. If it is not unwound, the reserves could pour into the economy, causing inflation. In that event, the Fed will have effectively turned the government debt and mortgage-backed securities it purchased into money that will have an explosive impact. If reserves are unwound too quickly, banks may find it hard to adjust and pull back on loans. Unwinding would be hard to manage now, but will become ever harder the more the balance sheet rises.

The issue is not merely how much we spend, but how wisely, how effectively. Did you know that the federal government had 46 separate job-training programs? Yet a 47th for green jobs was added, and the success rate was so poor that the Department of Labor inspector general said it should be shut down. We need to get much better results from current programs, serving a more carefully targeted set of people with more effective programs that increase their opportunities.

Did you know that funding for federal regulatory agencies and their employment levels are at all-time highs? In 2010, the number of *Federal Register* pages devoted to proposed new rules broke its previous all-time record for the second consecutive year. It's up by 25 percent compared to 2008. These regulations alone will impose large costs and create heightened uncertainty for business and especially small business.

This is all bad enough, but where we are headed is even worse.

President Obama's budget will raise the federal debt-to-GDP ratio to 80.4 percent in two years, about double its level at the end of 2008, and a larger percentage point increase than Greece from the end of 2008 to the beginning of this year.

Under the president's budget, for example, the debt expands rapidly to $18.8 trillion from $10.8 trillion in 10 years. The interest costs alone will reach $743 billion a year, more than we are currently spending on Social Security, Medicare or national defense, even under the benign assumption of no inflationary increase or adverse bond-market reaction. For every one percentage point increase in interest rates above this projection, interest costs rise by more than $100 billion, more than current spending on veterans' health and the National Institutes of Health combined.

Worse, the unfunded long-run liabilities of Social Security, Medicare and Medicaid add tens of trillions of dollars to the debt, mostly due to rising real benefits per beneficiary. Before long, all the government will be able to do is finance the debt and pay pension and medical benefits. This spending will crowd out all other necessary government functions.

What does this spending and debt mean in the long run if it is not controlled? One result will be ever-higher income and payroll taxes on all taxpayers that will reach over 80 percent at the top and 70 percent for many middle-income working couples.

Did you know that the federal government used the bankruptcy of two auto companies to transfer money that belonged to debt holders such as pension funds and paid it to friendly labor unions? This greatly increased uncertainty about creditor rights under bankruptcy law.

The Fed is adding to the uncertainty of current policy. Quantitative easing as a policy tool is very hard to manage. Traders speculate whether and when the Fed will intervene next. The Fed can intervene without limit in any credit market—not only mortgage-backed securities but also securities backed by automobile loans or student loans. This raises questions about why an independent agency of government should have this power.

When businesses and households confront large-scale uncertainty, they tend to wait for more clarity to emerge before making major commitments to spend, invest and hire. Right now, they confront a mountain of regulatory uncertainty and a fiscal cliff that, if unattended, means a sharp increase in taxes and a sharp decline in spending bound to have adverse effect on the economy. Are you surprised that so much cash is waiting on the sidelines?

What's at stake?

We cannot count on problems elsewhere in the world to make Treasury securities a safe haven forever. We risk eventually losing the privilege and great benefit of lower interest rates from the dollar's role as the global reserve currency. In short, we risk passing an economic, fiscal and financial point of no return.

Suppose you were offered the job of Treasury secretary a few months from now. Would you accept? You would confront problems that are so daunting even Alexander Hamilton would have trouble preserving the full faith and credit of the United States. Our first Treasury secretary famously argued that one of a nation's greatest assets is its ability to issue debt, especially in a crisis. We needed to honor our Revolutionary War debt, he said, because the debt "foreign and domestic, was the price of liberty."

History has reconfirmed Hamilton's wisdom. As historian John Steele Gordon has written, our nation's ability to issue debt helped preserve the Union in the 1860s and defeat totalitarian governments in the 1940s. Today, government officials are issuing debt to finance pet projects and payoffs to interest groups, not some vital, let alone existential, national purpose.

The problems are close to being unmanageable now. If we stay on the current path, they will wind up being completely unmanageable, culminating in an unwelcome explosion and crisis.

The fixes are blindingly obvious. Economic theory, empirical studies and historical experience teach that the solutions are the lowest possible tax rates on the broadest base, sufficient to fund the necessary functions of government on balance over the business cycle; sound monetary policy; trade liberalization; spending control and entitlement reform; and regulatory, litigation and education reform. The need is clear. Why wait for disaster? The future is now.

A Better Energy Future

How to Gain a Climate Consensus
George P. Shultz
September 5, 2007

We in the United States—and we as global citizens—live in what is, in many respects, a golden moment. Economic growth is globally strong, and, if security threats can be contained, this expansion, with some ups and downs, can be sustained.

Strong growth means increased use of energy at a pace that can strain the capacity to supply what is needed at a reasonable price. This highlights two urgent questions: how to use energy without producing excess greenhouse gases that create disruptive conditions on a global scale; and how to reduce the threat to national security from excess dependence on oil.

The greenhouse gas problem is more broadly recognized today than it was during the Kyoto Protocol negotiations. Moreover, the protocol is running its course, so a new treaty is needed. That treaty should have a different structure—one that ultimately achieves universality.

During the Reagan administration, we faced the problem of depletion of the ozone layer, and negotiations resulted in the Montreal Protocol. To be sure, the problem then was less complex than that of today. However, there are parallels, and lessons from the Montreal Protocol can be useful.

The reductions called for in ozone-depleting substances were aggressive but realistic in that they could be undertaken without severe economic damage, in part because demand triggered the development by private industry of needed chemicals and appliances.

Because we in the United States were ready to take action, we could ask others to act as well.

The protocol also recognized the importance of a little wiggle room, so provision was made for the possibility of special arrangements among countries.

The countries with low per capita incomes were integral to the process and were given special treatment in terms of trading rules and the establishment of a fund that could help them meet their obligations.

What can we learn from this? Here are some guiding principles:

- The process benefited greatly from strong US leadership. We were the science leader, the moral leader and the diplomatic leader. Yes, those of us working for an agreement, notably John Negroponte, now deputy secretary of state, faced internal opposition; there were doubts about the reality of the problem and that reasonable solutions could be identified and implemented. But at all the crunch points, Ronald Reagan was there for us. The president cleared the way, and in the end he called the result a "monumental achievement." The Senate readily gave its consent to ratification.

- Universality of coverage is a necessary goal. The world must be represented at the table. Interests and capabilities vary widely. Patience and flexibility are key. We must focus on the countries that matter most and explore shared interests, identify respective vulnerabilities and adaptive options, and share views on scientific and technological advances. We could explore the possibility of industry-specific solutions within such groups as air transport, automotive, steel and electric utilities. One caution: Holdouts must not be allowed to get special treatment.

- The negotiating structure must involve constituencies because, in the end, they will bear the weight of necessary actions. At all costs, we must avoid what happened at Kyoto, where we signed the protocol after the Senate, by unanimous vote, advised President Bill Clinton not to conclude a treaty that lacked commitments by developing countries. In other words, our negotiator had lost touch with his constituency.

- The use of economic incentives (caps and trading rights, and carbon taxes) is essential to avoid disastrously high costs of control. The cap-and-trade system has been highly successful in reducing sulfur dioxide emissions by electricity utilities in the United States. That system relies on a scientifically valid and accepted emission-measurement system used by a clearly identified and homogeneous set of utilities. Fortunately, such a careful system of measurement exists for a viable greenhouse gas regimen. The product of collaboration between the World Resources Institute and the World Business Council for Sustainable Development, these standards for accounting and reporting greenhouse gases should be duly understood and adopted. Even with clear units of account, however, large problems arise as the coverage and heterogeneity of the system grow. And for trading across borders, the system needs to be accepted among the trading partners. Scams are easy to imagine. No nation should be allowed to trade without a verifiable, transparent system of measuring and monitoring of reductions, and holding emitters accountable. In many respects, a straight-out carbon tax is simpler and likelier to produce the desired result. If the tax were offset by cuts elsewhere to make it revenue-neutral, acceptability would be enhanced.

- Do not expect China, India and other developing countries to accept what amounts to a cap on economic growth. They will not—and cannot—do that. We must create market incentives for them to cut emissions while continuing to grow and find actions that are economically feasible in a relatively low-income environment. We may also need to give them extra time, even allowing some short-term emissions growth, before requiring them to reduce their emissions. This is similar to the way we accommodated developing countries under the Montreal Protocol.

- Another imperative, a derivative of the previous point, is the need to deal effectively with issues of intellectual property. The obligation to reward innovators must be reconciled with the needs of low-income societies.

- The negotiations should not conclude until important first steps are identified and agreed upon so that everyone takes some action.

As we consider a new treaty, we must recognize that one size will not fit the world, even though some technologies may have wide, even universal, application. The Montreal Protocol, as a successful environmental treaty, provides a model for establishing a process with wide agreement to take important action.

Why We Support a Revenue-Neutral Carbon Tax

George P. Shultz and Gary S. Becker

April 7, 2013

Americans like to compete on a level playing field. All the players should have an equal opportunity to win based on their competitive merits, not on some artificial imbalance that gives someone or some group a special advantage.

We think this idea should be applied to energy producers. They all should bear the full costs of the use of the energy they provide. Most of these costs are included in what it takes to produce the energy in the first place, but they vary greatly in the price imposed on society by the pollution they emit and its impact on human health and well-being, the air we breathe and the climate we create. We should identify these costs and see that they are attributed to the form of energy that causes them.

At the same time, we should seek out the many forms of subsidy that run through the entire energy enterprise and eliminate them. In their place we propose a measure that could go a long way toward leveling the playing field: a revenue-neutral tax on carbon, a major pollutant. A carbon tax would encourage producers and consumers to shift toward energy sources that emit less carbon—such as toward gas-fired power plants and away from coal-fired plants—and generate greater demand for electric and flex-fuel cars and lesser demand for conventional gasoline-powered cars.

We argue for revenue neutrality on the grounds that this tax should be exclusively for the purpose of leveling the playing field, not for financing some other government programs or for expanding the government sector. And revenue neutrality means that it will not have fiscal drag on economic growth.

The imposition of such a tax raises questions about how it should be levied and what measures should be used to see that the revenues collected are refunded to the public so that the tax is clearly revenue-neutral.

The tax might be imposed at a variety of stages in the production and distribution of energy. You can make an argument for imposing it at the point most visible to the population at large, which would be the point of consumption such as gasoline stations and electricity bills. An administratively more efficient way of imposing the tax, however, would be to collect it at the level of production, which would reduce greatly the number of collection points.

Revenue neutrality comes from distribution of the proceeds, which could be done in many ways. On the grounds of ease of administration and visibility, we advocate having the tax collected and distributed by an existing unit of government, either the Internal Revenue Service or the Social Security Administration. In either case, we think the principle of transparency should be observed. Money collected should go into an identified fund and the amounts flowing in and out should be clearly visible. This flow of funds should not be included in the unified budget, so as to keep the money from being spent on general government purposes, as happened to the earlier excess of inflows over outflows in the Social Security system.

In the case of administration by the IRS, an annual distribution could be made to every taxpayer and recipient of the Earned Income Tax Credit. In the case of the SSA, the distribution could be made, in terms proportionate to the dollars involved, to everyone either paying into the system or receiving benefits from it. In any case, checks to recipients should be identified as "Your carbon dividend."

The right level of the tax for the United States deserves careful study, but the principle of a lower starting rate with scheduled increases to an identified level has proven to be a good one in the five-year experience of a similar carbon tax in British Columbia. This gives time for producers and consumers to get accustomed to a carbon tax, and to discover how they can respond efficiently.

The tax should also further increase over time if the apparent severity of the climate effects is growing and, alternatively, the tax should fall over time if the severity appears to be decreasing. Finally, to equalize the present and future burdens, the carbon rate should rise over time approximately at the real interest rate (say, the real return on 10-year Treasurys), so that the present value of the burden would be the same to future consumers and producers as it is to present ones.

A revenue-neutral carbon tax should be supplemented by a reasonable and sustained support for research and development in the energy area. However, we would eliminate any program (loan guarantees, etc.) that tempts the government to get into commercial activities. Clearly, a revenue-neutral carbon tax would benefit all Americans by eliminating the need for costly energy subsidies while promoting a level playing field for energy producers.

APPENDIX FIVE

Drugs: The War with No Winner

A Real Debate About Drug Policy

George P. Shultz and Paul A. Volcker

June 11, 2011

"The global war on drugs has failed, with devastating consequences for individuals and societies around the world."

That is the opening sentence of a report issued last week by the Global Commission on Drug Policy. Both of us have signed on to this report. Why?

We believe that drug addiction is harmful to individuals, impairs health and has adverse societal effects. So we want an effective program to deal with this problem.

The question is: What is the best way to go about it? For 40 years now, our nation's approach has been to criminalize the entire process of producing, transporting, selling and using drugs, with the exception of tobacco and alcohol. Our judgment, shared by other members of the commission, is that this approach has not worked, just as our national experiment with the prohibition of alcohol failed. Drugs are still readily available, and crime rates remain high. But drug use in the US is no lower than, and sometimes surpasses, drug use in countries with very different approaches to the problem.

At the same time, the costs of the drug war have become astronomical. Inmates arrested for consuming drugs and for possessing small quantities of them now crowd our prisons, where too often they learn how to become real criminals. The dollar costs are huge, but they pale in comparison to the lives being lost in our neighborhoods and throughout the world. The number of drug-related casualties in Mexico is on the same order as the number of US lives lost in the Vietnam and Korean wars.

Throughout our hemisphere, governance and economic development have suffered because of drugs. It is no accident that the initiative for this global commission came from former presidents of Latin American nations. These countries, sometimes with American support, have made strong efforts to reduce drug supplies. But they have increasingly concluded that drug policies in the US are making it more difficult for their people to enjoy security and prosperity.

The problem starts with the demand for drugs. As Milton Friedman put it forcibly over 20 years ago in the pages of this paper: "It is demand that must operate through repressed and illegal channels. Illegality creates obscene profits that finance the murderous tactics of the drug lords; illegality leads to the corruption of law enforcement officials."

We do not support the simple legalization of all drugs. What we do advocate is an open and honest debate on the subject. We want to find our way to a less costly and more effective method of discouraging drug use, cutting down the power of organized crime, providing better treatment and minimizing negative societal effects.

Other countries that have tried different approaches include Britain, the Netherlands, Switzerland, Portugal and Australia. What can we learn from these varied experiences, some more successful than others? What can we learn from our own experience in reducing sharply the smoking of cigarettes or in the handling of alcohol after the end of Prohibition?

Simple legalization is by no means the only or safest approach. One possibility is to decriminalize the individual use of drugs while maintaining laws against supplying them, thus allowing law-enforcement efforts to focus on the drug peddlers. Some of the money that is saved can be spent on treatment centers, which drug users are more likely to seek out if doing so does not expose them to the risk of arrest.

The situation that confronts us today is dangerous. After 40 years of concentrating on one approach that has been unsuccessful, we should be willing to take a look at other ways of working to solve this pressing problem. As the Global Commission on Drug Policy concludes: "Break the taboo on debate and reform. The time for action is now."

Effective Diplomacy Applied to Issues of Foreign Policy

US Foreign Policy: Realism and Progress
New York, NY
September 30, 1982

Following is an address by Secretary Shultz before the 37th UN General Assembly in New York, September 30, 1982.

I begin by paying tribute to our new Secretary General, who has brought great distinction to the office during his brief tenure. Dag Hammarskjold once told the General Assembly that "independence, impartiality, objectivity—they all describe essential aspects of what, without exception, must be in the attitude of the Secretary General." Javier Perez de Cuellar, a man of the Third World and, I am proud to note, of the New World as well, has already demonstrated his strict adherence to this most exacting standard. In so doing, he has earned the esteem of my government and the gratitude of all who believe in the purposes of the charter.

I congratulate, as well, Mr. Hollai [Imre Hollai, Deputy Foreign Minister] of Hungary upon his election as President of the 37th Session of the General Assembly.

As I stand before you today, I cannot help but reflect on my relation to this city and to this hall. I was born about four miles from here. I was reared and educated not far away, just across the Hudson River. And I took a tour through this building just after it opened in 1952 marveling at the reality of a temple erected in the hope, at least, of abolishing war.

When I took that tour back in the early fifties, there was great public interest in what was called "the Meditation Room." I understand the room is still here. But in the years since then, this institution has become more famous for talk than for meditation. This hall has heard great ideas eloquently expressed. It has also heard doubletalk, platitudes, and ringing

United States Department of State, Bureau of Public Affairs, Washington, DC.

protestations of innocence—all too often aimed at camouflaging outrageous and inhuman acts.

But we must not ridicule words. I believe that the greatest advance in human history was not the wheel, the use of electricity, or the internal combustion engine. Indispensable to progress as these have been, our most remarkable achievement was the slow, clumsy but triumphant creation of language. It is words that released our ancestors from the prison of the solitary. Words gave us the means to transmit to our children and the future the crowning jewel of human existence: knowledge. The Code of Hammurabi, the Bible, the Analects of Confucius, the teachings of the Buddha, the Koran, the insights of Shakespeare, the creed of Mahatma Gandhi or Martin Luther King—all these are arrangements of words.

Is it not profoundly revealing that the first victims of tyrants are—words? No people better know the meaning of freedom than those who have been arrested, beaten, imprisoned, or exiled because of what they said. A single man speaking out—a Lech Walesa, for example—is more dangerous than an armored division.

All of us here—whether we arrived after a short one-hour flight, as I did, or came from the other side of the globe, as many of you did—enter this auditorium for one main purpose: to talk about what our governments see as the problems ahead and how they should be solved. On one point, at least, we can all agree: The problems are many and difficult. I shall not try, in the minutes allotted me, to deal with each—or even most—of those issues in detail. Instead, I want to give you some sense of the principles and general approach the United States will take toward our common problems.

Americans are, by history and by inclination, a practical and pragmatic people—yet a people with a vision. It is the vision—usually simple and sometimes naive—that has so often led us to dare and to achieve. President Reagan's approach to foreign policy is grounded squarely on standards drawn from the pragmatic American experience. As de Tocqueville pointed out, "To achieve its objective, America relies on personal interest, and gives full rein to the strength and reason of the individual." That is as true now as when it was said 150 years ago. Our principal instrument, now as then, is freedom. Our adversaries are the oppressors, the totalitarians, the tacticians of fear and pressure.

On this foundation, President Reagan's ideas and the structure of his foreign policy are so straightforward that those of us enmeshed in day-to-day details may easily lose sight of them. The President never does; he consistently brings us back to fundamentals. Today, I will talk about those fundamentals. They consist of four ideas that guide our actions.

- We will start from realism.
- We will act from strength, both in power and purpose.
- We will stress the indispensable need to generate consent, build agreements, and negotiate on key issues.
- We will conduct ourselves in the belief that progress is possible, even though the road to achievement is long and hard.

Reality

If we are to change the world we must first understand it. We must face reality—with all its anguish and all its opportunities. Our era needs those who, as Pericles said, have the clearest vision of what is before them, glory and danger alike, and, notwithstanding, go out to meet it.

Reality is not an illusion nor a sleight of hand, though many would have us believe otherwise. The enormous, grinding machinery of Soviet propaganda daily seeks to distort reality, to bend truth for its own purposes. Our world is occupied by far too many governments which seek to conceal truth from their own people. They wish to imprison reality by controlling what can be read or spoken or heard. They would have us believe that black is white and up is down.

Much of present day reality is unpleasant. To describe conditions as we see them, as I do today and as President Reagan has over the course of his presidency, is not to seek confrontation. Far from it. Our purpose is to avoid misunderstanding and to create the necessary preconditions for change. And so, when we see aggression, we will call it aggression. When we see subversion, we will call it subversion. When we see repression, we will call it repression.

- Events in Poland, for example, cannot be ignored or explained away. The Polish people want to be their own master. Years of systematic tyranny could not repress this desire, and neither will martial law. But in Poland today, truth must hide in corners.

- Nor can we simply turn our heads and look the other way as Soviet divisions brutalize an entire population in Afghanistan. The resistance of the Afghan people is a valiant saga of our times. We demean that valor if we do not recognize its source.

- And Soviet surrogates intervene in many countries, creating a new era of colonialism at the moment in history when peoples around the globe had lifted that burden from their backs.

- Nor will we shy away from speaking of other problems affecting the free and developing worlds. Much of the developing world is threatened by a crisis of confidence in financial institutions and the stultifying effects of state-controlled economies. The naturally vibrant economies of many Western nations and trade between the world's major trading partners are threatened by recession and rising protectionism.

  The great alliances that shore up world stability and growth—our hemispheric partnership and NATO, and the Western and Japanese industrial democracies—are challenged by new as well as chronic strains.

- Finally, the shadow of war still darkens the future of us all. There is no ultimate safety in a nuclear balance of terror constantly contested. There is no peace of mind at a time when increasing numbers of nations appear willing to launch their armies into battles for causes which seem local but have ramifications for regional and even global harmony.

The list of troubles is long; the danger of despair great. But there is another side to the present reality; it is a reality of hope. We are living in a fantastic time of opportunity.

Historians in the future will surely marvel over the accomplishments achieved by human beings in the last half of this century. We have expanded the frontiers of thought—in science, biology, and engineering;

in painting, music, and mathematics; in technology and architecture—far beyond the point anyone could have dared predict, much less hoped for. We know much today about the oceans and forests and the geological strata that lock in the story of our past. We know more about a baby—or the brain—than was accumulated in 10 millenia before our time. We are learning to produce food for all of us; we are no longer helpless before the threat of disease; we explore our universe as a matter of course. We are confronting the nature of nature itself. The opportunities are grand. This, too, is a clear reality.

Thus, realism shows us a world deeply troubled, yet with reason for hope. There is one necessary condition: The only way we can enhance and amplify the human potential is by preserving, defending, and extending those most precious of conditions—freedom and peace.

Strength

America's yearning for peace does not lead us to be hesitant in developing our strength or in using it when necessary. Indeed, clarity about the magnitude of the problems we face leads inevitably to a realistic appreciation of the importance of American strength. The strength of the free world imposes restraint, invites accommodation, and reassures those who would share in the creative work that is the wonderful consequence of liberty.

Strength means military forces to insure that no other nation can threaten us, our interests, or our friends. But when I speak of strength, I do not mean military power alone. To Americans, strength derives as well from a solid economic base and social vitality at home and with our partners. And, most fundamentally, the true wellspring of strength lies in America's moral commitment.

The bulwark of America's strength is military power for peace.   The American people have never accepted weakness, nor hesitancy, nor abdication. We will not put our destiny into the hands of the ruthless. Americans today are emphatically united on the necessity of a strong defense. This year's defense budget will insure that the United States will help its friends and allies defend themselves—to make sure that peace is seen clearly by all to be the only feasible course in world affairs.

Along with military readiness and capability must come the willingness to employ it in the cause of peace, justice, and security. Today in Beirut the US Marines—together with our allies Italy and France—are helping the Lebanese government and armed forces assure the safety of the peoples of that tormented capital. Our Marines represent an extension of American power, not for war but to secure the peace. They are there to speed the moment when all foreign forces depart from Lebanon. There must be early agreement on a timetable for the full application of Lebanon's independence, sovereignty, and territorial integrity. Lebanon deserves the world's help—to secure peace and to rebuild a thriving society.

America will continue to use its strength with prudence, firmness, and balance. We intend to command the respect of adversaries and to deserve the confidence of allies and partners.

The engine of America's strength is a sound economy. In a time of recession, industrialized and less developed nations alike are bedeviled by excessive inflation, restricted markets, unused capacity, stagnating trade, growing pressure for protectionism, and the most potent enemy of expansion—pervasive uncertainty.

The United States, with its vast human and scientific resources, can survive an era of economic strife and decay. But our moral commitment and our self-interest require us to use our technological and productive abilities to build lasting prosperity at home and to contribute to a sound economic situation abroad.

President Reagan has instituted a bold program to get the American economy moving. Our rate of inflation is down markedly, and we will keep it down. This will add stability to the value of the dollar and give greater confidence to international financial markets.

The recent drop in US interest rates will stimulate new investments within and beyond our shores. Conservation through market pricing of energy has reduced US demand for world energy supplies. We are putting the recession behind us. A growing and open American economy will provide new markets for goods and services produced elsewhere and new opportunities for foreign investment. Just as we have a stake in worldwide recovery, others will prosper as our recovery develops.

For wider prosperity to take hold, we must cooperatively attend these international issues.

- The lure of protectionist trade policies must be resisted—whether in the form of overt import restrictions and export subsidies or by more subtle domestic programs. These can only distort world trade and impair growth everywhere. Let us determine to make the November ministerial meeting of the GATT [General Agreement on Tariffs and Trade] a time to stem these protectionist pressures and reinvigorate positive efforts for a more open trading system.

- The implications of the external debt of many nations must be understood. Immediate debt problems are manageable if we use good sense and avoid destabilizing actions. But the magnitude of external debt will almost inevitably reduce resources available for future lending for development purposes. Economic adjustment is imperative. The International Monetary Fund can provide critical help and guidance in any country's efforts to smooth the adjustment process. The new borrowing arrangement proposed by the United States can be crucial to this effort.

- And the necessity of reducing government interference in the market must be recognized. Every nation has the right to organize society as its inhabitants wish, but economic facts cannot be ignored. Those facts clearly demonstrate that the world's command economies have failed abysmally to meet the needs of their peoples. The newly prosperous industrialized nations are those with the most free and open markets.

The bedrock of our strength is our moral and spiritual character. The sources of true strength lie deeper than economic or military power—in the dedication of a free people which knows its responsibility. America's institutions are those of freedom accessible to every person and of government as the accountable servant of the people. Equal opportunity; due process of law; open trial by jury; freedom of belief, speech, and assembly—our Bill of Rights, our guarantees of liberty and limited government—were hammered out in centuries of ordeal. Because we care about these human values for ourselves, so must we then be concerned, and legitimately so, with abuses of freedom, justice, and humanitarian principles beyond our borders. This is why we will speak and act for prisoners of conscience, against terrorism, and against the brutal silencing of the Soviet Helsinki Watch Committee. This is why we are anxious to participate in periodic reviews of the human rights performance of ourselves as well as others. We welcome scrutiny of our own system. We are not perfect, and we know it, but we have nothing to hide.

Our belief in liberty guides our policies here in the United Nations as elsewhere. Therefore, in this forum the United States will continue to insist upon fairness, balance, and truth. We take the debate on human rights seriously. We insist upon honesty in the use of language; we will point out inconsistencies, double standards, and lies. We will not compromise our commitment to truth.

Readiness To Solve Problems

The world has work to do for the realists, the pragmatists, and the free. With a clear understanding of the troubled circumstances of the hour and with a strengthened ability to act, we need, as well, the vision to see beyond the immediate present.

All of us here represent nations which must understand and accept the imperative of fair engagement on the issues before us and, beyond that, of common effort toward shared goals. Whether we are seeking to bring peace to regional conflict or a resolution of commercial differences, the time of imposed solutions has passed. Conquest, pressure, acquiescence under duress were common in decades not long past, but not today. Not everybody who wants his concerns addressed will find us automatically receptive. But when negotiations are in order, America is prepared to go to work on the global agenda and to do so in a way that all may emerge better off and more secure than before.

We manage our problems more intelligently, and with greater mutual understanding, when we can bring ourselves to recognize them as expressions of mankind's basic dilemma. We are seldom confronted with simple issues of right and wrong, between good and evil. Only those who do not bear the direct burden of responsibility for decision and action can indulge themselves in the denial of that reality. The task of statesmanship is to mediate between two—or several—causes, each of which often has a legitimate claim.

It is on this foundation that the United States stands ready to try to solve the problems of our time—to overcome chaos, deprivation, and the heightened dangers of an era in which ideas and cultures too often tend to clash and technologies threaten to outpace our institutions of control.

We are engaged in negotiations and efforts to find answers to issues affecting every part of the globe and every aspect of our lives upon it.

The Middle East.   The agony of the Middle East now exceeds the ability of news bulletins or speeches to express; it is a searing wound on our consciousness. The region is in constant ferment. Unrest flares into violence, terror, insurrection, and civil strife. War follows war. It is clear to everyone in this hall that international peace, security, and cooperative progress cannot be truly achieved until this terrible regional conflict is settled.

All of us have witnessed in the past several months a graphic reminder of the need for practical peace negotiations in the Middle East. Of the nations in the world which need and deserve peace, Israel surely holds a preeminent place. Of the peoples of the world who need and deserve a place with which they can truly identify, the Palestinian claim is undeniable.

But Israel can only have permanent peace in a context in which the Palestinian people also realize their legitimate rights. Similarly, the Palestinian people will be able to achieve their legitimate rights only in a context which gives to Israel what it so clearly has a right to demand—to exist, and to exist in peace and security.

This most complex of international conflicts cannot be resolved by force. Neither the might of armies nor the violence of terrorists can succeed in imposing the will of the strong upon the weak. Nor can it be settled simply by the rhetoric of even the most carefully worded document. It can only be resolved through the give and take of direct negotiations leading to the establishment of practical arrangements on the ground.

In other words, it can only be resolved through hard work. For those who believe that there is no contradiction between permanent peace for Israel and the legitimate rights of the Palestinian people—and for those who believe that both are essential for peace and that neither can be achieved without the other—the task can truly be a labor of love.

On September 1, President Reagan challenged the parties to the Arab-Israeli conflict to make a fresh start on the road to peace in the Middle East. The Camp David agreements, resting squarely on UN Security Council Resolution 242, with its formula of peace for territory, remain available to those who would accept the challenge to make this journey with us. The road will not be easy but, in his statement, President Reagan made a number of proposals which, for those who are willing to join the effort, make the journey safer and easier. I call on all concerned to accept President Reagan's challenge and hasten the realization of true peace in the Middle East.

Arms Control.   In addition to the imperative need to resolve regional problems, there is an equally significant global imperative: to halt, and reverse, the global arms buildup. As an American, I am aware that arms control and disarmament are a special responsibility of the world's most powerful nations—the United States and the Soviet Union. And as an American, I can report that we are fulfilling our responsibility to seek to limit and reduce conventional and nuclear arms to the lowest possible levels.

With this goal in mind, President Reagan has initiated a comprehensive program for negotiated arms reductions. In Central Europe, the most heavily armed region on this planet, the Western allies are seeking substantial reductions in NATO and Warsaw Pact troops to equal levels. To achieve this goal, we have recently introduced a new proposal designed to revitalize the talks in Vienna on mutual and balanced reductions in military manpower.

In the area of strategic arms, the United States has also taken the initiative by calling for a one-third reduction in the number of nuclear warheads that American and Soviet ballistic missiles can deliver. And in the talks in Geneva on intermediate-range nuclear forces, the United States has gone even further, by asking the Soviet Union to agree to a bold proposal for eliminating an entire category of weapons from the arsenals of the two sides.

But as important as these negotiations are, the problem of arms control cannot be left to the two superpowers. The threat of nuclear proliferation extends to every region in the world and demands the attention and energy of every government. This is not solely, or even primarily, a concern of the superpowers. The non-nuclear countries will not be safer if nuclear intimidation is added to already deadly regional conflicts. The developing nations will not be more prosperous if scarce resources and scientific talent are diverted to nuclear weapons and delivery systems.

Unfortunately, as the task becomes more important, it also becomes more difficult. Greater quantities of dangerous materials are produced, and new suppliers emerge who lack a clear commitment to nonproliferation. But the technology that helped to create the problems can supply answers as well. Vigorous action to strengthen the barriers to aggression and to resolve disputes peacefully can remove the insecurities that are the root of the problem. The United States, for its part, will work to tighten export controls, to promote broader acceptance of safeguards, to urge meaningful actions when agreements are violated, and to strengthen the International Atomic Energy Agency. As our action last week in Vienna should make clear, we will not accept attempts to politicize—and, therefore, emasculate—such vital institutions.

Progress

Perhaps the most common phrase spoken by the American people in our more than two centuries of national life has been: "You can't stop progress." Our people have always been imbued with the conviction that the future of a free people would be good.

America continues to offer that vision to the world. With that vision and with the freedom to act creatively, there is nothing that people of good will need fear.

I am not here to assert, however, that the way is easy, quick, or that the future is bound to be bright. There is a poem by Carl Sandburg in which a traveler asks the sphinx to speak and reveal the distilled wisdom of all the ages. The sphinx does speak. Its words are: "Don't expect too much."

That is good counsel for all of us here. It does not mean that great accomplishments are beyond our reach. We can help shape more constructive international relations and give our children a better chance at life. It does mean, however, that risk, pain, expense, and, above all, endurance are needed to bring those achievements into our grasp.

We must recognize the complex and vexing character of this world. We should not indulge ourselves in fantasies of perfection or unfulfillable plans or solutions gained by pressure. It is the responsibility of leaders not to feed the growing appetite for easy promises and grand assurances. The plain truth is this: We face the prospect of all too few decisive or dramatic breakthroughs; we face the necessity of dedicating our energies and creativity to a protracted struggle toward eventual success.

Conclusion

That is the approach of my country—because we see not only the necessity, but the possibility, of making important progress on a broad front.

- Despite deep-seated differences between us and the Soviet Union, negotiators of both sides are now at work in a serious, businesslike effort at arms control.
- President Reagan has issued an important call for an international conference on military expenditure. The achievement of a common system for accounting and reporting is the prerequisite for subsequent agreement to limit or curtail defense budgets.
- The Caribbean Basin Initiative establishes the crucial bond between economic development and economic freedom. It can be a model for fair and productive cooperation between economies vastly different in size and character.
- And the diplomatic way is open to build stability and progress in southern Africa through independence for Namibia under internationally acceptable terms.

Realism and a readiness to work long and hard for fair and freely agreed solutions—that is our recipe for optimism. That is the message and the offer which my government brings to you today.

I began my remarks here today with an informal personal word. Let me end in the same spirit. We must be determined and confident. We must be prepared for trouble but always optimistic. In this way the vast bounties produced by the human mind and imagination can be shared by all the races and nations we represent here in this hall.

A predecessor of mine as Secretary of State, whose portrait hangs in my office, conveyed the essence of America's approach to the world's dangers and dilemmas. He said we would act with "a stout heart and a clear conscience, and never despair."

That is what John Quincy Adams said nearly a century and a half ago. I give you my personal pledge today that we will continue in that spirit, with that determination, and with that confidence in the future.

America and the Struggle for Freedom
San Francisco, CA
February 22, 1985

Following is an address by Secretary Shultz before the Commonwealth Club of California, San Francisco, California, February 22, 1985.

A revolution is sweeping the world today—a democratic revolution. This should not be a surprise. Yet it is noteworthy because many people in the West lost faith, for a time, in the relevance of the idea of democracy. It was fashionable in some quarters to argue that democracy was culture bound; that it was a luxury only industrial societies could afford; that other institutional structures were needed to meet the challenges of development; that to try to encourage others to adopt our system was ethnocentric and arrogant.

In fact, what began in the United States of America over two centuries ago as a bold new experiment in representative government has today captured the imagination and the passions of peoples on every continent. The Solidarity movement in Poland; resistance forces in Afghanistan, in Cambodia, in Nicaragua, in Ethiopia and Angola; dissidents in the Soviet Union and Eastern Europe; advocates of peaceful democratic change in South Africa, Chile, the Republic of Korea, and the Philippines—all these brave men and women have something in common: they seek independence, freedom, and human rights—ideals which are at the core of democracy and which the United States has always championed.

The American Tradition
All Americans can be proud that the example of our Founding Fathers has helped to inspire millions around the globe. Throughout our own history,

United States Department of State, Bureau of Public Affairs, Washington, DC.

we have always believed that freedom is the birthright of all peoples and that we could not be true to ourselves or our principles unless we stood for freedom and democracy not only for ourselves but for others.

And so, time and again in the last 200 years, we have lent our support—moral and otherwise—to those around the world struggling for freedom and independence. In the 19th century Americans smuggled guns and powder to Simon Bolivar, the Great Liberator; we supported the Polish patriots and others seeking freedom. We well remembered how other nations, like France, had come to our aid during our own revolution.

In the 20th century, as our power as a nation increased, we accepted a greater role in protecting and promoting freedom and democracy around the world. Our commitment to these ideals has been strong and bipartisan in both word and deed. During World War I, the Polish pianist Paderewski and the Czech statesman Masaryk raised funds in the United States; then Woodrow Wilson led the way at war's end in achieving the independence of Poland, Czechoslovakia, and other states.

At the height of World War II, Franklin Roosevelt set forth a vision of democracy for the postwar world in the Atlantic Charter and Four Freedoms. The United States actively promoted decolonization. Harry Truman worked hard and successfully at protecting democratic institutions in postwar Western Europe and at helping democracy take root in West Germany and Japan. At the United Nations in 1948 we supported the Universal Declaration of Human Rights—which declares the right of every nation to a free press, free assembly and association, periodic and genuine elections, and free trade unions. John F. Kennedy drew upon the very essence of America with his call to "pay any price . . . to assure the survival and success of liberty."

The March of Democracy

The struggle for liberty is not always successful. But those who once despaired, who saw democracy on the decline, and who argued that we must lower our expectations were, at best, premature. Civilizations decline when they stop believing in themselves; ours has thrived because we have never lost our conviction that our values are worth defending.

When Indira Gandhi, the Prime Minister of the world's largest democracy, was assassinated, we were shocked and saddened. But our confidence in the resilience of democracy was renewed as millions of India's people went to the polls freely to elect her successor. As Rajiv Gandhi leads his nation to new greatness, he demonstrates more clearly than any words or abstract scientific models that democracy is neither outmoded nor is it the exclusive possession of a few, rich, Western nations. It has worked for decades in countries as diverse as Costa Rica and Japan.

In the Western Hemisphere, over 90 percent of the population of Latin America and the Caribbean today live under governments that are either democratic or clearly on the road to democracy—in contrast to only one-third in 1979. In less than six years, popularly elected democrats have replaced dictators in Argentina, Bolivia, Ecuador, El Salvador, Honduras, Panama, Peru, and Grenada. Brazil and Uruguay will inaugurate civilian presidents in March. After a long twilight of dictatorship, this hemispheric trend toward free elections and representative government is something to be applauded and supported.

The Challenge to the Brezhnev Doctrine

Democracy is an old idea, but today we witness a new phenomenon. For many years we saw our adversaries act without restraint to back insurgencies around the world to spread communist dictatorships. The Soviet Union and its proxies, like Cuba and Vietnam, have consistently supplied money, arms, and training in efforts to destabilize or overthrow noncommunist governments. "Wars of national liberation" became the pretext for subverting any noncommunist country in the name of so-called "socialist internationalism."

At the same time, any victory of communism was held to be irreversible. This was the infamous Brezhnev doctrine, first proclaimed at the time of the invasion of Czechoslovakia in 1968. Its meaning is simple and chilling: once you're in the so-called "socialist camp," you're not allowed to leave. Thus the Soviets say to the rest of the world: "What's mine is mine. What's yours is up for grabs."

In recent years, Soviet activities and pretensions have run head-on into the democratic revolution. People are insisting on their right to independence, on their right to choose their government free of outside control. Where once the Soviets may have thought that all discontent was ripe for turning into communist insurgencies, today we see a new and different kind of struggle: people around the world risking their lives against communist despotism. We see brave men and women fighting to challenge the Brezhnev doctrine.

In December 1979, the Soviets invaded **Afghanistan** to preserve a communist system installed by force a year and a half earlier. But their invasion met stiff resistance, and the puppet government they installed has proved incapable of commanding popular support. Today, the Soviets have expanded their occupation army and are trying to devastate the population and the nation they cannot subdue. They are demolishing entire Afghan villages and have driven one out of every four Afghans to flee the country. They have threatened neighboring countries like Pakistan and have been unwilling to negotiate seriously for a political solution.

In the face of this Soviet invasion, the Afghans who are fighting and dying for the liberation of their country have made a remarkable stand. Their will has not flagged; indeed, their capacity to resist has grown. The countryside is now largely in the hands of the popular resistance, and not even in the major cities can the Soviets claim complete control. Clearly, the Afghans do not share the belief of some in the West that fighting back is pointless, that the only option is to let one's country be "quietly erased," to use the memorable phrase of the Czech writer, Milan Kundera.

In **Cambodia,** the forces open to democracy, once all but annihilated by the Khmer Rouge, are now waging a similar battle against occupation and a puppet regime imposed by a Soviet ally, communist Vietnam. Although Vietnam is too poor to feed, house, or care for the health of its own population adequately, the Stalinist dictators of Hanoi are bent on imperial domination of Indochina—much as many had predicted before, during, and after the Vietnam war. But six years after its invasion, Vietnam does not control Cambodia. Resistance forces total over 50,000; of these, noncommunist forces have grown from zero to over 20,000. The Vietnamese still need an occupation army of 170,000 to keep order in the country; they even had to bring in two new divisions to mount the recent offensive. That offensive, while more brutal than previous attacks, will prove no more conclusive than those before.

In **Africa,** as well, the Brezhnev doctrine is being challenged by the drive for independence and freedom. In Ethiopia, a Soviet-backed Marxist-Leninist dictatorship has shown indifference to the desperate poverty and suffering of its people. The effects of a natural disaster have been compounded by the regime's obsession with ideology and power. In classical Stalinist fashion, it has ruined agricultural production through forced collectivization; denied food to starving people for political reasons; subjected many thousands to forced resettlement; and spent vast sums of money on arms and "revolutionary" spectacles. But the rulers cannot hide the dimensions of the tragedy from their people. Armed insurgencies continue, while the regime persists in relying on military solutions and on expanding the power and scope of the police and security apparatus.

In Angola, a Marxist regime came into power in 1975 backed and sustained by 30,000 Cuban troops and substantial numbers of Soviet and East European "advisers." The continuation of this Soviet/Cuban intervention has been a major impediment to the achievement of independence for Namibia under the terms of UN Security Council Resolution 435; it is also a continuing challenge to African independence and regional peace and security—thus our sustained diplomatic effort to achieve a regional settlement addressing the issues of both Angola and Namibia. In Angola, UNITA [National Union for the Total Independence of Angola] has waged an armed struggle against the regime's monopoly of power and in recent years has steadily expanded the territory under its control. Foreign forces, whether Cuban or South African, must leave. At some point there will be an internal political settlement in Angola that reflects Angolan political reality, not external intervention.

Finally, an important struggle is being waged today closer to home in **Central America.** Its countries are in transition, trying to resolve the inequities and tensions of the past through workable reforms and democratic institutions. But violent antidemocratic minorities, tied ideologically and militarily to the Soviet Union and Cuba, are trying to prevent democratic reform and to seize or hold power by force. The outcome of this struggle will affect not only the future of peace and democracy in this hemisphere but our own vital interests.

In Nicaragua, in 1979 the Sandinista leaders pledged to the Organization of American States (OAS) and to their own people to bring freedom to their country after decades of tyranny under Anastasio Somoza. The Sandinistas have betrayed these pledges and the hopes of the Nicaraguan people; instead, they have imposed a new and brutal tyranny that respects no frontiers. Basing themselves on strong military ties to Cuba and the Soviet Union, the Sandinistas are attempting, as rapidly as they can, to force Nicaragua into a totalitarian mold whose pattern is all too familiar. They are suppressing internal dissent; clamping down on the press; persecuting the church; linking up with the terrorists of Iran, Libya, and the PLO [Palestine Liberation Organization]; and seeking to undermine the legitimate and increasingly democratic governments of their neighbors.

This betrayal has forced many Nicaraguans who supported the anti-Somoza revolution back into opposition. And while many resist peacefully, thousands now see no choice but to take up arms again, to risk everything so that their hopes for freedom and democracy will not once again be denied.

The Sandinistas denounce their opponents as mercenaries or former National Guardsmen loyal to the memory of Somoza. Some in this country seem all too willing to take these charges at face value, even though they come from the same Sandinista leaders whose word has meant so little up to now. But all you have to do is count the numbers: more people have taken up arms against the Sandinistas than ever belonged to Somoza's National Guard. In fact, most of the leaders of the armed resistance fought in the revolution against Somoza; and some even served in the new government until it became clear that the *comandantes* were bent on communism, not freedom; terror, not reform; and aggression, not peace. The new fighters for freedom include peasants and farmers, shopkeepers and vendors, teachers and professionals. What unites them to each other and to the other thousands of Nicaraguans who resist without arms is disillusionment with Sandinista militarism, corruption, and fanaticism.

Despite uncertain and sporadic support from outside, the resistance in Nicaragua is growing. The Sandinistas have strengthened their Soviet and Cuban military ties, but their popularity at home has declined sharply. The struggle in Nicaragua for democracy and freedom, and against dictatorship, is far from over, and right now may well be a pivotal moment that decides the future.

America's Moral Duty

This new phenomenon we are witnessing around the world—popular insurgencies *against* communist domination—is not an American creation. In every region the people have made their own decision to stand and fight rather than see their cultures and freedoms "quietly erased." They have made clear their readiness to fight with or without outside support, using every available means and enduring severe hardships, alone if need be.

But America also has a moral responsibility. The lesson of the postwar era is that America must be the leader of the free world; there is no one else to take our place. The nature and extent of our support—whether moral support or something more—necessarily varies from case to case. But there should be no doubt about where our sympathies lie.

It is more than mere coincidence that the last four years have been a time of both renewed American strength and leadership and a resurgence of democracy and freedom. As we are the strongest democratic nation on earth, the actions we take—or do not take—have both a direct and an indirect impact on those who share our ideals and hopes all around the globe. If we shrink from leadership, we create a vacuum into which our adversaries can move. Our national security suffers, our global interests suffer, and, yes, the worldwide struggle for democracy suffers.

The Soviets are fond of talking about the "correlation of forces," and for a few years it may have seemed that the correlation of forces favored communist minorities backed by Soviet military power. Today, however, the Soviet empire is weakening under the strain of its own internal problems and external entanglements. And the United States has shown the will and the strength to defend its interests, to resist the spread of Soviet influence, and to protect freedom. Our actions, such as the rescue of Grenada, have again begun to offer inspiration and hope to others.

The importance of American power and leadership to the strength of democracy has not been the only lesson of recent history. In many ways, the reverse has also proven true: the spread of democracy serves American interests.

Historically, there have been times when the failure of democracy in certain parts of the world did not affect our national security. In the 18th and 19th centuries, the failure of democracy to take root elsewhere was unfortunate and even troubling to us, but it did not necessarily pose a threat to our own democracy. In the second half of the 20th century, that is less and less true. In almost every case in the postwar period, the imposition of communist tyrannies has led to an increase in Soviet global power and influence. Promoting insurgencies against noncommunist governments in important strategic areas has become a low-cost way for the Soviets to extend the reach of their power and to weaken their adversaries, whether they be China or the democracies of the West and Japan. This is true in Southeast Asia, Southwest Asia, Africa, and Central America.

When the United States supports those resisting totalitarianism, therefore, we do so not only out of our historical sympathy for democracy and freedom but also, in many cases, in the interests of national security. As President Reagan said in his second inaugural address: "America must remain freedom's staunchest friend, for freedom is our best ally and it is the world's only hope to conquer poverty and preserve peace."

In many parts of the world we have no choice but to act, on both moral and strategic grounds.

How To Respond?

The question is: How should we act? What should America do to further both its security interests and the cause of freedom and democracy? A prudent strategy must combine different elements, suited to different circumstances.

First, as a matter of fundamental principle, the United States supports human rights and peaceful democratic change throughout the world, including in noncommunist, pro-Western countries. Democratic institutions are the best guarantor of stability and peace, as well as of human rights. Therefore, we have an interest in seeing peaceful progress toward democracy in friendly countries.

Such a transition is often complex and delicate, and it can only come about in a way consistent with a country's history, culture, and political realities. We will not succeed if we fail to recognize positive change when it does occur—whether in South Africa, or the Republic of Korea, or the Philippines. Nor will we achieve our goal if we ignore the even greater threat to the freedom of such countries as South Korea and the Philippines from external or internal forces of totalitarianism. We must heed the cautionary lessons of both Iran and Nicaragua, in which pressures against right-wing authoritarian regimes were not well thought out and helped lead to even more repressive dictatorship.

Our influence with friendly governments is a precious resource; we use it for constructive ends. The President has said that "human rights means working at problems, not walking away from them." Therefore, we stay engaged. We stay in contact with all democratic political forces, in opposition as well as in government. The historic number of transitions from authoritarian regimes to democracy in the last decade, from southern Europe to Latin America, demonstrates the effectiveness of this approach—as well as the essential difference between authoritarian and totalitarian regimes. There are no examples of a communist system, once consolidated, evolving into a democracy.

In June 1982, addressing the British Parliament, President Reagan endorsed a new effort—including leaders of business, labor, and both the Democratic and Republican Parties—to enlist the energies of American private citizens in helping to develop the skills, institutions, and practices of democracy around the world. Today, the National Endowment for Democracy, the concrete result of that initiative, is assisting democratic groups in a wide variety of countries. The endowment represents practical American support for people abroad working for our common ideals.

Second, we have a moral obligation to support friendly democratic governments by providing economic and security assistance against a variety of threats.   When democratic friends are threatened by externally supported insurgencies, when hostile neighbors try to intimidate them by acquiring offensive arms or sponsor terrorism in an effort to topple their governments, international security is jeopardized. The more we can lend appropriate help to others to protect themselves, the less need there will be for more direct American involvement to keep the peace.

Americans have always responded with courage when overwhelming danger called for an immediate, all-out national effort. But the harder task is to recognize and meet challenges before they erupt into major crises, before they represent an immediate threat, and before they require an all-out effort. We have many possible responses that fall between the extremes of inaction and the direct use of military force—but we must be willing to use them, or else we will inevitably face the agonizing choice between those two extremes.

Economic and security assistance is one of those crucial means of avoiding and deterring bigger threats. It is also vital support to those friendly nations on the front line—like Pakistan, Thailand, or Honduras and Costa Rica—whose security is threatened by Soviet and proxy efforts to export their system.

Third, we should support the forces of freedom in communist totalitarian states.   We must not succumb to the fashionable thinking that democracy has enemies only on the right, that pressures and sanctions are fine against right-wing dictators but not against left-wing totalitarians. We should support the aspirations for freedom of peoples in communist states just as we want freedom for people anywhere else. For example, without raising false hopes, we have a duty to make it clear—especially on the anniversary of the Yalta conference—that the United States will never accept the artificial division of Europe into free and not free. This has nothing to do with boundaries and everything to do with ideas and governance. Our radios will continue to broadcast the truth to people in closed societies.

Fourth, and finally, our moral principles compel us to support those struggling against the imposition of communist tyranny. From the founding of this nation, Americans have believed that people have the right to seek freedom and independence—and that we have both a legal right and a moral obligation to help them.

In contrast to the Soviets and their allies, the United States is committed to the principles of international law. The UN and OAS Charters reaffirm the inherent right of individual and collective self-defense against aggression—aggression of the kind committed by the Soviets in Afghanistan, by Nicaragua in Central America, and by Vietnam in Cambodia. Material assistance to those opposing such aggression can be a lawful form of collective self-defense. Moral and political support, of course, is a long-standing and honorable American tradition—as is our humanitarian assistance for civilians and refugees in war-torn areas.

Most of what we do to promote freedom is, and should continue to be, entirely open. Equally, there are efforts that are most effective when handled quietly. Our Founding Fathers were sophisticated men who understood the necessity for discreet actions; after the controversies of the 1970s, we now have a set of procedures agreed between the President and Congress for overseeing such special programs. In a democracy, clearly, the people have a right to know and to shape the overall framework and objectives that guide all areas of policy. In those few cases where national security requires that the details are better kept confidential, Congress and the President can work together to ensure that what is done remains consistent with basic American principles.

Do we really have a choice? In the 1970s, a European leader proposed to Brezhnev that peaceful coexistence should extend to the ideological sphere. Brezhnev responded firmly that this was impossible, that the ideological struggle continued even in an era of détente, and that the Soviet Union would forever support "national liberation" movements. The practical meaning of that is clear. When Soviet Politburo member Gorbachev was in London recently, he affirmed that Nicaragua had gained independence only with the Sandinista takeover. The Soviets and their proxies thus proceed on the theory that any country not Marxist-

Leninist is not truly independent, and, therefore, the supply of money, arms, and training to overthrow its government is legitimate.

Again: "What's mine is mine. What's yours is up for grabs." This is the Brezhnev doctrine.

So long as communist dictatorships feel free to aid and abet insurgencies in the name of "socialist internationalism," why must the democracies, the target of this threat, be inhibited from defending their own interests and the cause of democracy itself?

How can we as a country say to a young Afghan, Nicaraguan, or Cambodian: "Learn to live with oppression; only those of us who already have freedom deserve to pass it on to our children"? How can we say to those Salvadorans who stood so bravely in line to vote: "We may give you some economic and military aid for self-defense, but we will also give a free hand to the Sandinistas who seek to undermine your new democratic institutions"?

Some try to evade this moral issue by the relativistic notion that "one man's freedom fighter is another man's terrorist." This is nonsense. There is a self-evident difference between those fighting to impose tyranny and those fighting to resist it. In El Salvador, pro-communist guerrillas backed by the Soviet bloc are waging war against a democratically elected government; in Nicaragua and elsewhere, groups seeking democracy are resisting the tightening grip of totalitarians seeking to suppress democracy. The essence of democracy is to offer means for peaceful change, legitimate political competition, and redress of grievances. Violence directed against democracy is, therefore, fundamentally lacking in legitimacy.

What we should do in each situation must, of necessity, vary. But it must always be clear whose side we are on—the side of those who want to see a world based on respect for national independence, for freedom and the rule of law, and for human rights. Wherever possible, the path to that world should be through peaceful and political means; but where dictatorships use brute power to oppress their own people and threaten their neighbors, the forces of freedom cannot place their trust in declarations alone.

Central America

Nowhere are both the strategic and the moral stakes clearer than in Central America.

The Sandinista leaders in Nicaragua are moving quickly, with Soviet-bloc and Cuban help, to consolidate their totalitarian power. Should they achieve this primary goal, we could confront a second Cuba in this hemisphere, this time on the Central American mainland—with all the strategic dangers that this implies. If history is any guide, the Sandinistas would then intensify their efforts to undermine neighboring governments in the name of their revolutionary principles—principles which Fidel Castro himself flatly reaffirmed on American television a few weeks ago. Needless to say, the first casualty of the consolidation of Sandinista power would be the freedom and hopes for democracy of the Nicaraguan people. The second casualty would be the security of Nicaragua's neighbors and the security of the entire region.

I do not believe anyone in the United States wants to see this dangerous scenario unfold. Yet there are those who would look the other way, imagining that the problem will disappear by itself. There are those who would grant the Sandinistas a peculiar kind of immunity in our legislation—in effect, enacting the Brezhnev doctrine into American law.

The logic of the situation in Central America is inescapable.

- The Sandinistas are committed Marxist-Leninists; it would be foolish of us and insulting to them to imagine that they do not believe in their proclaimed goals. They will not modify or bargain away their position unless there is compelling incentive for them to do so.
- The only incentive that has proved effective thus far comes from the vigorous armed opposition of the many Nicaraguans who seek freedom and democratic government.
- The pressures of the armed resistance have diverted Sandinista energies and resources away from aggression against its neighbor El Salvador, thus helping to disrupt guerrilla plans for a major offensive there last fall.
- If the pressure of the armed resistance is removed, the Sandinistas will have no reason to compromise; all US diplomatic efforts—and those of the Contadora Group—will be undermined.

Central America's hopes for peace, security, democracy, and economic progress will not be realized unless there is a fundamental change in Nicaraguan behavior in four areas.

First, Nicaragua must stop playing the role of surrogate for the Soviet Union and Cuba. As long as there are large numbers of Soviet and Cuban security and military personnel in Nicaragua, Central America will be embroiled in the East-West conflict.

Second, Nicaragua must reduce its armed forces, now in excess of 100,000, to a level commensurate with its legitimate security needs— a level comparable to those of its neighbors. The current imbalance is incompatible with regional stability.

Third, Nicaragua must absolutely and definitively stop its support for insurgents and terrorists in the region. All of Nicaragua's neighbors, and particularly El Salvador, have felt the brunt of Sandinista efforts to destabilize their governments. No country in Central America will be secure as long as this continues.

And fourth, the Sandinistas must live up to their commitments to democratic pluralism made to the OAS in 1979. The internal Nicaraguan opposition groups, armed and unarmed, represent a genuine political force that is entitled to participate in the political processes of the country. It is up to the government of Nicaragua to provide the political opening that will allow their participation.

We will note and welcome such a change in Nicaraguan behavior no matter how it is obtained. Whether it is achieved through the multilateral Contadora negotiations, through unilateral actions taken by the Sandinistas alone or in concert with their domestic opponents, or through the collapse of the Sandinista regime is immaterial to us. But without such a change of behavior, lasting peace in Central America will be impossible.

The democratic forces in Nicaragua are on the front line in the struggle for progress, security, and freedom in Central America. Our active help for them is the best insurance that their efforts will be directed consistently and effectively toward these objectives.

But the bottom line is this: those who would cut off these freedom fighters from the rest of the democratic world are, in effect, consigning Nicaragua to the endless darkness of communist tyranny. And they are leading the United States down a path of greater danger. For if we do not take the appropriate steps now to pressure the Sandinistas to live up to their past promises—to cease their arms buildup, to stop exporting tyranny across their borders, to open Nicaragua to the competition of freedom and democracy—then we may find later, when we can no longer avoid acting, that the stakes will be higher and the costs greater.

Whatever options we choose, we must be true to our principles and our history. As President Reagan said recently:

> It behooves all of us who believe in democratic government, in free elections, in the respect for human rights to stand side by side with those who share our ideals, especially in Central America. We must not permit those heavily armed by a faraway dictatorship to undermine their neighbors and to stamp out democratic alternatives at home. We must have the same solidarity with those who struggle for democracy as our adversaries do with those who would impose communist dictatorship.

We must, in short, stand firmly in the defense of our interests and principles and the rights of peoples to live in freedom. The forces of democracy around the world merit our standing with them. To abandon them would be a shameful betrayal—a betrayal not only of brave men and women but of our highest ideals.

The Future of American Foreign Policy: New Realities and New Ways of Thinking
Washington, DC
January 31, 1985

Following is a statement by Secretary Shultz before the Senate Foreign Relations Committee, Washington, DC, January 31, 1985.

I am honored to lead off this important series of hearings on the future of American foreign policy. This is an auspicious moment: the beginning of a new presidential term, of a new Congress, and of the term of a distinguished new chairman [Senator Richard G. Lugar]. It is, for many reasons, a time of great promise and opportunity for the United States in world affairs.

Therefore, I commend the chairman for focusing the attention of the Congress and the American people on the fundamental issues we will face—not just the day-to-day issues that make the news but the underlying trends at work and the most important goals we pursue.

My presentation today is thus of a special kind. I would like to step back a bit and look at the present situation in perspective—the perspective of recent history, the perspective of the intellectual currents of our time, and the perspective of America's ideals and their relevance to the world's future.

The Changing International System

Soon after the dawn of the nuclear age, Albert Einstein observed that everything had changed except our ways of thinking. Even so dramatic a development as the nuclear revolution took a long time to be fully understood; how much longer has it usually taken to understand the

United States Department of State, Bureau of Public Affairs, Washington, DC.

implications of more subtle, intangible historical changes taking place around us.

Nineteen forty-five, everyone knows, marked a major turning point. An international system that had lasted for more than a century had broken down under the weight of two world wars and a great depression. An international order centered on Europe and dominated by Europe was replaced in the early postwar period by a new arrangement—a world dominated by two new superpowers, torn by ideological conflict, and overshadowed by nuclear weapons that made a new world war potentially suicidal. At the same time, an integrated international economic system established by America's initiative—based on the dollar and on a strong commitment to the freest possible flow of trade and investment—replaced the unbridled economic nationalism that had helped undermine international peace between the wars.

But history never stops. The postwar order, too, evolved and changed its shape. The breakup of colonial empires brought scores of new states onto the world stage. The so-called Third World became the scene of a growing number of local and regional conflicts. America, after Vietnam, retreated for a time from its active role of leadership. Europe, China, and Japan came into their own again as important economic and political actors; the energy crisis dramatized both the diffusion of economic power and the vulnerability of the postwar economic system. The United States and the Soviet Union attempted a political dialogue to stabilize relations and control nuclear arms; then the dialogue broke down under the weight of the Soviet military buildup and geopolitical offensive.

Today, the cycle is turning again. Change is constant. America has recovered its strength and self-confidence. Power continues to be dispersed and the structure of political relations more complex, even as the interdependence of states increases. And as we head toward the 21st century, is a stable new pattern of international relations emerging? Einstein's observation takes on new relevance: our ways of thinking must adapt to new realities; we must grasp the new trends and understand their implications.

But we are not just observers; we are participants, and we are engaged. America is again in a position to have a major influence over the trend of events—and America's traditional goals and values have *not* changed. Our duty must be to help shape the evolving trends in accordance with our ideals and interests; to help build a new structure of international stability that will ensure peace, prosperity, and freedom for coming generations. This is the real challenge of our foreign policy over the coming years.

What are the forces of change? And what are the possible elements of a new and more secure international system?

Relations Between the Superpowers

Relations between the superpowers remain crucial, even though their political predominance is less than it was a few decades ago. Over 50 years' experience of US-Soviet relations has given us by now a mature understanding of what is possible and what is not possible in this relationship. Yet conditions are evolving and the problem remains a conceptual challenge.

True friendship and cooperation will remain out of reach so long as the Soviet system is driven by ideology and national ambition to seek to aggrandize its power and undermine the interests of the democracies. We must resist this Soviet power drive vigorously if there is to be any hope for lasting stability. At the same time, in the thermonuclear age the common interest in survival gives both sides an incentive to moderate the rivalry and to seek, in particular, ways to control nuclear weapons and reduce the risks of war.[1] We cannot know whether such a steady Western policy will, over time, lead to a mellowing of the Soviet system; perhaps not. But the West has the same responsibility in either case: to resist Soviet encroachments firmly while holding the door open to more constructive possibilities.

After the failure of their political campaign to divide NATO, their propaganda to thwart deployment of intermediate-range nuclear missiles in Europe, and their boycott of talks, the Soviets have now returned to the arms control dialogue. We welcome this. My meeting in Geneva with

---

1. See Current Policy No. 577, "Realism and Responsibility: The US Approach to Arms Control," Detroit, May 14, 1984.

Soviet Foreign Minister Gromyko was a constructive beginning of what the United States hopes will be a fruitful negotiation.

My able interlocutor, Andrei Gromyko, is, in a sense, the living embodiment of some of the Soviet Union's great advantages—continuity, patience, the ability to fashion a long-term strategy and stick to it. When the Soviets shift tactics, it is more often than not an adjustment to objective conditions without basic diversion from their long-term aims.

The democracies, in contrast, have long had difficulty maintaining the same consistency, coherence, discipline, and sense of strategy. Free societies are often impatient. Western attitudes have fluctuated between extremes of gloom and pessimism, on the one hand, and susceptibility to a Soviet smile on the other. Our ways of thinking have tended too often to focus either on increasing our strength or on pursuing negotiations; we have found it hard to do both simultaneously—which is clearly the most sensible course and probably the only way we can sustain either our defense programs or our ability to negotiate.

It is vital, for example, to carry through with the modernization of our strategic forces—in particular, the MX—to avoid undercutting our negotiators just as they begin the quest for real reductions in nuclear arms. The Soviets will have little incentive to negotiate seriously for reductions to lower, equal levels if we hand them on a silver platter their long-cherished goal of *unilateral* American reductions. Likewise, as we pursue such agreements, we are obliged to bear in mind the Soviets' record of violating previous accords and to insist on effective verification provisions in any new agreements.

In the last four years, the underlying conditions that affect US-Soviet relations have changed dramatically. A decade or so ago, when the United States was beset by economic difficulties, neglecting its defenses, and hesitant about its role of leadership, the Soviets exploited these conditions. They continued their relentless military buildup; they and their clients moved more boldly in the geopolitical arena, intervening in such places as Angola, Cambodia, Ethiopia, and Afghanistan, believing that the West was incapable of resisting. They had reason for confidence that what they call the global "correlation of forces" was shifting in their favor.

Today, the West is more united than ever before. The United States is restoring its military strength and economic vigor and has regained its self-assurance; we have a President with a fresh mandate from the people for an active role of leadership. The Soviets, in contrast, face profound structural economic difficulties, a continuing succession problem, and restless allies; its diplomacy and its clients are on the defensive in many parts of the world. We have reason to be confident that the "correlation of forces" is shifting back in *our* favor.

Nevertheless, history won't do our work for us. The Soviets can be counted upon periodically to do something, somewhere, that is abhorrent or inimical to our interests. The question is how the West can respond in a way that could help discipline Soviet international behavior but does not leave our own strategy vulnerable to periodic disruption by such external shocks. We must never let ourselves be so wedded to improving relations with the Soviets that we turn a blind eye to actions that undermine the very foundation of stable relations; symbolic responses to outrageous Soviet behavior have their place, and so do penalties and sanctions. At the same time, experience shows we cannot deter or undo Soviet geopolitical encroachments except by helping, in one way or another, those resisting directly on the ground. And many negotiations and endeavors we undertake with the Soviets serve mutual interests— indeed, they *all* should.

This leaves us with tough choices. Whether important negotiations ought to be interrupted after some Soviet outrage will always be a complex calculation. When the Soviets shot down the Korean Air Lines passenger plane in 1983, President Reagan made sure the world knew the full unvarnished truth about the atrocity; nevertheless, he also sent our arms control negotiators back to Geneva because he believed that a reduction in nuclear weapons was a critical priority.

In short, our "way of thinking" must seek a sustainable strategy geared to American goals and interests in the light of Soviet behavior but not just in reaction to it. Such a strategy requires a continuing willingness to solve problems through negotiation where this serves our interests (and presumably mutual interests). Our leverage will come from creating objective realities that will give the Soviets a growing stake in better relations with us across the board by modernizing our defenses, assisting our friends, and confronting Soviet challenges. We must learn to pursue a strategy geared to long-term thinking and based on both negotiation and strength simultaneously if we are to build a stable US-Soviet relationship for the next century.[2]

The intellectual challenge of a new era faces us in a related dimension, namely arms control. The continuous revolution in technology means that the strategic balance—and the requirements of deterrence—are never static. Unfortunately, conventional ways of thinking about many of these questions continue to lag behind reality.

For decades, standard strategic doctrine in the West has ultimately relied on the balance of terror—the confrontation of offensive arsenals by which the two sides threaten each other with mass extermination. Certainly deterrence has worked under these conditions; nevertheless, for political, strategic, and even moral reasons, we should seek to do better than the proposition that our defense strategy *must* rely on offensive threats and *must* leave our people unprotected against attack. The Soviets, for their part, have *always* attached enormous importance to strategic defense, including not only air defense and civil defense but a deployed and modernized antiballistic missile system around Moscow—and intensive research into new defensive technologies.

The pace of technological advance now opens possibilities for new ways of strategic thinking—never an easy process. The vehemence of some of the criticism of the President's Strategic Defense Initiative (SDI) seems to come less from the argument over technical feasibility—which future research will answer one way or another in an objective manner—than from the passionate defense of orthodox doctrine in the face of changing strategic realities. We are proceeding with SDI research because we see a positive and, indeed, revolutionary potential: defensive measures may become available that could render obsolete the threat of

2. See Current Policy No. 492, "US-Soviet Relations in the Context of US Foreign Policy," testimony to the Senate Foreign Relations Committee, June 15, 1983; Current Policy No. 624, "Managing the US-Soviet Relationship Over the Long Term," Los Angeles, October 18, 1984.

an offensive first strike. A new strategic equilibrium based on defensive technologies and sharply reduced offensive deployments is likely to be the most stable and secure arrangement of all.

Our concept can be described as follows: during the next 10 years, the US objective is a radical reduction in the power of existing and planned offensive nuclear arms as well as the stabilization of the relationship between offensive and defensive nuclear arms, whether on earth or in space. We are even now looking forward to a period of transition to a more stable world, with greatly reduced levels of nuclear arms and an enhanced ability to deter war based upon an increasing contribution of non-nuclear defenses against offensive nuclear arms. This period of transition could lead to the eventual elimination of all nuclear arms, both offensive and defensive. A world free of nuclear arms is an ultimate objective to which we, the Soviet Union, and all other nations can agree.

The Growing Unity and Strength of Friends and Allies

As the political dominance of the superpowers began to erode in the last few decades, some saw a five-power world emerging—with the United States, the Soviet Union, Western Europe, China, and Japan as the major players. After the energy crisis of the early 1970s, others emphasized the increasing importance of the North-South relationship. The fact is, none of these concepts adequately describes the evolving pattern of world politics. In my view, the most striking trend is something else: the growing dynamism, cohesion, and cooperation of like-minded nations that share an important set of positive goals.

Equilibrium is not enough. American foreign policy is driven by positive goals—peace, democracy, liberty, and human rights; racial justice; economic and social progress; the strengthening of cooperation and the rule of law. These are not Soviet goals. Yet they are at the core of any durable international system because they are the goals that inspire peoples and nations around the world.[3]

3. See Current Policy No. 551, "Human Rights and the Moral Dimension of US Foreign Policy," Peoria, IL, February 22, 1984.

The new spirit and unity of peoples that share these goals is a new trend we can see in many regions of the world and in many dimensions of foreign policy.

We see a new spirit of collaboration and friendship in our ties with our immediate neighbors, **Canada and Mexico**—ties whose importance is self-evident and which are a priority interest of the President.

In the **Atlantic community,** our time is marked by a new degree of political harmony and intimate collaboration among the Western allies. Just as striking, Japan, too, has emerged as a partner on key political and security issues. There is a new awareness, for example, of the importance of strengthening conventional defenses as a way of bolstering Europe's security while reducing NATO's reliance on nuclear weapons. A strong Western deterrence posture is the most solid basis for engaging the East in constructive negotiations. Under Lord Carrington's wise leadership, NATO is taking steps for the short run to improve its readiness and infrastructure. For the longer run, the alliance is addressing other critical deficiencies, including the fundamental challenge of improving the efficiency of allied defense procurement.

Amid all the changes in the world, the security and well-being of Western Europe continue to be a vital interest of the United States. We have always supported West European unity, knowing that a strong Europe, while it would be a competitor in some ways, was in the overall interest of the free world. We wish the European Community well; we encourage our European friends to make further progress in developing a true European-wide market and in breaking down structural rigidities that impede both economic expansion and effective economic cooperation with us.

We see also, in Europe, new and creative thinking about the continuing pursuit of political unity and about strengthening West European cooperation in the defense field. We support both these goals. The West can only benefit from a major European role in world affairs. And the peoples of Western Europe should see defense as an endeavor they undertake for their own future, not as a favor to the United States. With statesmanship and a spirit of collaboration on both sides of the Atlantic, this evolution will strengthen the common defense and heighten the sense of common political purpose among the democracies.

As we think about Europe's evolution, we cannot forget **Eastern Europe.** Since the days of the Marshall Plan, when the West invited the East to join, we have always wanted the success of Western Europe to be a beacon to *all* of Europe. The present political division of the continent is wholly artificial. It exists only because it has been imposed by brute Soviet power; the United States has never recognized it as legitimate or permanent. Behind this cruel barrier lie political repression and economic stagnation. In certain countries, there are efforts at liberalization. But *all* the peoples of Eastern Europe are capable of something better, deserve something better, and yearn for something better. We have witnessed in recent years the powerful aspiration for free trade unions, for economic reform, for political and religious freedom, for true peace and security, for human rights as promised by the Helsinki accords.[4] We hope to see the day when the Soviet Union learns to think anew of its own security in terms compatible with the freedom, security, and independence of its neighbors.

In **East Asia and the Pacific,** another new reality is changing our thinking about the world. The economic dynamism of this region is taking on increasing importance, not only as a factor in America's foreign trade but as an economic model for the developing world and as a unique and attractive vision of the future. We see the countries of free Asia growing at 7 percent a year over the past decade; for the past five years, our trade with East Asia and the Pacific has been greater than our trade with any other region and is expanding at an accelerating rate. ASEAN [Association of South East Asian Nations] has become one of the world's most impressive examples of economic development and regional political cooperation. The Republic of Korea is a spectacular economic success story. Japan is playing a larger role—responsibly, positively, and cooperatively—commensurate with its growing strength. Experience is proving that economic openness is the formula for prosperity.

Pragmatism is now the watchword in the People's Republic of China, where the hopes for economic modernization have been invested—

4. See Current Policy No. 508, "The Challenge of the Helsinki Process," Madrid, September 9, 1983.

wisely—in a bold program of reform. China's long march to market is a truly historic event—a great nation throwing off outmoded economic doctrines and liberating the energies of a billion talented people. We wish China well in this exciting endeavor.

There are, of course, problems that pose dangers to this bright economic future: the Soviet military buildup in the region; aggression by the Soviet Union and its clients in Afghanistan and Cambodia; unresolved tensions on the Korean Peninsula; internal problems in various countries. East Asia has a rich heritage of civilization—and also a turbulent history of bitter conflict. The tragedy that two of Asia's great ancient monuments—Angkor Wat and Borobudur—have suffered damage from modern violence is both a paradox and a warning.

The United States is conscious of its responsibility to contribute, in its way, to security and stability in East Asia and the Pacific. Our diplomacy seeks peaceful solutions to Asia's problems so that the fullest potential of its promise can be realized. We welcome, in particular, the role of ASEAN, including the frontline state of Thailand, which is working effectively to curb Vietnamese expansionism and aggression and to achieve a just settlement of the Cambodian conflict.

Overall, we are enormously encouraged by the new trend we see toward wider collaboration among many Asian nations with an extraordinary diversity of cultures, races, and political systems. A sense of Pacific community is emerging. There is an expanding practice of regional consultation and a developing sense of common interest in regional security. In this sense, a decade after Vietnam, the United States has more than restored its position in Asia. We can be proud of the vitality of our alliances, friendships, and productive ties in this promising region. If nations act with wisdom and statesmanship, we may well be at the threshold of a new era in international relations in the Pacific Basin.[5]

In **Latin America,** another kind of trend is apparent—the steady advance of democracy. Democracy is hardly a new idea, but this new development *is* revising some earlier assumptions in some quarters about

5. See Current Policy No. 598, "Asia-Pacific and the Future," Honolulu, July 18, 1984.

the world's political future. A few years back, pessimists maintained that the industrial democracies were doomed to permanent minority status in the world community. Today, there is mounting evidence that the ideal of liberty is alive and well. In the Western Hemisphere, almost 95 percent of the population of Latin America and the Caribbean today live under governments that are either democratic or clearly on the road to democracy—in contrast to only one-third in 1979. Over the last five years, popularly elected leaders have replaced military rulers or dictators in Argentina, Bolivia, Ecuador, El Salvador, Honduras, Panama, Peru, and Grenada. Brazil and Uruguay will inaugurate new civilian presidents in March. Guatemala is in transition to democracy. After a long twilight of dictatorship, the trend toward free elections and popular sovereignty in this hemisphere is something to cheer about.[6]

The United States has always been a champion of democracy. Democratic institutions are the best guarantor of human rights and also the best long-term guarantor of stability. The National Endowment for Democracy, with bipartisan support, is one reflection of this American commitment. On every continent, we see a trend toward democracy or else a yearning for democracy; both are vivid demonstrations that the idea of liberty is far from a culture-bound aspiration or monopoly of the industrialized West.

In fact, after years of guerrilla insurgencies led by communists against pro-Western governments, we now see dramatic and heartening examples of popular insurgencies *against* communist regimes. Today, in a variety of different circumstances—in Nicaragua, in Afghanistan, in Cambodia, in Ethiopia, and elsewhere in Africa—Marxist-Leninist rulers have found that the aspiration for representative government is not so easy to suppress. Americans have a long and honorable tradition of supporting the struggle of other peoples for freedom, democracy, independence, and liberation from tyranny. In the 19th century we supported Simon Bolivar, Polish patriots, and others seeking freedom—reciprocating, in a way, the aid given to us in our own revolution by other nations like France.

---

6. See Current Policy No. 550, "Democratic Solidarity in the Americas," Bridgetown, Barbados, February 8, 1984.

As the President put it a week ago: "[W]e, who are committed to free government and democratic institutions, must maintain a sense of fraternity between ourselves and other freedom-loving peoples." This is a proud heritage and a moral responsibility and it poses some practical questions that we must face up to early in the 99th Congress.

The future of democracy is precisely what is at stake in **Central America.** US policy is to promote democracy, reform, and human rights; to support economic development; to help provide a security shield against those who seek to spread tyranny by force; and to support dialogue and negotiation both within and among the countries of the region. Acting directly and through Cuba, the Soviet Union is abetting the establishment of a new communist dictatorship in Nicaragua.

We are backing democratic governments and democratic political forces throughout Central America against extremists of both the left and the right. If we abandon those seeking democracy, the extremists will gain and the forces of moderation and decency will be the victims. This is why the administration has worked so hard, and will continue to work hard, for effective negotiations, for economic and security assistance, and for the bipartisan plan that emerged from the Kissinger commission [National Bipartisan Commission on Central America]. If the forces of dictatorship continue to feel free to aid and abet insurgencies in the name of "proletarian internationalism," it would be absurd if the democracies felt inhibited about promoting the cause of democracy, even by collective self-defense against such actions. Our nation's vital interests *and* moral responsibility require us to stand by our friends in their struggle for freedom.[7]

The Dynamic of Change

The process of change is inexorable. In **southern Africa** we have a role to play in working for democratic change. We are also key to efforts to help create a climate of regional security that will enable and encourage countries to get on with the priority of building decent and prosperous

7. See Current Policy No. 478, "Struggle for Democracy in Central America," Dallas, April 15, 1983.

societies. In short, US policy must pursue the dual objectives of racial justice and regional security. These two goals are not in conflict; they reinforce each other. But achieving them requires responsible, prudent, and dedicated diplomacy.

These twin challenges call for serious analysis and sober thinking, not emotional responses. We have already accomplished much, but our influence is not infinite. Today, there is less cross-border violence in southern Africa than at any time in more than a decade. Progress is being made toward a Namibia settlement. We have strengthened ties with Mozambique and other regional states. And South Africa itself has developed cooperative relations with many of its neighbors.

President Reagan has made clear that we regard South African apartheid as repugnant. He spoke loud and clear on December 10 when he said:

> We . . . call upon the government of South Africa to reach out to its black majority by ending the forced removal of blacks from their communities and the detention, without trial, and lengthy imprisonment of black leaders. . . . [W]e ask that the constructive changes of recent years be broadened to address the aspirations of all South Africans. . . . We urge both the government and the people of South Africa to move toward a more just society.

Within South Africa, a dynamic of change is already at work: more positive change is occurring now than in the 1970s or 1960s or 1950s. The positive influence of our relationship—our diplomacy, our companies, our assistance programs for black South Africans—is helping to build the basis for further change. Apartheid must go. But the only course consistent with American values is to engage ourselves as a force for constructive, peaceful change while there is still a chance. It cannot be our choice to cheer on, from the sidelines, the forces of polarization that could erupt in a race war; it is not our job to exacerbate hardship, which could lead to the same result.

Another region of change is the **Middle East.** Recent events have reminded us that the Arab-Israeli conflict is far from the only source of tension in that part of the world. There are other deep-seated national, ethnic, and religious conflicts like the Iran-Iraq war; there are diverse sources of radical extremism ranging from Marxist-Leninist ideology, to Islamic fundamentalism, to Muammar Qadhafi's bizarre personal brand of fanaticism; the Soviets seek to reinforce rejectionist elements and to exploit regional tensions for their own advantage.

The United States will continue its efforts to promote peaceful solutions in this vital area. This mediation is, of course, a traditional American role, but new conditions always call for new ways of thinking about how to pursue it. We are committed to the support of diplomatic efforts to end the conflicts in the gulf, in Lebanon, and in the Sahara. We are committed to the President's September 1 initiative as the most promising route to a solution of the Palestinian problem. We will be intensively engaged this year in consultations with our Arab and Israeli friends to explore opportunities for progress.[8]

In the global economy, an important shift of another kind is taking place—an intellectual shift, reflecting some lessons from experience. Lord Keynes's point about practical men being in thrall to some defunct economist may be less true now than in the past. Or perhaps the views first expressed by Adam Smith over two centuries ago on the creation of the "wealth of nations" are once again gaining practical prominence. At any rate, reality is intruding on some long-held notions about economic policy.

In both industrialized and developing countries, the economic difficulties of recent years are reminding us of some old truths about the real sources of economic progress. Some of us never forgot those truths. But recent experience has fueled a broad and long-overdue skepticism about statist solutions, central planning, and government direction.

This intellectual shift is partly the product of the extraordinary vigor of the American recovery. The United States has revised its tax system to provide real incentives to work, to save, to invest, to take risks, to be efficient. We have reduced government regulation, intervention, and control. We have opened opportunities for freer competition in trans-

8. See Current Policy No. 528, "Promoting Peace in the Middle East," Atlanta, GA, November 19, 1983.

portation, finance, communication, manufacturing, and distribution. Last year's real growth in GNP [gross national product] was the sharpest increase since 1951; inflation was the lowest since 1967. The overall result has been the extraordinary creation of over 7 million new jobs in two years.

Success inspires emulation. Not only in East Asia, as I noted, but on every continent—Europe, Latin America, Africa, and elsewhere in Asia—we see movement to decentralize, to deregulate, to denationalize, to reduce rigidity, and to enlarge the scope for individual producers and consumers to cooperate freely through markets. In Africa, for example, if there is to be a long-term solution to the problem of hunger, it will have to come not just from relief efforts but from training, productive investment, and liberalizing reforms in agriculture; our aid policy is encouraging the efforts of African countries to move further in this direction.[9]

A worldwide revolution in economic thought and economic policy is under way. And it is coming just in time because it coincides with yet another revolution—a revolution in the technological base of the global economy. This is what Walter Wriston has called "the onrushing age of information technology"—the combination of microchip computers, advanced telecommunications, and continuing innovation that is transforming almost every aspect of human endeavor.

The implications of this revolution are not only economic. First of all, the very existence of these technologies is yet another testimony to the crucial importance of entrepreneurship—and government policies that give free rein to entrepreneurship—as the wellspring of technological creativity and economic growth. The closed societies of the East are likely to fall far behind in these areas—and Western societies that maintain too many restrictions on economic activity run the same risk.

Second, any government that resorts to heavy-handed measures to control or regulate or tax the flow of electronic information will find itself stifling growth of the world economy as well as its own progress. This is one of the reasons why the United States is pressing for a new

9. See Current Policy No. 487, "The US and the Developing World: Our Joint Stake in the World Economy," New York, May 26, 1983.

round of trade negotiations in these service fields of data processing and transfer of information.

Third, the advance of technology in this dimension is bound to challenge many cherished notions of sovereignty. But here, too, the West has the advantage because the free flow of information is inherently compatible with our political system and values. The communist states, in contrast, fear this information revolution perhaps even more than they fear Western military strength. If knowledge is power, then the communications revolution threatens to undermine their most important monopoly—their effort to stifle their people's information, thought, and independence of judgment. We all remember the power of the Ayatollah's message disseminated on tape cassettes in Iran; what could have a more profound impact in the Soviet bloc than similar cassettes, outside radio broadcasting, direct broadcast satellites, personal computers, or Xerox machines?

Totalitarian societies face a dilemma: either they try to stifle these technologies and thereby fall further behind in the new industrial revolution or they permit these technologies and see their totalitarian control inevitably eroded. In fact, they do not have a choice because they will never be able to block entirely the tide of technological advance however hard they try.

The march of technology also compels us to continue our efforts to prevent the spread of nuclear weapons. The United States has long been the leader of an international effort to establish a regime of institutional arrangements, legal commitments, and technological safeguards to control the proliferation of nuclear weapons capabilities. This program has, in fact, had considerable success in that the number of states that have acquired the means to produce nuclear explosives is far lower than doomsayers predicted 20 years ago. At the same time, the potential dangers of nuclear weapons proliferation remain as serious and menacing to international stability as has long been predicted.

The Reagan administration will pursue this essential endeavor with a realistic appreciation of its complexities. Our thinking on this issue takes account of the growing international reliance on peaceful nuclear energy, the security concerns that give rise to the incentive to seek nuclear weapons, and the need for broad multilateral collaboration among nuclear suppliers if a nonproliferation regime is to be effective. We have made progress in restoring a relationship of confidence and a reputation for reliability with our nuclear-trading partners. We have had fruitful talks with the Soviet Union on this subject; we have worked to promote comprehensive safeguards and stricter export controls.[10]

New Challenges to Our Ways of Thinking

These broad trends I have described are mostly positive trends, but not all. We see social dislocation arising from economic change; we see urban alienation, political turbulence, and the many potential sources and forms of disorder I have mentioned. The changes in the international system will follow the positive trends only if we—the United States and the free world—meet our responsibility to defend our interests and seek to shape events in accordance with our own ideals and goals.

In at least one respect, the modern world—with its spreading technology and prosperity and democratic aspirations—is ironically also becoming more and more vulnerable. I am thinking, of course, about terrorism. Even as the world becomes more secure from the danger of major war, paradoxically the democratic world now faces an increasing threat from this new form of warfare.

Terrorism these days is becoming less an isolated phenomenon of local fanatics and increasingly part of a new international strategy resorted to by the enemies of freedom. It is a vicious weapon used deliberately against democracies—against the interests, policies, and friends of democracies, and against completely innocent people. There are disturbing links, as well, to international drug trafficking. Terrorism is a problem that, more than many others, is forcing us into new ways of thinking about how to safeguard our future. During the year ahead we must be prepared for serious terrorist threats in Western Europe, in the Middle East, and in Latin America, much of it supported by or encouraged by a handful of ruthless governments.

10. See Current Policy No. 631, "Preventing the Proliferation of Nuclear Weapons," New York, November 1, 1984.

As you know, I have been speaking out frequently on this subject to stimulate public consideration and discussion of the complex issues involved.[11] A counterstrategy for combating terrorism, in my view, must encompass many things.

- We and our allies must work still harder to improve security, share information, coordinate police efforts, and collaborate in other ways to defeat international terrorism. Much has been done in the past year, but much more remains to be done.
- We in this country must think hard about the moral stakes involved. If we truly believe in our democratic values and our way of life, we must be willing to defend them. Passive measures are unlikely to suffice; means of more active defense and deterrence must be considered and given the necessary political support.
- Finally, while working tirelessly to deny terrorists their opportunities and their means, we can—and must—be absolutely firm in denying them their goals. They seek to blackmail us into changing our foreign policies or to drive us out of countries and regions where we have important interests. This we *cannot* permit; we cannot yield position or abandon friends or responsibilities under this kind of pressure. If we allow terrorists even one such victory, we embolden them further; we demoralize all who rely on us, and we make the world an even more dangerous place.

There is, of course, a broader issue here, which I have also been discussing in several public statements. This is the basic question of the use of American power in the defense of our interests and the relevance of our power as the backstop to our diplomacy. It is reflected, for example, in what are often called "gray-area challenges"—namely, the kind of regional or local conflicts and crises that are likely to persist in a turbulent world, below the threshold of major war but nonetheless affecting

11. See Current Policy No. 589, "Terrorism: The Challenge to the Democracies," Washington, DC, June 24, 1984; Current Policy No. 629, "Terrorism and the Modern World," New York, October 25, 1984; Current Policy No. 642, "The Ethics of Power," New York, December 9, 1984.

important Western interests. Most of the major conflicts since 1945, indeed, have originated in such conflicts in the developing world. The end of the colonial order has not brought universal peace and justice; much of the developing world is torn by the continuing struggle between the forces of moderation and the forces of radicalism—a struggle actively exploited and exacerbated by the Soviet Union.

It is absurd to think that America can walk away from such challenges. This is a world of great potential instability and many potential dangers. We live, as is commonly said, on a shrinking planet and in a world of increasing interdependence. We have an important stake in the health of the world economy and in the overall conditions of global security; the freedom and safety of our fellow human beings will always impinge on our moral consciousness. Not all these challenges threaten vital interests, but at the same time an accumulation of successful challenges can add up to a major adverse change in the geopolitical balance.

We must be wise and prudent in deciding how and where to use our power. Economic and security assistance to allies and friends is clearly the preferred course—and is of crucial importance to our foreign policy; the direct American use of force must always be a last resort. The United States will always seek political solutions to problems, but such solutions will never succeed unless aggression is resisted and diplomacy is backed by strength. We are reasonably well prepared to deter all-out Soviet nuclear aggression—provided we continue with our strategic modernization—but we must be sure we are also well prepared physically and psychologically for this intermediate range of challenges.[12]

Peace, Progress, and Freedom

I have touched on a wide variety of topics, but two very important, and very basic, conclusions can be drawn from them.

First, the agenda for the immediate future seems to me to be an agenda on which the American people are essentially united. These are goals that are widely shared and tasks that are likely to reinforce another important

---

12. See Current Policy No. 561, "Power and Diplomacy in the 1980s," Washington, DC, April 3, 1984.

trend: namely, the reemergence of a national consensus on the main elements of our foreign policy.[13] This, indeed, may be the most important positive trend of all because so many of our difficulties in recent decades have been very much the product of our own domestic divisions. I hope that our two parties and our two branches of government will find ways to cooperate in this spirit, which would enormously strengthen our country in the face of the new opportunities and challenges I have described.

Second, all the diverse topics I have touched upon are, in the end, closely interrelated. President Reagan made this point in his speech to the United Nations last September.[14] The United States seeks peace and security; we seek economic progress; we seek to promote freedom, democracy, and human rights. The conventional way of thinking is to treat these as discrete categories of activity. In fact, as we have seen, it is now more and more widely recognized that there is a truly profound connection among them. And this has important implications for the future.

It is no accident, for example, that America's closest and most lasting international relationships are its alliances with its fellow democracies. These ties with the Atlantic community, Japan, and other democratic friends have an enduring quality precisely because they rest on a moral base, not only a base of strategic interest. When George Washington advised his countrymen to steer clear of permanent alliances, his attitude was colored by the fact that there were hardly any other fellow democracies in those days. We were among the first, and we had good reason to be wary of entanglements with countries that did not share our democratic principles. In any case, we now *define* our strategic interests in terms that embrace the safety and well-being of the democratic world.

Similarly, as I have already discussed, it is more and more understood that economic progress is related to a political environment of openness and freedom. It used to be thought in some quarters that socialism was the appropriate model for developing countries because central planning was better able to mobilize and allocate resources in conditions of scar-

13. See Current Policy No. 625, "A Forward Look at Foreign Policy," Los Angeles, October 19, 1984.

14. See Current Policy No. 615, "Reducing World Tensions," the President's address before the UN General Assembly, New York, September 24, 1984.

city. The historical experience of Western Europe and North America, which industrialized in an era of limited government, was not thought to be relevant.

Yet the more recent experience of the Third World shows that a dominant government role in developing economies has done more to stifle the natural forces of production and productivity and to distort the efficient allocation of resources. The real engine of growth, in developing as well as industrialized countries, turns out to be the natural dynamism of societies that minimize central planning, open themselves to trade with the world, and give free rein to the talents and efforts and risk-taking and investment decisions of individuals.

Finally, there is almost certainly also a relationship between economic progress, freedom, and world peace. Andrei Sakharov has written:

> I am convinced that international trust, mutual understanding, disarmament, and international security are inconceivable without an open society with freedom of information, freedom of conscience, the right to publish, and the right to travel and choose the country in which one wishes to live. I am also convinced that freedom of conscience, together with other civic rights, provides both the basis for scientific progress and a guarantee against its misuse to harm mankind.

The implication of all this is profound: it is that the Western values of liberty and democracy—which some have been quick to write off as culture bound or irrelevant or passé—are not to be so easily dismissed. Their obituary is premature. These values are the source of our strength, economic as well as moral, and they turn out to be more central to the world's future than many may have realized.

After more than a century of fashionable Marxist mythology about economic determinism and the "crisis of capitalism," the key to human progress turns out to be those very Western concepts of political and economic freedom that Marxists claimed were obsolete. They were wrong. Today, the supreme irony: it is the communist system that looks bankrupt, morally as well as economically. The West is resilient and resurgent.

And so, in the end, the most important new way of thinking that is called for in this decade is our way of thinking about ourselves. Civilizations thrive when they believe in themselves; they decline when they lose this faith. All civilizations confront massive problems, but a society is more likely to master its challenges rather than be overwhelmed by them if it retains this bedrock self-confidence that its values are worth defending. This is the essence of the Reagan revolution and of the leadership the President has sought to provide in America.

The West has been through a difficult period in the last decade or more. But now we see a new turn. The next phase of the industrial revolution—like all previous phases—comes from the democratic world, where innovation and creativity are allowed to spring from the unfettered human spirit. By working together, we can spread the benefit of the technological revolution to all. And on every continent—from Nicaragua to Cambodia, from Poland to South Africa to Afghanistan—we see that the yearning for freedom is the most powerful political force all across the planet.

So, as we head toward the 21st century, it is time for the democracies to celebrate their system, their beliefs, and their success. We face challenges but we are well poised to master them. Opinions are being revised about which system is the wave of the future. The free nations, if they maintain their unity and their faith in themselves, have the advantage—economically, technologically, morally.

History is on freedom's side.

Terrorism and the Modern World
New York, NY
October 25, 1984

Following is an address by Secretary Shultz before the Park Avenue Synagogue, New York, October 25, 1984.

Someday terrorism will no longer be a timely subject for a speech, but that day has not arrived. Less than two weeks ago, one of the oldest and greatest nations of the Western world almost lost its Prime Minister, Margaret Thatcher, to the modern barbarism that we call terrorism. A month ago the American Embassy Annex in East Beirut was nearly destroyed by a terrorist truck bomb, the third major attack on Americans in Lebanon within the past two years. To list all the other acts of brutality that terrorists have visited upon civilized society in recent years would be impossible here because that list is too long. It is too long to name and too long to tolerate.

But I am here to talk about terrorism as a phenomenon in our modern world—about what terrorism is and what it is not. We have learned a great deal about terrorism in recent years. We have learned much about the terrorists themselves, their supporters, their diverse methods, their underlying motives, and their eventual goals. What once may have seemed the random, senseless, violent acts of a few crazed individuals has come into clearer focus. A pattern of terrorist violence has emerged. It is an alarming pattern, but it is something that we can identify and, therefore, a threat that we can devise concrete measures to combat. The knowledge we have accumulated about terrorism over the years can provide the basis for a coherent strategy to deal with the phenomenon, if we have the will to turn our understanding into action.

United States Department of State, Bureau of Public Affairs, Washington, DC.

The Meaning of Terrorism

We have learned that terrorism is, above all, a form of political violence. It is neither random nor without purpose. Today, we are confronted with a wide assortment of terrorist groups which, alone or in concert, orchestrate acts of violence to achieve distinctly political ends. Their stated objectives may range from separatist causes to revenge for ethnic grievances to social and political revolution. Their methods may be just as diverse: from planting homemade explosives in public places to suicide car bombings to kidnappings and political assassinations. But the overarching goal of all terrorists is the same: they are trying to impose their will by force—a special kind of force designed to create an atmosphere of fear. The horrors they inflict are not simply a new manifestation of traditional social conflict; they are depraved opponents of civilization itself, aided by the technology of modern weaponry. The terrorists want people to feel helpless and defenseless; they want people to lose faith in their government's capacity to protect them and thereby to undermine the legitimacy of the government itself, or its policies, or both.

The terrorists profit from the anarchy caused by their violence. They succeed when governments change their policies out of intimidation. But the terrorist can even be satisfied if a government responds to terror by clamping down on individual rights and freedoms. Governments that overreact, even in self-defense, may only undermine their own legitimacy, as they unwittingly serve the terrorist's goals. The terrorist succeeds if a government responds to violence with repressive, polarizing behavior that alienates the government from the people.

The Threat to Democracy

We must understand, however, that terrorism, wherever it takes place, is directed in an important sense against *us*, the democracies—against our most basic values and often our fundamental strategic interests. Because terrorism relies on brutal violence as its only tool, it will always be the enemy of democracy. For democracy rejects the indiscriminate or improper use of force and relies instead on the peaceful settlement of disputes through legitimate political processes.

The moral bases of democracy—the principles of individual rights, freedom of thought and expression, freedom of religion—are powerful barriers against those who seek to impose their will, their ideologies, or their religious beliefs by force. Whether in Israel or Lebanon or Turkey or Italy or West Germany or Northern Ireland, a terrorist has no patience for the orderly processes of democratic society, and, therefore, he seeks to destroy it. Indeed, terrorism seeks to destroy what all of us here are seeking to build.

The United States and the other democracies are morally committed to certain ideals and to a humane vision of the future. Nor is our vision limited to within our borders. In our foreign policies, as well, we try to foster the kind of world that promotes peaceful settlement of disputes, one that welcomes beneficial change. We do not practice terrorism, and we seek to build a world which holds no place for terrorist violence, a world in which human rights are respected by all governments, a world based on the rule of law.

And there is yet another reason why we are attacked. If freedom and democracy are the targets of terrorism, it is clear that totalitarianism is its ally. The number of terrorist incidents in totalitarian states is minimal, and those against their personnel abroad are markedly fewer than against the West. And this is not only because police states offer less room for terrorists to carry out acts of violence. States that support and sponsor terrorist actions have managed in recent years to co-opt and manipulate the terrorist phenomenon in pursuit of their own strategic goals.

It is not a coincidence that most acts of terrorism occur in areas of importance to the West. More than 80 percent of the world's terrorist attacks in 1983 occurred in Western Europe, Latin America, and the Middle East. Terrorism in this context is not just criminal activity but an unbridled form of warfare.

Today, international links among terrorist groups are more clearly understood. And Soviet and Soviet-bloc support is also more clearly understood. We face a diverse family of dangers. Iran and the Soviet Union are hardly allies, but they both share a fundamental hostility to the West. When Libya and the PLO [Palestine Liberation Organization] provide arms and training to the communists in Central America, they are aiding Soviet-supported Cuban efforts to undermine our security in that vital region. When the Red Brigades in Italy and the Red Army Faction in Germany assault free countries in the name of communist ideology, they hope to shake the West's self-confidence, unity, and will to resist intimidation. The terrorists who assault Israel—and, indeed, the Marxist Provisional IRA [Irish Republican Army] in Northern Ireland—are ideological enemies of the United States. We cannot and we will not succumb to the likes of Khomeini and Qadhafi.

We also now see a close connection between terrorism and international narcotics trafficking. Cuba and Nicaragua, in particular, have used narcotics smugglers to funnel guns and money to terrorists and insurgents in Colombia. Other communist countries, like Bulgaria, have also been part of the growing link between drugs and terrorism.

We should understand the Soviet role in international terrorism without exaggeration or distortion. One does not have to believe that the Soviets are puppeteers and the terrorists marionettes; violent or fanatic individuals and groups can exist in almost any society.

But in many countries, terrorism would long since have withered away had it not been for significant support from outside. When Israel went into Lebanon in 1982, Israeli forces uncovered irrefutable evidence that the Soviet Union had been arming and training the PLO and other groups. Today, there is no reason to think that Soviet support for terrorist groups around the world has diminished. Here as elsewhere, there is a wide gap between Soviet words and Soviet deeds, a gap that is very clear, for instance, when you put Soviet support for terrorist groups up against the empty rhetoric of the resolution against so-called "state terrorism" which the USSR has submitted to this year's UN General Assembly. The Soviets condemn terrorism, but in practice they connive with terrorist groups when they think it serves their own purposes, and their goal is always the same: to weaken liberal democracy and undermine world stability.

The Moral and Strategic Stakes

The stakes in our war against terrorists, therefore, are high. We have already seen the horrible cost in innocent lives that terrorist violence has incurred. But perhaps even more horrible is the damage that terrorism threatens to wreak on our modern civilization. For centuries mankind has strived to build a world in which the highest human aspirations can be fulfilled.

We have pulled ourselves out of a state of barbarism and removed the affronts to human freedom and dignity that are inherent in that condition. We have sought to free ourselves from that primitive existence described by Hobbes where life is lived in "continual fear and danger of violent death . . . nasty, brutish, and short." We have sought to create, instead, a world where universal respect for human rights and democratic values makes a better life possible. We in the democracies can attest to all that man is capable of achieving if he renounces violence and brute force, if he is free to think, write, vote, and worship as he pleases. Yet all of these hard-won gains are threatened by terrorism.

Terrorism is a step backward; it is a step toward anarchy and decay. In the broadest sense, terrorism represents a return to barbarism in the modern age. If the modern world cannot face up to the challenge, then terrorism, and the lawlessness and inhumanity that come with it, will gradually undermine all that the modern world has achieved and make further progress impossible.

Obstacles to Meeting the Challenge

The magnitude of the threat posed by terrorism is so great that we cannot afford to confront it with half-hearted and poorly organized measures. Terrorism is a contagious disease that will inevitably spread if it goes untreated. We need a strategy to cope with terrorism in all of its varied manifestations. We need to summon the necessary resources and determination to fight it and, with international cooperation, eventually stamp it out. And we have to recognize that the burden falls on us, the democracies—no one else will cure the disease for us.

Yet clearly we face obstacles, some of which arise precisely because we are democracies. The nature of the terrorist assault is, in many ways, alien to us. Democracies like to act on the basis of known facts and shared knowledge. Terrorism is clandestine and mysterious by nature. Terrorists rely on secrecy, and, therefore, it is hard to know for certain who has committed an atrocity.

Democracies also rely on reason and persuasive logic to make decisions. It is hard for us to understand the fanaticism and apparent irrationality of many terrorists, especially those who kill and commit suicide in the belief that they will be rewarded in the afterlife. The psychopathic ruthlessness and brutality of terrorism is an aberration in our culture and alien to our heritage.

And it is an unfortunate irony that the very qualities that make democracies so hateful to the terrorists—our respect for the rights and freedoms of the individual—also make us particularly vulnerable. Precisely because we maintain the most open societies, terrorists have unparalleled opportunity to strike at us. Terrorists seek to make democracies embattled and afraid, to break down democratic accountability, due process, and order; they hope we will turn toward repression or succumb to chaos.

These are the challenges we must live with. We will certainly not alter the democratic values that we so cherish in order to fight terrorism. We will have to find ways to fight back without undermining everything we stand for.

Combating Moral Confusion

There is another obstacle that we have created for ourselves that we should overcome—that we must overcome—if we are to fight terrorism effectively. The obstacle I am referring to is confusion.

We cannot begin to address this monumental challenge to decent, civilized society until we clear our heads of the confusion about terrorism, in many ways the *moral* confusion, that still seems to plague us. Confusion can lead to paralysis, and it is a luxury that we simply cannot afford.

The confusion about terrorism has taken many forms. In recent years, we have heard some ridiculous distortions, even about what the word "terrorism" means. The idea, for instance, that denying food stamps to some is a form of terrorism cannot be entertained by serious people. And those who would argue, as recently some in Great Britain have, that physical violence by strikers can be equated with "the violence of unemployment" are, in the words of The Economist, "a menace to democracy everywhere." In a real democracy, violence is unequivocally bad. Such distortions are dangerous, because words are important. When we distort our language, we may distort our thinking, and we hamper our efforts to find solutions to the grave problems we face.

There has been, however, a more serious kind of confusion surrounding the issue of terrorism: the confusion between the terrorist act itself and the political goals that the terrorists claim to seek.

The grievances that terrorists supposedly seek to redress through acts of violence may or may not be legitimate. The terrorist acts themselves, however, can never be legitimate. And legitimate causes can never justify or excuse terrorism. Terrorist means discredit their ends.

We have all heard the insidious claim that "one man's terrorist is another man's freedom fighter." When I spoke on the subject of terrorism this past June, I quoted the powerful rebuttal to this kind of moral relativism made by the late Senator Henry Jackson. His statement bears repeating today: "The idea that one person's 'terrorist' is another's 'freedom fighter,'" he said, "cannot be sanctioned. Freedom fighters or revolutionaries don't blow up buses containing non-combatants; terrorist murderers do. Freedom fighters don't set out to capture and slaughter school children; terrorist murderers do. Freedom fighters don't assassinate innocent businessmen, or hijack and hold hostage innocent men, women, and children; terrorist murderers do. It is a disgrace that democracies would allow the treasured word 'freedom' to be associated with acts of terrorists." So spoke Scoop Jackson.

We cannot afford to let an Orwellian corruption of language obscure our understanding of terrorism. We know the difference between terrorists and freedom fighters, and as we look around the world, we have no trouble telling one from the other.

How tragic it would be if democratic societies so lost confidence in their own moral legitimacy that they lost sight of the obvious: that violence directed against democracy or the hopes for democracy lacks fundamental justification. Democracy offers the opportunity for peaceful change, legitimate political competition, and redress of grievances. We must oppose terrorists no matter what banner they may fly. For terrorism in *any* cause is the enemy of freedom.

And we must not fall into the deadly trap of giving justification to the unacceptable acts of terrorists by acknowledging the worthy-sounding motives they may claim. Organizations such as the Provisional IRA, for instance, play on popular grievances, and political and religious emotions, to disguise their deadly purpose. They find ways to work through local political and religious leaders to enlist support for their brutal actions. As a result, we even find Americans contributing, we hope unwittingly, to an organization which has killed—in cold blood and without the slightest remorse—hundreds of innocent men, women, and children in Great Britain and Ireland; an organization which has assassinated senior officials and tried to assassinate the British Prime Minister and her entire cabinet; a professed Marxist organization which also gets support from Libya's Qadhafi and has close links with other international terrorists. The government of the United States stands firmly with the government of the United Kingdom and the government of Ireland in opposing any action that lends aid or support to the Provisional IRA.

Moral confusion about terrorism can take many forms. When 2 Americans and 12 Lebanese were killed at our Embassy Annex in East Beirut last month, for instance, we were told by some that this mass murder was an expression, albeit an extreme expression, of Arab hostility to American policy in the Middle East. We were told that this bombing happened because of a vote we cast in the United Nations, or because of our policies in Lebanon, or because of the overall state of our relations with the Arab nations, or because of our support for Israel.

We were advised by some that if we want to stop terrorism—if we want to put an end to these vicious murders—then what we need to do is change our policies. In effect, we have been told that terrorism is in some measure our own fault, and we deserved to be bombed. I can tell you here and now that the United States will not be driven off or stayed from our course or change our policy by terrorist brutality.

We cannot permit ourselves any uncertainty as to the real meaning of terrorist violence in the Middle East or anywhere else. Those who truly seek peace in the Middle East know that war and violence are no answer. Those who oppose radicalism and support negotiation are themselves the target of terrorism, whether they are Arabs or Israelis. One of the great tragedies of the Middle East, in fact, is that the many moderates on the Arab side—who are ready to live in peace with Israel—are threatened by the radicals and their terrorist henchmen and are thus stymied in their own efforts for peace.

The terrorists' principal goal in the Middle East is to destroy any progress toward a negotiated peace. And the more our policies succeed, the closer we come toward achieving our goals in the Middle East, the harder terrorists will try to stop us. The simple fact is, the terrorists are more upset about *progress* in the Middle East than they are about any alleged failures to achieve progress. Let us not forget that President Sadat was murdered because he made peace, and that threats continue to be issued daily in that region because of the fear—yes, fear—that others might favor a negotiated path toward peace.

Whom would we serve by changing our policies in the Middle East in the face of the terrorist threat? Not Israel, not the moderate Arabs, not the Palestinian people, and certainly not the cause for peace. Indeed, the worst thing we could do is change our principled policies under the threat of violence. What we *must* do is support our friends and remain firm in our goals.

We have to rid ourselves of this moral confusion which lays the blame for terrorist actions on us or on our policies. We are attacked not because of what we are doing wrong but because of what we are doing right. We are right to support the security of Israel, and there is no terrorist act or threat that will change that firm determination. We are attacked not because of some mistake we are making but because of who we are and what we believe in. We must not abandon our principles, or our role in the world, or our responsibilities as the champion of freedom and peace.

The Response to Terrorism

While terrorism threatens many countries, the United States has a special responsibility. It is time for this country to make a broad national commitment to treat the challenge of terrorism with the sense of urgency and priority it deserves.

The essence of our response is simple to state: violence and aggression must be met by firm resistance. This principle holds true whether we are responding to full-scale military attacks or to the kinds of low-level conflicts that are more common in the modern world.

We are on the way to being well prepared to deter an all-out war or a Soviet attack on our principal allies; that is why these are the least likely contingencies. It is not self-evident that we are as well prepared and organized to deter and counter the "gray area" of intermediate challenges that we are more likely to face—the low-intensity conflict of which terrorism is a part.

We have worked hard to deter large-scale aggression by strengthening our strategic and conventional defenses, by restoring the pride and confidence of the men and women in our military and by displaying the kind of national resolve to confront aggression that can deter potential adversaries. We have been more successful than in the past in dealing with many forms of low-level aggression. We have checked communist aggression and subversion in Central America and the Caribbean and opened the way for peaceful, democratic processes in that region. And we successfully liberated Grenada from Marxist control and returned that tiny island to freedom and self-determination.

But terrorism, which is also a form of low-level aggression, has so far posed an even more difficult challenge, for the technology of security has been outstripped by the technology of murder. And, of course, the United States is not the only nation that faces difficulties in responding to terrorism. To update President Reagan's report in the debate last Sunday, since September 1, 41 acts of terrorism have been perpetrated by no less than 14 terrorist groups against the people and property of 21 countries. Even Israel has not rid itself of the terrorist threat, despite its brave and prodigious efforts.

But no nation had more experience with terrorism than Israel, and no nation has made a greater contribution to our understanding of the problem and the best ways to confront it. By supporting organizations like the Jonathan Institute, named after the brave Israeli soldier who led and died at Entebbe, the Israeli people have helped raise international awareness of the global scope of the terrorist threat.

And Israel's contribution goes beyond the theoretical. Israel has won major battles in the war against terrorism in actions across its borders, in other continents, and in the land of Israel itself. To its great credit, the Israeli government has moved within Israel to apprehend and bring to trial its own citizens accused of terrorism.

Much of Israel's success in fighting terrorism has been due to broad public support for Israel's antiterrorist policies. Israel's people have shown the will, and they have provided their government the resources, to fight terrorism. They entertain no illusions about the meaning or the danger of terrorism. Perhaps because they confront the threat every day, they recognize that they are at war with terrorism. The rest of us would do well to follow Israel's example.

But part of our problem here in the United States has been our seeming inability to understand terrorism clearly. Each successive terrorist incident has brought too much self-condemnation and dismay, accompanied by calls for a change in our policies or our principles or calls for withdrawal and retreat. We *should* be alarmed. We *should* be outraged. We *should* investigate and strive to improve. But widespread public anguish and self-condemnation only convince the terrorists that they are on the right track. It only encourages them to commit more acts of barbarism in the hope that American resolve will weaken.

This is a particular danger in the period before our election. If our reaction to terrorist acts is to turn on ourselves instead of against the perpetrators, we give them redoubled incentive to do it again and to try to influence our political processes.

We have to be stronger, steadier, determined, and united in the face of the terrorist threat. We must not reward the terrorists by changing our policies or questioning our own principles or wallowing in self-flagellation or self-doubt. Instead, we should understand that terrorism is aggression and, like all aggression, must be forcefully resisted.

The Requirements for an Active Strategy

We must reach a consensus in this country that our responses should go beyond passive defense to consider means of active prevention, preemption, and retaliation. Our goal must be to prevent and deter future terrorist acts, and experience has taught us over the years that one of the best deterrents to terrorism is the certainty that swift and sure measures will be taken against those who engage in it. We should take steps toward carrying out such measures. There should be no moral confusion on this issue. Our aim is not to seek revenge but to put an end to violent attacks against innocent people, to make the world a safer place to live for all of us. Clearly, the democracies have a moral right, indeed a duty, to defend themselves.

A successful strategy for combating terrorism will require us to face up to some hard questions and to come up with some clear-cut answers. The questions involve our intelligence capability, the doctrine under which we would employ force, and, most important of all, our public's attitude toward this challenge. Our nation cannot summon the will to act without firm public understanding and support.

First, our intelligence capabilities, particularly our human intelligence, are being strengthened. Determination and capacity to act are of little value unless we can come close to answering the questions: who, where, and when. We have to do a better job of finding out who the terrorists are; where they are; and the nature, composition, and patterns of behavior of terrorist organizations. Our intelligence services are organizing themselves to do the job, and they must be given the mandate and the flexibility to develop techniques of detection and contribute to deterrence and response.

Second, there is no question about our ability to use force where and when it is needed to counter terrorism. Our nation has forces prepared for action—from small teams able to operate virtually undetected, to the full weight of our conventional military might. But serious issues are involved—questions that need to be debated, understood, and agreed if we are to be able to utilize our forces wisely and effectively.

If terrorists strike here at home, it is a matter for police action and domestic law enforcement. In most cases overseas, acts of terrorism against our people and installations can be dealt with best by the host government and its forces. It is worth remembering that just as it is the responsibility of the US government to provide security for foreign embassies in Washington, so the internationally agreed doctrine is that the security of our embassies abroad in the first instance is the duty of the host government, and we work with those governments cooperatively and with considerable success. The ultimate responsibility of course is ours, and we will carry it out with total determination and all the resources available to us. Congress, in a bipartisan effort, is giving us the legislative tools and the resources to strengthen the protection of our facilities and our people overseas—and they must continue to do so. But while we strengthen our defenses, defense alone is not enough.

The heart of the challenge lies in those cases where international rules and traditional practices do not apply. Terrorists will strike from areas where no governmental authority exists, or they will base themselves behind what they expect will be the sanctuary of an international border. And they will design their attacks to take place in precisely those "gray areas" where the full facts cannot be known, where the challenge will not bring with it an obvious or clear-cut choice of response.

In such cases we must use our intelligence resources carefully and completely. We will have to examine the full range of measures available to us to take. The outcome may be that we will face a choice between doing nothing or employing military force. We now recognize that terrorism is being used by our adversaries as a modern tool of warfare. It is no aberration. We can expect more terrorism directed at our strategic interests around the world in the years ahead. To combat it, we must be willing to use military force.

What will be required, however, is public understanding *before the fact* of the risks involved in combating terrorism with overt power.

- The public must understand *before the fact* that there is potential for loss of life of some of our fighting men and loss of life of some innocent people.
- The public must understand *before the fact* that some will seek to cast a preemptive or retaliatory action by us in the worst light and will attempt to make our military and our policy makers—rather than the terrorists—appear to be the culprits.
- The public must understand *before the fact* that occasions will come when their government must act before each and every fact is known— and the decisions cannot be tied to the opinion polls.

Public support for US military actions to stop terrorists before they commit some hideous act or in retaliation for an attack on our people is crucial if we are to deal with this challenge.

Our military has the capability and the techniques to use power to fight the war against terrorism. This capability will be used judiciously. To be successful over the long term, it will require solid support from the American people.

I can assure you that in this administration our actions will be governed by the rule of law; and the rule of law is congenial to action against terrorists. We will need the flexibility to respond to terrorist attacks in a variety of ways, at times and places of our own choosing. Clearly, we will not respond in the same manner to every terrorist act. Indeed, we will want to avoid engaging in a policy of automatic retaliation which might create a cycle of escalating violence beyond our control.

If we are going to respond or preempt effectively, our policies will have to have an element of unpredictability and surprise. And the prerequisite for such a policy must be a broad public consensus on the moral and strategic necessity of action. We will need the capability to act on a moment's notice. There will not be time for a renewed national debate after every terrorist attack. We may never have the kind of evidence that can stand up in an American court of law. But we cannot allow ourselves to become the Hamlet of nations, worrying endlessly over whether and how to respond. A great nation with global responsibilities cannot afford to be hamstrung by confusion and indecisiveness. Fighting terrorism will not be a clean or pleasant contest, but we have no choice but to play it.

We will also need a broader international effort. If terrorism is truly a threat to Western moral values, our morality must not paralyze us; it must give us the courage to face up to the threat. And if the enemies of these values are united, so, too, must the democratic countries be united in defending them. The leaders of the industrial democracies, meeting at the London summit in June, agreed in a joint declaration that they must redouble their cooperation against terrorism. There has been followup to that initial meeting, and the United States is committed to advance the process in every way possible. Since we, the democracies, are the most vulnerable, and our strategic interests are the most at stake, we must act together in the face of common dangers. For our part, we will work whenever possible in close cooperation with our friends in the democracies.

Sanctions, when exercised in concert with other nations, can help to isolate, weaken, or punish states that sponsor terrorism against us. Too often, countries are inhibited by fear of losing commercial opportunities or fear of provoking a bully. Economic sanctions and other forms of countervailing pressure impose costs and risks on the nations that apply them, but some sacrifices will be necessary if we are not to suffer even greater costs down the road. Some countries are clearly more vulnerable to extortion than others; surely this is an argument for banding together in mutual support, not an argument for appeasement.

If we truly believe in the values of our civilization, we have a duty to defend them. The democracies must have the self-confidence to tackle this menacing problem or else they will not be in much of a position to tackle other kinds of problems. If we are not willing to set limits to what kinds of behavior are tolerable, then our adversaries will conclude that there are no limits. As Thomas Jefferson once said, when we were confronted with the problem of piracy, "an insult unpunished is the parent of others." In a basic way, the democracies must show whether they believe in themselves.

We must confront the terrorist threat with the same resolve and determination that this nation has shown time and again throughout our history. There is no room for guilt or self-doubt about our right to defend a way of life that offers *all* nations hope for peace, progress, and human dignity. The sage Hillel expressed it well: "If I am not for myself, who will be? If I am for myself alone, who am I?"

As we fight this battle against terrorism, we must always keep in mind the values and way of life we are trying to protect. Clearly, we will not allow ourselves to descend to the level of barbarism that terrorism represents. We will not abandon our democratic traditions, our respect for individual rights, and freedom, for these are precisely what we are struggling to preserve and promote. Our values and our principles will give us the strength and the confidence to meet the great challenge posed by terrorism. If we show the courage and the will to protect our freedom and our way of life, we will prove ourselves again worthy of these blessings.

US-Soviet Relations in the Context
of US Foreign Policy
Washington, DC
June 15, 1983

Statement before the Senate Foreign Relations Committee, Washington, DC, June 15, 1983.

I appreciate the opportunity to meet with you and to discuss this subject of great importance. As you have suggested, it has all sorts of dimensions to it that weigh on peoples' minds; it is a subject that I've thought about a great deal, of course. The President has. You might say that the President has taken the time not only to talk with me about this, but he has read through this testimony and made a few suggestions, which I found it possible to accept, and has signed off on the testimony. So I feel very confident in saying that I am speaking not only for myself but for the President in this statement.

The management of our relations with the Soviet Union is of utmost importance. That relationship touches virtually every aspect of our international concerns and objectives—political, economic, and military—and every part of the world.

We must defend our interests and values against a powerful Soviet adversary that threatens both. And we must do so in a nuclear age, in which a global war would even more thoroughly threaten those interests and values. As President Reagan pointed out on March 31: "We must both defend freedom and preserve the peace. We must stand true to our principles and our friends while preventing a holocaust." It is, as he said, "one of the most complex moral challenges ever faced by any generation."

We and the Soviets have sharply divergent goals and philosophies of political and moral order; these differences will not soon go away. Any other assumption is unrealistic. At the same time, we have a fundamental common interest in the avoidance of war. This common interest impels us to work toward a relationship between our nations that can lead to a safer world for all mankind.

But a safer world will not be realized through good will. Our hopes for the future must be grounded in a realistic assessment of the challenges we face and in a determined effort to create the conditions that will make their achievement possible. We have made a start. Every postwar American president has come sooner or later to recognize that peace must be built on strength; President Reagan has long recognized this reality. In the past two years this nation—the President in partnership with the Congress—has made a fundamental commitment to restoring its military and economic power and moral and spiritual strength. And having begun to rebuild our strength, we now seek to engage the Soviet leaders in a constructive dialogue—a dialogue through which we hope to find political solutions to outstanding issues.

This is the central goal we have pursued since the outset of this administration. We do not want to—and need not—accept as inevitable the prospect of endless, dangerous confrontation with the Soviet Union. For if we do, then many of the great goals that the United States pursues in world affairs—peace, human rights, economic progress, national independence—will also be out of reach. We can—and must—do better.

With that introduction, let me briefly lay out for this committee what I see as the challenge posed by the Soviet Union's international behavior in recent years and the strategy which that challenge requires of us. Then I would like to discuss steps this administration has taken to implement that strategy. Finally, I will focus on the specific issues that make up the agenda for US-Soviet dialogue and negotiation.

Together, these elements constitute a policy that takes account of the facts of Soviet power and of Soviet conduct, mobilizes the resources needed to defend our interests, and offers an agenda for constructive dialogue to resolve concrete international problems. We believe that, if sustained, this policy will make international restraint Moscow's most realistic course and it can lay the foundation for a more constructive relationship between our peoples.

The Soviet Challenge

It is sometimes said that Americans have too simple a view of world affairs, that we start with the assumption that all problems can be solved. Certainly we have a simple view of how the world should be—free peoples choosing their own destinies, nurturing their prosperity, peaceably resolving conflicts. This is the vision that inspires America's role in the world. It does not, however, lead us to regard mutual hostility with the USSR as an immutable fact of international life.

Certainly there are many factors contributing to East-West tension. The Soviet Union's strategic Eurasian location places it in close proximity to important Western interests on two continents. Its aspirations for greater international influence lead it to challenge these interests. Its Marxist-Leninist ideology gives its leaders a perspective on history and a vision of the future fundamentally different from our own. But we are not so deterministic as to believe that geopolitics and ideological competition must ineluctably lead to permanent and dangerous confrontation. Nor is it permanently inevitable that contention between the United States and the Soviet Union must dominate and distort international politics.

A peaceful world order does not require that we and the Soviet Union agree on all the fundamentals of morals or politics. It does require, however, that Moscow's behavior be subject to the restraint appropriate to living together on this planet in the nuclear age. Not all the many external and internal factors affecting Soviet behavior can be influenced by us. But we take it as part of our obligation to peace to encourage the gradual evolution of the Soviet system toward a more pluralistic political and economic system and, above all, to counter Soviet expansionism through sustained and effective political, economic, and military competition.

In the past decade, regrettably, the changes in Soviet behavior have been for the worse. Soviet actions have come into conflict with many of our objectives. They have made the task of managing the Soviet-American relationship considerably harder and have needlessly drawn more and more international problems into the East-West rivalry. To be specific, it is the following developments which have caused us the most concern.

First is the continuing Soviet quest for military superiority even in the face of mounting domestic economic difficulties. In the late 1970s the allocation of resources for the Soviet military was not only at the expense of the Soviet consumer. It came even at the expense of industrial investment on which the long-term development of the economy depends. This decision to mortgage the industrial future of the country is a striking demonstration of the inordinate value the Soviets assign to maintaining the momentum of the relentless military buildup under way since the mid-1960s. This buildup consumed an estimated annual average of at least 12 percent of Soviet gross national product (GNP) throughout this entire period and has recently consumed even more as a result of the sharp decline in Soviet economic growth. During much of this same period, as you know, the share of our own GNP devoted to defense spending has actually declined.

The second disturbing development is the unconstructive Soviet involvement, direct and indirect, in unstable areas of the Third World. Arms have become a larger percentage of Soviet exports than of the export trade of any other country. The Soviets have too often attempted to play a spoiling or scavenging role in areas of concern to us, most recently in the Middle East.

Beyond this, the Soviets in the 1970s broke major new ground in the kinds of foreign military intervention they were willing to risk for themselves or their surrogates. This has escalated from the provision of large numbers of military advisers to the more extensive and aggressive use of proxy forces as in Angola, Ethiopia, and Indochina, and finally to the massive employment of the Soviet Union's own ground troops in the invasion of Afghanistan. In this way, the Soviet Union has tried to block peaceful solutions and has brought East-West tensions into areas of the world that were once free of them.

Third is the unrelenting effort to impose an alien Soviet "model" on nominally independent Soviet clients and allies. One of the most important recent achievements in East-West relations was the negotiation of the Helsinki Final Act, with its pledges concerning human rights and national independence in Europe. Poland's experience in the past two years can be considered a major test of the Soviet Union's respect—or lack of it—for these commitments. Moscow clearly remains unwilling to countenance meaningful national autonomy for its satellites, let alone real independence. Elsewhere in the world, the coming to power of Soviet-supported regimes has usually meant (as in Afghanistan) the forcible creation of Soviet-style institutions and the harsh regimentation and repression of free expression and free initiative—all at enormous human, cultural, and economic cost.

Fourth is Moscow's continuing practice of stretching a series of treaties and agreements to the brink of violation and beyond.   The Soviet Union's infringement of its promises and legal obligations is not confined to isolated incidents. We have had to express our concerns about Soviet infractions on one issue after another—human rights and the Helsinki Final Act, "yellow rain" and biological warfare. We are becoming increasingly concerned about Soviet practices—including the recent testing of ICBMs [intercontinental ballistic missiles]—that raise questions about the validity of their claim of compliance with existing SALT [strategic arms limitation talks] agreements. Little else is so corrosive of international trust as this persistent pattern of Soviet behavior.

The American Response:
Beyond Containment and Détente

This assessment of Soviet international behavior both dictates the approach we must take to East-West relations and indicates the magnitude of the task.

- If we are concerned about the Soviet commitment to military power, we have to take steps to *restore the military balance,* preferably on the basis of verifiable agreements that reduce arms on both sides but, if necessary, through our own and allied defense programs.
- If we are concerned about the Soviet propensity to use force and promote instability, we have to make clear that we will *resist encroachments* on our vital interests and those of our allies and friends.

- If we are concerned about the loss of liberty that results when Soviet clients come to power, then we have to *ensure that those who have a positive alternative to the Soviet model receive our support.*
- Finally, if we are concerned about Moscow's observance of its international obligations, we must *leave Moscow no opportunity to distort or misconstrue our own intentions.* We will defend our interests if Soviet conduct leaves us no alternative; at the same time, we will respect legitimate Soviet security interests and are ready to negotiate equitable solutions to outstanding political problems.

In designing a strategy to meet these goals, we have, of course, drawn in part on past strategies, from containment to détente. There is, after all, substantial continuity in US policy, a continuity that reflects the consistency of American values and American interests. However, we have not hesitated to jettison assumptions about US-Soviet relations that have been refuted by experience or overtaken by events.

Consider how the world has changed since the Truman administration developed the doctrine of containment. Soviet ambitions and capabilities have long since reached beyond the geographic bounds that this doctrine took for granted. Today Moscow conducts a fully global foreign and military policy that places global demands on any strategy that aims to counter it. Where it was once our goal to contain the Soviet presence within the limits of its immediate postwar reach, now our goal must be to advance our own objectives, where possible foreclosing and when necessary actively countering Soviet challenges wherever they threaten our interests.

The policy of détente, of course, represented an effort to induce Soviet restraint. While in some versions it recognized the need to resist Soviet geopolitical encroachments, it also hoped that the anticipation of benefits from expanding economic relations and arms control agreements would restrain Soviet behavior.

Unfortunately, experience has proved otherwise. The economic relationship may have eased some of the domestic Soviet economic constraints that might have at least marginally inhibited Moscow's behavior. It also raised the specter of a future Western dependence on Soviet-bloc trade that would inhibit Western freedom of action toward the East more than it would dictate prudence to the USSR. Similarly, the SALT I and SALT II processes did not curb the Soviet strategic arms buildup, while encouraging many in the West to imagine that security concerns could now be placed lower on the agenda.

Given these differences from the past, we have not been able merely to tinker with earlier approaches. Unlike containment, our policy begins with the clear recognition that the Soviet Union is and will remain a global superpower. In response to the lessons of this global superpower's conduct in recent years, our policy, unlike some versions of détente, assumes that the Soviet Union is more likely to be deterred by our actions that make clear the risks their aggression entails than by a delicate web of interdependence.

Our policy is not based on trust or on a Soviet change of heart. It is based on the expectation that, faced with demonstration of the West's renewed determination to strengthen its defenses, enhance its political and economic cohesion, and oppose adventurism, the Soviet Union will see restraint as its most attractive, or only, option. Perhaps, over time, this restraint will become an ingrained habit; perhaps not. Either way, our responsibility to be vigilant is the same.

Programs to Increase Our Strength

In a rapidly evolving international environment, there are many fundamental ways the democratic nations can, and must, advance their own goals in the face of the problem posed by the Soviet Union. We must build a durable political consensus at home and within the Atlantic alliance on the nature of the Soviet challenge. We must strengthen our defenses and those of our allies. We must build a common approach within the alliance on the strategic implications of East-West economic relations. And we must compete peacefully and even more effectively with the USSR for the political sympathies of the global electorate, especially through the promotion of economic dynamism and democracy throughout the world. Finally, we must continue rebuilding America's moral-spiritual strength. If sustained over time, these policies can foster a progressively more productive dialogue with the Soviet Union itself.

Building Consensus

From the beginning of this administration, the President recognized how essential it was to consolidate a new consensus here at home and among our traditional allies and friends. After 15 years in which foreign policy had been increasingly a divisive issue, he believed we had an opportunity to shape a new unity in America, expressing the American people's recovery of self-confidence. After the trauma of Vietnam, he sought to bolster a realistic pride in our country and to reinforce the civic courage and commitment on which the credibility of our military deterrent ultimately rests.

The President also felt that the possibility of greater cooperation with our allies depended importantly on a reaffirmation of our common moral values and interests. There were, as well, opportunities for cooperation with friendly governments of the developing world and new efforts to seek and achieve common objectives.

Redressing the Military Balance

President Reagan also began a major effort to modernize our military forces. The central goal of our national security policy is deterrence of war; restoring and maintaining the strategic balance is a necessary condition for that deterrence. But the strategic balance also shapes, to an important degree, the global environment in which the United States pursues its foreign policy objectives. Therefore, decisions on major strategic weapons systems can have profound political as well as military consequences.

As Secretary of State I am acutely conscious of the strength or weakness of American power and its effect on our influence over events. Perceptions of the strategic balance are bound to affect the judgments of not only our adversaries but also our allies and friends around the world who rely on us. As leader of the democratic nations, we have an inescapable responsibility to maintain this pillar of the military balance which only we can maintain. Our determination to do so is an important signal of our resolve and is essential to sustaining the confidence of allies and friends and the cohesion of our alliances. This is why the Congress's support of the Peacekeeper ICBM program has been such a valuable contribution to our foreign policy, as well as to our defense.

At the same time, we have begun an accelerated program to strengthen our conventional capabilities. We are pursuing major improvements of our ground, naval, and tactical air forces; we have also added a new Central Command in the Middle East that will enhance our ability to deploy forces rapidly if threats to our vital interests make this necessary. To deter or deal with any future crisis, we need to maintain both our conventional capabilities and our strategic deterrent.

We are also working closely with our allies to improve our collective defense. As shown in the security declaration of the Williamsburg summit and in the North Atlantic Council communiqué of just the other day, we and our allies are united in our approach in the INF [intermediate-range nuclear forces] negotiations in Geneva and remain on schedule for the deployment of Pershing II and ground-launched cruise missiles. That deployment will take place as planned unless we are able to reach a balanced and verifiable agreement at Geneva which makes deployment unnecessary.

Upgrading NATO's conventional forces is, of course, a collective alliance responsibility. At the NATO summit in Bonn a year ago, the President and the leaders of the Atlantic alliance reaffirmed that a credible conventional defense is essential to ensuring European security. We and our allies will continue our efforts toward this goal. At the same time, we have taken steps to ensure a more equitable sharing of the burden of that defense. As a measure of the value of such steps, we estimate that last year's agreement with the FRG [Federal Republic of Germany] on host-nation support will cost about 10 percent of what it would cost to provide the same capability with US reserves or 3 percent of what it would cost to provide that capability with active forces.

The Soviets apparently believe they can weaken or divide the Western alliance if they can dominate outlying strategic areas and resources. To deter threats to our vital interests outside Europe, we are developing our ability to move forces, supported by our allies, to key areas of the world such as Southwest Asia. The allies are also working with us to contribute to stability and security in certain volatile areas, including Lebanon and the Sinai.

In Asia we are modernizing our forces and are working with our allies, especially Japan and Korea, to improve their ability to fulfill agreed roles and missions.

Reassessing the Security Implications of East-West Economic Relations

The balance of power cannot be measured simply in terms of military forces or hardware; military power rests on a foundation of economic strength. Thus, we and our allies must not only strengthen our own economies but we must also develop a common approach to our economic relations with the Soviet Union that takes into account our broad strategic and security interests. In the past, the nations of the West have sometimes helped the Soviets to avoid difficult economic choices by allowing them to acquire militarily relevant technology and subsidized credits. Possible dependence on energy imports from the Soviet Union is another cause for concern.

In the past year, we have made substantial progress toward an allied consensus on East-West trade. The Williamsburg summit declaration stated clearly: "East-West economic relations should be compatible with our security interests." The NATO communiqué two days ago made a similar statement. Our allies agree with us that trade which makes a clear and direct contribution to the military strength of the Soviet Union should be prohibited. There is also general agreement that economic relations with the USSR should be conducted on the basis of a strict balance of mutual advantages.

Studies undertaken under NATO and OECD [Organization for Economic Cooperation and Development] auspices have for the first time laid the groundwork for common analyses. We expect in time to draw common policy conclusions from these studies. The communiqué of the OECD ministerial meeting on May 9–10 declared that "East-West trade and credit flows should be guided by the indications of the market. In the light of these indications, Governments should exercise financial prudence without granting preferential treatment." The United States seeks agreement that we not subsidize Soviet imports through the terms of government credits. Beyond this, we urge other Western governments to exercise restraint in providing or guaranteeing credit to the Soviet Union, allowing the commercial considerations of the market to govern credit.

Similarly, at the IEA [International Energy Agency] ministerial meeting in Paris on May 8, it was agreed that security concerns should be considered among the full costs of imported energy, such as gas; it was agreed that countries "would seek to avoid undue dependence on any one source of gas imports and to obtain future gas supplies from secure sources, with emphasis on indigenous OECD sources."

The fruitful cooperative discussions of these issues at the OECD, IEA, Williamsburg, and NATO are only a beginning. Economic relationships are a permanent element of the strategic equation. How the West should respond economically to the Soviet challenge will and should be a subject of continuing discussion in Western forums for years to come.

Peace and Stability in the Third World

Since the 1950s, the Soviet Union has found in the developing regions of the Third World its greatest opportunities for extending its influence through subversion and exploitation of local conflicts. A satisfactory East-West military balance will not by itself close off such opportunities. We must also respond to the economic, political, and security problems that contribute to these opportunities. Our approach has four key elements.

First, in the many areas where Soviet activities have added to instability, we are pursuing peaceful diplomatic solutions to regional problems, to raise the political costs of Soviet-backed military presence and to encourage the departure of Soviet-backed forces. Our achievements in the Middle East, while far from complete, are addressed to this goal; we are actively encouraging ASEAN [Association of South East Asian Nations] efforts to bring about Vietnamese withdrawal from Kampuchea; we strongly support the worldwide campaign for Soviet withdrawal from Afghanistan; and we have made considerable progress toward an internationally acceptable agreement on Namibia. In our own hemisphere, we are working with other regional states in support of a peaceful solution to the conflict and instability in Central America.

Second, we are building up the security capabilities of vulnerable governments in strategically important areas. We are helping our friends to help themselves and to help each other. For this purpose, we are asking the Congress for a larger, more flexible security assistance program for FY 1984.

Third, our program recognizes that economic crisis and political instability create fertile ground for Soviet-sponsored adventurism. We are seeking almost $4 billion in economic assistance to help developing countries lay the basis for economic and social progress. We are seeking congressional approval to raise IMF [International Monetary Fund] quotas and broaden IMF borrowing arrangements to address critical financial needs of some of the largest Third World nations. We urge the Congress to approve the full amount requested by the administration toward meeting the US commitment to the IDA [International Development Association].

Finally, there is the democracy initiative, an effort to assist our friends in the Third World to build a foundation for democracy. I might say it has been fascinating to me as this project, which is very small, has gotten started, to see the reaction to it. We held a meeting in the State Department with people from various parts of the world on the subject of free elections, and it was denounced by the Soviet Union. The interesting thing was, they noticed it. I was struck by the fact that in Mr. Chernenko's [Secretary of the Communist Party of the Soviet Union (CPSU)] speech yesterday one of the subjects that he brought out was the importance to them of destroying President Reagan's, in a sense, ideological initiatives. It seems we have their attention. But I think if we can put competition on the basis of ideological competition, of competition of economic systems, we'll walk away with it.

Negotiation and Dialogue: The US-Soviet Agenda

Together these programs increase our political, military, and economic strength and help create an international climate in which opportunities for Soviet adventurism are reduced. They are essential for the success of the final element of our strategy—engaging the Soviets in an active and productive dialogue on the concrete issues that concern the two sides. Strength and realism can deter war, but only direct dialogue and negotiation can open the path toward lasting peace. In this dialogue, our agenda is as follows:

- To seek improvement in Soviet performance on human rights, which you emphasized, Mr. Chairman [Senator Charles H. Percy], in your opening statement;
- To reduce the risk of war, reduce armaments through sound agreements, and ultimately ease the burdens of military spending;
- To manage and resolve regional conflicts; and
- To improve bilateral relations on the basis of reciprocity and mutual interest.

This is a rigorous and comprehensive agenda, and our approach to it is principled, practical, and patient. We have pressed each issue in a variety of forums, bilateral and multilateral. We have made clear that the concerns we raise are not ours alone, but are shared by our allies and friends in every region of the globe. We have made clear that each of our concerns is serious, and the Soviets know that we do not intend to abandon any of them merely because agreement cannot be reached quickly or because agreement has been reached on others.

Let me briefly review the state of our dialogue in each of these areas.

Human Rights

Human rights is a major issue on our agenda. To us it is a matter of real concern that Soviet emigration is at its lowest level since the 1960s and that Soviet constriction of emigration has coincided with a general crackdown against all forms of internal dissent. The Helsinki monitoring groups have all been dispersed, and their leaders have been imprisoned or expelled from the country. And the Soviet Union's first independent disarmament group has been harassed and persecuted.

We address such questions both multilaterally and bilaterally. In such forums as the UN Human Rights Commission, the International Labor Organization, and especially the review conference of CSCE [Conference on Security and Cooperation in Europe]—I might say where Max

Kampelman [chairman of the US delegation] is doing an absolutely out-standing job—we have made clear that human rights cannot be relegated to the margins of international politics. Our Soviet interlocutors have a different view; they seek to dismiss human rights as a "tenth-rate issue," not worthy of high-level attention.

But our approach will not change. Americans know that national rights and individual rights cannot realistically be kept separate. We believe, for example, that the elements of the postwar European "settle-ment" that were adopted by the parties to the Helsinki Final Act in 1975 form an integral whole; no one part will survive alone. Guided by this conviction, we and our allies have held at the Madrid review conference that movement in one "basket" of this settlement—such as the convening of a European disarmament conference—must be matched by progress in the other "baskets," especially human rights.

We insist on this balance because we believe that international obliga-tions must be taken seriously by the governments that assume them. But there is also a deeper reason that directly concerns the question of secu-rity. In Europe, as elsewhere, governments that are not at peace with their own people are unlikely to be on good terms with their neighbors. The only significant use of military force on the continent of Europe since 1945 has been by the Soviet Union against its East European "allies." As long as this unnatural relationship continues between the USSR and its East European neighbors, it is bound to be a source of instability in Europe.

We have been just as concerned about human rights issues on a bilat-eral as on a multilateral basis. The need for steady improvement of Soviet performance in the most important human rights categories is as cen-tral to the Soviet-American dialogue as any other theme. Sometimes we advance this dialogue best through public expressions of our concerns, at other times through quiet diplomacy. What counts, and the Soviets know this, is whether we see results.

Arms Control

Let me turn to arms control. We believe the only arms control agree-ments that count are those that provide for real reductions, equality, verifiability, and enhanced stability in the East-West balance. Success in our negotiations will not, of course, bring East-West competition to an end. But sustainable agreements will enable us to meet the Soviet challenge in a setting of greater stability and safety.

The United States is now applying these principles in an ambitious program of arms control negotiations including INF, START [strategic arms reduction talks], MBFR [mutual and balanced force reductions], and the ongoing discussions in the UN Committee on Disarmament in Geneva. If we can reach a balanced agreement in the CSCE at Madrid, we would be prepared to participate also in a conference on disarmament in Europe.

No previous administration has put so many elements of the East-West military equation on the negotiating table. You are aware of the US position in the various talks, so I need not go into great detail. I will, however, touch on a few main points.

START   In the strategic arms reduction talks, the United States has focused on the most destabilizing strategic systems—land-based ballistic missiles. Our objective is to strengthen deterrence while enhancing strategic stability through reductions. The President has proposed reductions in ballistic missile warheads by one-third. In presenting a comprehensive proposal, he has indicated that all strategic weapons are "on the table." Although our respective positions are far apart, the Soviets apparently accept the proposition that an agreement must involve significant reductions. This is progress.

We have recently undertaken a full review of the US position, which included an assessment of the Scowcroft commission's recommendations and some thoughtful suggestions from the Congress. One week ago, the President announced that he is willing to raise the deployed-missile ceiling in accordance with the Scowcroft recommendations. He also announced that he has given our negotiators new flexibility to explore all appropriate avenues for achieving reductions. It is now up to the Soviet Union to reciprocate our flexibility.

Confidence-Building Measures   We have also tabled a draft agreement on confidence-building measures that calls for exchange of information and advance notification of ballistic missile launches and major exercises. We want to move forward promptly to negotiate separate agreements on these very important measures, which would enhance stability in a crisis as well as symbolizing the common interest in preventing war. Yet another effort to prevent misperception of military activities on either side, and thus to lower the risk of war, is the President's recent proposal to expand and upgrade crisis communications between Washington and Moscow. Here, too, we hope for early agreement.

INF   In the negotiations on intermediate-range nuclear forces, "equal rights and limits" between the United States and the Soviet Union is one of our key principles. President Reagan's proposal of November 1981 sought to achieve the complete elimination of those systems on each side about which the other side has expressed the greatest concern—that is, longer-range, land-based INF missiles.

We still regard this as the most desirable outcome. Yet after more than a year of talks, the Soviets continue to resist this equitable and effective solution. In fact, their position has not substantially changed since it was first put forward nearly a year ago. The proposal made by Mr. Andropov [General Secretary of the CPSU] last December would allow the Soviet Union to maintain its overwhelming monopoly of longer-range INF (LRINF) missiles while prohibiting the deployment of even one comparable US missile.

In an effort to break this stalemate, the President has proposed an interim agreement as a route to the eventual elimination of LRINF systems. Under such an agreement, we would reduce the number of missiles we plan to deploy in Europe if the Soviet Union will reduce the total number of warheads it has already deployed to an equal level. This would result in equal limits for both sides on a global basis. Reflecting the concerns of our Asian allies and friends, we have made it clear that no agreement can come at their expense. We hope that in the current round of negotiations the Soviets will move to negotiate in good faith on the President's proposal, which was unanimously supported by our partners at the Williamsburg summit.

MBFR   In the mutual and balanced force reductions talks in Vienna, NATO and the Warsaw Pact are discussing an agreement on conventional forces in Central Europe, the most heavily armed region of the world, where Warsaw Pact forces greatly exceed NATO's. Last year, the President announced a new Western position in the form of a draft treaty calling for substantial reductions to equal manpower levels. Although the Soviets and their allies have agreed to the principle of parity, progress has been prevented by inability to resolve disagreement over existing Warsaw Pact force levels and by problems of verification.

Chemical Weapons   In the 40-nation Committee on Disarmament in Geneva, the United States has introduced a far-reaching proposal for a comprehensive ban on chemical weapons—an agreement which would eliminate these terrible weapons from world arsenals. This initiative has been vigorously supported by our allies and friends, as well as by many nonaligned nations. Our emphasis on the importance of mandatory on-site inspections has been widely applauded. An independent, impartial verification system, observed by and responsive to all parties, is essential to create confidence that the ban is being respected.

Nuclear Testing and Nonproliferation   In other areas, we have proposed to the Soviet Union improvements in the verification provisions of two agreements to limit underground nuclear testing. So far the Soviet response has been negative. We have also initiated a dialogue with the Soviets in one area where our respective approaches very often coincide: nuclear nonproliferation.

We should not anticipate early agreement in any of these negotiations. The Soviets have their own positions, and they are tough, patient negotiators. But we believe that our positions are fair and even-handed and that our objectives are realistic.

Regional Issues

Let me now turn to regional issues which in the sweep of things historically have been the matters that are most upsetting to our relationship with the Soviet Union. Important as it is, arms control has not been—and cannot be—the dominant subject of our dialogue with the Soviets. We must also address the threat to peace posed by the Soviet exploitation of regional instability and conflict. Indeed, these issues—arms control and political instability—are closely related: the increased stability that we try to build into the superpower relationship through arms control can be undone by irresponsible Soviet policies elsewhere. In our numerous discussions with the Soviet leadership, we have repeatedly expressed our strong interest in reaching understandings with the Soviets that would minimize superpower involvement in conflicts beyond their borders.

The list of problem areas is formidable, but we have insisted that regional issues are central to progress. We have made clear our commitment to relieve repression and economic distress in Poland, to achieve a settlement in southern Africa, to restore independence to Afghanistan, to end the occupation of Kampuchea, and to halt Soviet- and Cuban-supported subversion in Central America. In each instance, we have conveyed our views forcefully to the Soviets in an attempt to remove the obstacles that Soviet conduct puts in the way of resolving these problems.

Last year, for example, Ambassador Arthur Hartman [US Ambassador to the USSR] conducted a round of exploratory talks on Afghanistan between US and Soviet officials in Moscow. Any solution to the Afghanistan problem must meet four requirements: complete withdrawal of Soviet forces, restoration of Afghanistan's independent and nonaligned status, formation of a government acceptable to the Afghan people, and honorable return of the refugees. This is not the view of the United States alone. These principles underlie the discussions now under way under the auspices of the UN Secretary General, which we support.

On southern African problems, Assistant Secretary Chester Crocker has held a number of detailed exchanges with his Soviet counterpart. Southern Africa has been a point of tension and periodic friction between the United States and the Soviet Union for many years. We want to see tensions in the area reduced. But this more peaceful future will not be achieved unless all parties interested in the region show restraint, external military forces are withdrawn, and Namibia is permitted to achieve independence. If the Soviets are at all concerned with the interests of Africans, they should have an equal interest in achieving these objectives.

As in our arms control negotiations, we have made it absolutely clear to the Soviets in these discussions that we are not interested in cosmetic solutions. We are interested in solving problems fundamental to maintenance of the international order.

It is also our view that Soviet participation in international efforts to resolve regional conflicts—in southern Africa or the Middle East, for example—depends on Soviet conduct. If the Soviets seek to benefit from tension and support those who promote disorder, they can hardly expect to have a role in the amelioration of those problems. Nor should we expect them to act responsibly merely because they gain a role. At the same time, we have also made it clear that we will not exploit and, in fact, are prepared to respond positively to Soviet restraint. The decision in each case is theirs.

Bilateral Relations

The final part of our agenda with the Soviets comprises economic and other bilateral relations. In our dialogue, we have spelled out our view of these matters in a candid and forthright way. As we see it, economic transactions can confer important strategic benefits, and we must be mindful of the implications for our security. Therefore, as I have already indicated, we believe economic relations with the East deserve more careful scrutiny than in the past. But our policy is not one of economic warfare against the USSR. East-West trade in nonstrategic areas—in the words of the NATO communiqué—"conducted on the basis of commercially sound terms and mutual advantage, that avoids preferential treatment of the Soviet Union, contributes to constructive East-West relations."

Despite the strains of the past few years in our overall relationship, we have maintained the key elements in the structure for bilateral trade. We have recently agreed with the USSR to extend our bilateral fisheries agreement for one year and have begun to negotiate a new long-term US-Soviet grain agreement. Our grain sales are on commercial terms and are not made with government-supported credits or guarantees of any kind.

As for contacts between people, we have cut back on largely symbolic exchanges but maintained a framework of cooperation in scientific, technical, and humanitarian fields. A major consideration as we pursue such exchanges must be reciprocity. If the Soviet Union is to enjoy virtually unlimited opportunities for access to our free society, US access to Soviet society must increase. We have made progress toward gaining Soviet acceptance of this principle as is indicated by the airing in Moscow this past weekend of an interview with Deputy Secretary Ken Dam.

Eight bilateral cooperative agreements are now in effect, and exchanges between the Academies of Science continue, as do exchanges of young scholars and Fulbright fellows. *America Illustrated* magazine continues to be distributed in the Soviet Union in return for distribution here of *Soviet Life,* in spite of the absence of a cultural exchanges agreement. Toward the private sector we have maintained an attitude of neither encouraging nor discouraging exchanges, and a steady flow of tourists and conference participants goes on in both directions. The number of US news bureaus in Moscow has actually increased in the last year.

Prospects

Let me just say a word about prospects. It is sometimes said that Soviet-American relations are "worse than ever." This committee's staff, for example, has made such a judgment in a recent report. Certainly the issues dividing our two countries are serious. But let us not be misled by "atmospherics," whether sunny or, as they now seem to be, stormy.

In the mid-1950s, for example, despite the rhetoric and tension of the Cold War—and in the midst of a leadership transition—the Soviet Union chose to conclude the Austrian State Treaty. It was an important agreement, which contributed to the security of Central Europe, and it carries an important lesson for us today. The Soviet leadership did not negotiate seriously merely because Western rhetoric was firm and principled, nor should we expect rhetoric to suffice now or in the future. But adverse "atmospherics" did not prevent agreement; Soviet policy was instead affected by the pattern of Western actions, by our resolve and clarity of purpose. And the result was progress.

There is no certainty that our current negotiations with the Soviets will lead to acceptable agreements. What is certain is that we will not find ourselves in the position in which we found ourselves in the aftermath of détente. We have not staked so much on the prospect of a successful negotiating outcome that we have neglected to secure ourselves against the possibility of failure. Unlike the immediate postwar period, when negotiating progress was a remote prospect, we attach the highest importance to articulating the requirements for an improved relationship and to exploring every serious avenue for progress. Our parallel pursuit of strength and negotiation prepares us both to resist continued Soviet aggrandizement and to recognize and respond to positive Soviet moves.

We have spelled out our requirements—and our hope—for a more constructive relationship with the Soviet Union. The direction in which that relationship evolves will ultimately be determined by the decisions of the Soviet leadership. President Brezhnev's successors will have to weigh the increased costs and risks of relentless competition against the benefits of a less tense international environment in which they could more adequately address the rising expectations of their own citizens. While we can define their alternatives, we cannot decipher their intentions. To a degree unequaled anywhere else, Russia in this respect remains a secret.

Its history, of which this secrecy is such an integral part, provides no basis for expecting a dramatic change. And yet it also teaches that gradual change is possible. For our part, we seek to encourage change by a firm but flexible US strategy, resting on a broad consensus, that we can sustain over the long term whether the Soviet Union changes or not. If the democracies can meet this challenge, they can achieve the goals of which President Reagan spoke at Los Angeles: both defend freedom and preserve the peace.

"Tear Down This Wall," Twenty Years Later
Address before the American Academy in Berlin
Berlin, Germany
June 5, 2007

General Secretary Gorbachev, if you seek peace, if you seek prosperity for the Soviet Union and Eastern Europe, if you seek liberalization: Come here to this gate! Mr. Gorbachev, open this gate! Mr. Gorbachev, tear down this wall!

So spoke President Ronald Reagan 20 years ago. In the background was the Brandenburg Gate, all too visible behind the wall. Reagan's stirring words, though noted at the time, came dramatically alive when the wall was literally and joyously torn down some two and one-half years later.

Here in Berlin, on the 20th anniversary of President Reagan's speech and, incidentally, on the 60th anniversary of the announcement by then Secretary of State George Marshall of the plan that bears his name, we must ask ourselves: Why did the wall come down and what can we learn from this historic event? These questions are important because the disappearance of the wall is a metaphor for the end of the Cold War, which occurred largely without bloodshed. And the lessons we should learn are potentially useful because security concerns once again threaten the freedom and prosperity of our world.

I will speak particularly about the Reagan years since they were an important part of the picture and because I know them from personal experience. But I recognize one of the most important reasons for success: we in the West had a strategy that we were able to sustain for almost half a century. The basic architecture was put in place and solidified in the Truman and Eisenhower years and that architecture, particularly the NATO alliance, served us well throughout the Cold War period.

Let me talk first about a few ideas that underlay our success.

The strategy of containment was central. The West undertook to resist any expansion of the Soviet empire with the expectation that, sooner or later, the internal contradictions in the empire would cause it to look inward and, in the end, to change. As time went on, this guiding idea shifted into what was called détente: we're here, you're there, that's life, so the name of the game is peaceful coexistence. Well, that's a lot better than war, especially nuclear war.

But Ronald Reagan preferred the initial idea. He denounced détente and stood by his belief that the Soviet Union would change because, as he said in his "Tear Down This Wall" speech, "In the West today, we see a free world that has achieved a level of prosperity and well-being unprecedented in all human history. In the Communist world, we see failure, technological backwardness, declining standards of health, even want of the most basic kind—too little food."

He made some people nervous with his views and his rhetoric, but the idea that change is possible turned out to be an energizing and motivating stimulant, true to the original concept of containment.

A second idea, the concept of linkage, characterized the pre-Reagan approach to our relationship with the Soviet Union. The Reagan administration inherited the result of the application of this idea. When the Soviets invaded Afghanistan, President Carter was surprised, distressed, and angered. In reaction, he shut down everything from participation by US athletes in the Moscow Olympics to negotiations on arms control and even the annual visit of Foreign Minister Gromyko to Washington prior to the opening of the UN General Assembly.

As I took office, my friend, the West German Chancellor, Helmut Schmidt, counseled me: "George, the situation is dangerous; there is no human contact." To put it another way, linkage had been vastly overdone. President Reagan understood that linkage could work against the right outcome. Linkage could encourage the Soviets to do something bad just so they could agree to give it up in order to get something else they wanted. And if the Soviets did something good, linkage put pressure on us to go along with something else they were doing wrong. Above all, Ronald Reagan was determined to pursue freedom and make an effort to reduce nuclear armaments no matter what else was going on.

We confronted this issue most dramatically in September 1983, when the Soviets shot down a Korean airliner. The Boeing 747, with its unique profile, was carrying 269 passengers and crew. We obtained and released a recording of the fighter pilot's ground controller authorizing him to fire. Of course, we and the rest of the world were outraged.

But rather than cut ties, as his predecessor had done, and over the objections of a great many members of his administration, President Reagan authorized me to go ahead with an earlier-scheduled meeting with Foreign Minister Gromyko. Talk at the meeting was harsh and blunt, and, at one point, Gromyko started to leave but then came back. Our longtime interpreter told me that it was the most difficult and tumultuous meeting he had ever observed. I thought it was good for Gromyko to hear directly how appalled we were, as were people throughout the world.

Even more important, and, once again, over many objections, President Reagan sent our arms control negotiators back to Geneva to continue their quest for an agreement. So, it is not evidence of weakness that you meet with your counterpart. The important point is what you say.

We in the West also understood the importance of strength and its many dimensions. Free societies and free economies, with some help from the Marshall Plan, produced prosperity. These successes, in turn, produced confidence. The achievements could be made known through organizations such as Radio Liberty and Radio Free Europe, along with the British Broadcasting Corporation and Voice of America. So strength has many dimensions, including, of course, military capability. NATO was formed and held together. There were many difficult moments. Who can forget the Berlin Airlift and the resolute Berliners, as we in the NATO countries stood with them?

I believe the vital turning point in the Cold War was the deployment of Pershing missiles in Germany in late 1983. That deployment did not come easily, even though it was the implementation of a long-known NATO agreement. The run-up to deployment was accompanied by a drumbeat of threats from the Soviet Union. War, they implied, was in the offing. And the threats from the Soviet Union had an effect on the West. The 1983 nuclear freeze protest in New York City's Central Park still stands as one of the largest public demonstrations in American history, while massive and repeated demonstrations took place throughout the United Kingdom. Protesters filled the streets. Some politicians went wobbly. Nevertheless, a coherent NATO was on display. The hero of that turning point is right here today: former Chancellor Helmut Kohl. For despite the opposition to the 1983 deployment that manifested itself in the United States and the United Kingdom, no one in the West came under pressure as intense as that faced by the Chancellor of the Federal Republic of Germany—no one. I tip my hat to you, sir. If that deployment had not gone forward, our strength and our willpower could have been shattered and the outcome of the Cold War might well have been different.

But now I note that the strength we put on display was never used. What preceded the deployment was intense diplomacy with the Soviets and a continuing and even more intense consultative process among the Allies. In the end, that process made the deployment possible and the deployment—a magnificent display of the strength, determination, and cohesion of NATO—in turn made possible the diplomacy that followed and, in the end, tore down that wall. And by containing the Soviets—by making it clear that we would not permit them to isolate Berlin—NATO established the conditions in which brave people throughout the Warsaw Pact could bring the Cold War to a peaceful end. President Reagan called on Mr. Gorbachev to tear down the wall, but in the end it was the German people who did so.

So we see on display here a set of important ideas:

- Change toward freedom and openness is possible.
- Economic development goes in tandem with political openness.
- Strength of purpose and capability are essential.
- Strength works in tandem with diplomacy.
- A deep and continuing consultative process among like-minded people creates the understanding necessary to make hard choices.
- A successful strategy must be based on realism and sustainability.

Well, the Cold War is over, the world now proceeds on a global basis, and economic expansion is taking place almost everywhere at an unprecedented pace. The world is, in many ways, at a golden moment. But we know all too well what constitutes the main threat to the continuation of this prosperity and the political openness that tends to be its handmaiden.

The threat posed by Islamic extremists using the weapon of terror—even, potentially, nuclear terror—is all too real. We have seen the face of terror in the Americas, in Asia, in Europe, in the Middle East—in every corner of the world. There are Islamists who would build a kind of wall of ideology in an effort to shut in vast multitudes of believers in Islam who nevertheless wish for a better life consistent with the teachings of their religion. These radical jihadists promulgate a culture of hate and division.

What lessons can we draw from our earlier experiences as we combat and seek to isolate the forces of division and find accommodation with more moderate and tolerant Islam?

The notion of containment can also work against terrorism as it did against the Soviet Union. If we can prevent the spread of hateful ideology, then we have taken the first essential step. If you look at Indonesia and Malaysia, countries with large numbers of Muslims, you will see some signs that the strategy of containment can work. And remember that the strategy of containment includes the idea that change is possible. So look at Algeria today, where, as reported recently by the *New York Times*, 60 percent of the enrollment in colleges is by women, and they are filling an increasing array of jobs, including 70 percent of Algeria's lawyers and 60 percent of its judges.

Economic development based on human effort, not just the exploitation of oil wealth, can lead to more open political systems. Why not encourage that kind of development in Islamic lands and communities?

Strength is always a key: the military capability, willpower, and self-confidence to act when necessary. A special challenge is created by the potentially devastating consequences of a terrorist attack: huge numbers of lives lost, in addition to destruction of property and economic damage and dislocation. The need for sharply improved intelligence capability is obvious. Knowledge about attacks before they take place is essential. Then we have an uncomfortable decision to make, especially when the culprit group or individuals are in a country where terrorists are tolerated or even assisted. The failure to use preventive force in such circumstances can have consequences that are simply not acceptable.

Other ideas can also be effective.

Consultation and diplomatic engagement are essential. To paraphrase Helmut Schmidt, there is no substitute for human contact. The point is to be careful what you say and to be sure that your diplomacy is supported by strength.

Perhaps we can also gain some momentum for this agenda and strength, cooperation, containment, and diplomacy from the pursuit of two big ideas on a global scale. Each one is drawn from the Ronald Reagan playbook.

First, can we find our way to a world free of nuclear weapons? I'm working hard on this problem on a nonpartisan basis with Henry Kissinger, Sam Nunn, and William Perry, along with many others. We take a cue from development of that idea at the Reykjavik meeting between President Reagan and General Secretary Gorbachev some months before the speech we commemorate here. At Reykjavik, President Reagan and General Secretary Gorbachev came close, very close, to an agreement that would have led to the abolition of most kinds of nuclear weapons. Immediately afterwards, we all felt dejected. But within a few hours, we recognized the import of what had taken place. As I told President Reagan when we returned to Washington, Reykjavik had been a success, not a failure, because it demonstrated the possibility of a world free of the nuclear threat.

Many steps need to be taken and with great care. At the same time, the world might be rallied to this grand endeavor. The use of nuclear weapons has never made sense. Now, as they spread, the likelihood that they will be used rather than merely relied on for their deterrent value grows, with potentially disastrous consequences.

Second, can we find our way to a global structure that allows us to attack the issues of global warming? The Kyoto Protocol could not work because the concept behind it had no chance of global acceptance. The Montreal Protocol, which we developed during the Reagan period, was the 1987 international agreement to phase out the production of materials that were depleting the ozone layer of the atmosphere. When Montreal was completed, Ronald Reagan called it a "magnificent achievement." The Protocol has been implemented so widely that former UN Secretary General Kofi Annan called it "Perhaps the single most successful international agreement to date." It worked, in part, because every state was part of the problem and took part in the solution. In this respect, Montreal has a lot to teach post-Kyoto. We can put ideas that work into play once again.

The pursuit of big ideas on a world scale might well generate just the sense of cohesion that would help like-minded nations face down other problems that threaten our peace and our prosperity.

I am deeply honored and moved by the opportunity to speak here in Berlin on this special anniversary. The occasion reminds us that unpleasant realities can change if we confront them with strength, cohesion, and sustained diplomatic effort.

APPENDIX SEVEN

Toward a World Without Nuclear Weapons

Preventing the Proliferation of Nuclear Weapons
New York, NY
November 1, 1984

Following is an address by Secretary Shultz before the United Nations Association of the USA, New York, November 1, 1984.

In the early 1960s, during the presidency of John F. Kennedy, it was the consensus of defense policy experts that by the mid-1980s—today—between 15 and 25 countries would have nuclear weapons. Serious commentators then accepted, almost without question, the idea that the spread of nuclear weapons was inexorable, advancing like a Greek tragedy to some disastrous preordained conclusion.

Well, I'm happy to say they were wrong. It's 1984, and despite the steady and rapid development of nuclear energy around the world, the number of acknowledged nuclear-weapons states has held at five since China tested its first atomic bomb 20 years ago. Only one additional country, India, has carried out any kind of nuclear explosion—and that was 10 years ago.

Clearly, the potential danger is still with us. Regional rivalries and grandiose ambitions continue to tempt some countries to flirt with the dangerous and misguided notion that their security could be enhanced by obtaining nuclear weapons or at least by creating the perception that they can do so.

But these temptations can and are being held in check. The prophets of gloom were wrong in their prediction that nuclear proliferation was inevitable, because they did not foresee the determined efforts that would be undertaken by the international community to deter the spread of these deadly weapons. Without this undertaking, the

United States Department of State, Bureau of Public Affairs, Washington, DC.

nightmare of rampant nuclear proliferation might well have become reality.

While superpower negotiations to limit the growth of nuclear arsenals have garnered the headlines, the effort to prevent the spread of nuclear explosives has gone on largely out of the glare of publicity. Through seven administrations, the United States has led a concerted international campaign to control this threat to world peace. The endeavor has fostered a web of institutional arrangements, legal commitments, technological safeguards, and alternative means for addressing security concerns.

The ongoing antiproliferation campaign is an example of constructive diplomacy and international cooperation at its finest. In this enterprise we have found common ground not only between industrialized and developing countries, and between nuclear suppliers and nuclear consumers, but between ourselves and the Soviet Union. What we all share is the recognition that nuclear proliferation would aggravate political tensions among nations, heighten regional insecurities, and contribute to vastly greater instability in the world.

Since the day he took office, President Reagan has sought, as a fundamental objective, to reduce the dangers to world peace and global stability posed by nuclear weapons. The President's well-known efforts to achieve reductions in strategic and intermediate-range nuclear weapons have been one part of this enterprise. Prevention of nuclear proliferation has been another essential element.

In our efforts to control nuclear proliferation, like those directed toward reducing nuclear weapons, we must be guided by realism. We cannot wish the atom away, nor should we try to. Its secrets have been unlocked, and they have brought great benefit to mankind. Peaceful use of the atom has yielded not only an economical and reliable energy source but a wealth of applications in the fields of medicine and agriculture. We are only just beginning to realize the potential of peaceful nuclear technology for raising the living standards and improving the lives of millions of the world's people.

But we cannot be blind to the potential harm that misuse of this powerful force could bring. Diversion of nuclear technology to explosive purposes could pose a threat to peace and could at the very least undermine global stability.

Many of you undoubtedly saw press accounts of the Carnegie Endowment study on the nuclear proliferation problem that was released a couple of days ago. The study publicized a fact that those of us who deal with this issue have long been acutely aware of: that as long as international tension and conflict exist, there will be insecure or irresponsible leaders who seek to shift the balance of regional power dramatically by acquiring a "secret weapon."

We and other responsible members of the international community are ceaselessly at work to deter those who might be tempted to transform the promise of nuclear energy into the peril of nuclear weapons. Although we cannot be sure that further proliferation of nuclear explosives can be prevented for all time, there is a great deal we can do to retard its pace and make it much more difficult.

Nor can the United States realistically expect to deter proliferation all by itself. America no longer dominates the nuclear field—scientifically or commercially—as it once did. As mastery of the technology has spread, it has been harder to persuade others simply to follow our lead, let alone to dictate their actions and choices. Now more than ever, a successful nonproliferation effort requires cooperative undertakings involving both suppliers and users of nuclear technology, taking into account their energy needs, commercial interests, and concerns about their sovereignty.

Equally important, we must address the underlying causes of nuclear proliferation, not just its symptoms. Although the search for nuclear weapons might arise out of the simple megalomania of a national leader, a country is far more likely to "go nuclear" out of feelings of insecurity, usually arising from regional rivalries. The truth is that any "security" that might be gained by developing a nuclear-weapons capability is likely to be illusory. Proliferation begets proliferation; it is synonymous with instability and is destructive of everyone's security.

Nevertheless, as long as that sense of insecurity exists, the threat of sanctions, although an important deterrent, may not always suffice to discourage countries with the potential to build weapons from trying to do so. If the drive to acquire nuclear weapons is to be curbed, the sources of tension and insecurity also must be addressed. We can do this by providing political, economic, and security assistance to friendly countries anxious about their security. And we can continue to lend our efforts, as we have in the Middle East and southern Africa, for example, to resolution of the conflicts that are at the root of the problem.

In my experience as Secretary of State, I have found the problem of preventing nuclear proliferation to be as complicated and as challenging— intellectually, politically, and diplomatically—as any I've had to deal with. Just as we have discovered in dealing with other intricate, morally challenging foreign policy problems, like arms reduction and human rights, effective solutions often require us to make very tough choices.

Keeping our hands clean by trying to disengage from the problem, or by shunning all relations with potential offenders, is not the answer. We must deal with the causes of the problem and offer alternatives for its solution if we are to maintain our influence with potential proliferators and not jeopardize the other, often critical, interests we may have in common. Balancing these diverse and sometimes contradictory policy considerations can involve difficult trade-offs.

By the same token, if we are to maintain the cooperation of other nations whose participation is absolutely essential to any nonproliferation regime, we must respect their needs, their interests, and their sovereignty.

These are some of the considerations that have gone into shaping the nonproliferation policy of the Reagan administration.

Evolution of Nonproliferation Policy

Over the last three decades, America's nonproliferation policy has benefited from a remarkable continuity and steadfastness of purpose. In 1953, soon after he was elected, President Eisenhower took a historic step in inaugurating the Atoms for Peace program. By this act, the United States volunteered to share its peaceful nuclear technologies for the good of all mankind.

The International Atomic Energy Agency (IAEA), which was also proposed by President Eisenhower, was established in 1957 as an international institution through which to pursue those same goals. The IAEA was given a dual mission: to promote the peaceful use of nuclear energy and to effectuate a system of international safeguards against diversion of nuclear materials for nonpeaceful purposes. Through the intervening years, the IAEA has assumed even greater importance as a key instrument in the nonproliferation regime. It is an agency that the United States ranks among the most important of the international institutions.

The nuclear Non-Proliferation Treaty (NPT), signed in 1968, provided a juridical framework for the same effort. In adhering to the NPT, non-nuclear-weapon states undertook not to develop or acquire nuclear explosives and to accept safeguards on all their nuclear activities. At the same time, these states were assured access to peaceful nuclear technology, while nuclear suppliers committed themselves to ensuring that their nuclear exports were covered by IAEA safeguards. The parties to the treaty also agreed to make good-faith efforts to slow the nuclear arms race.

The early 1970s—particularly after the 1973 energy crisis—were perhaps the halcyon days for nuclear power. Nuclear generation of electricity was increasing rapidly, and the nonproliferation regime was expanding and appeared sound. But the explosion of a nuclear device by India in 1974, notwithstanding its "peaceful use" commitments under bilateral nuclear cooperation agreements, shocked the nuclear suppliers and caused them to reassess their nonproliferation policies.

Even before the Indian blast, there was a growing realization that variations in the export policies of the different nuclear suppliers made it difficult to apply uniform measures to deter proliferation. To close these gaps, the major nuclear suppliers convened in London in 1974 to discuss common multilateral export policies. Under the guidelines first adopted in 1976, members of the London Suppliers' Group agreed to transfer certain technology, equipment, and material only if the customer nation agreed to apply IAEA safeguards to the item supplied and to ensure its peaceful use.

For nearly three decades, the United States and other nations that share our views have relied on this combination of political incentives, international safeguards, bilateral export controls, and technological constraints to hold nuclear proliferation in check. But nonproliferation strategies have had to be continuously adapted to deal with evolving technologies and changing political circumstances.

When the Carter administration took office, its policy was fundamentally shaped by the view that nuclear energy development worldwide created significant proliferation risks. Decisions were made to defer reprocessing and plutonium use in this country. These domestic policies were paralleled by unilateral attempts to curtail the supply of nuclear technology abroad and particularly to discourage the use of plutonium-based technologies by other major industrial nations.

Rather than "setting a good example," as it was intended to do, this negative attitude toward nuclear power was seen by some of our friends as a challenge to their desire for energy independence. Thereby it reduced our influence in the international nuclear arena and eroded trust in the United States as a reliable nuclear supplier.

The enactment of the Nuclear Non-Proliferation Act during the Carter administration represented a serious effort to promote a more stringent and uniform set of international standards for nuclear exports. At the same time, however, it precluded us from carrying out certain supply contracts and agreements to cooperate in the nuclear area, thus impairing our ability to provide incentives for countries to act in ways consistent with nonproliferation goals. As a result, we were less able to win the support of those nations on critical supply, safeguards, and other nonproliferation issues.

Reagan Administration Policies and Achievements

President Reagan, therefore, shaped an approach that was designed to facilitate cooperation with our allies and friends and to ensure us an effective leadership role in international nuclear affairs.

Supporting Nuclear Power   As I said at the outset, we are realistic. In coming decades, nuclear energy will necessarily play a major role in providing environmentally safe and economically efficient electric power in the United States. Likewise, it is clear that nuclear-generated energy will be increasingly important for the economic development and energy security of many nations around the world. For these countries—Japan, for example, and much of Western Europe—nuclear power is critical to national well-being and energy security.

Making Rational Distinctions   We must make rational distinctions between close friends and allies who pose no great proliferation risk and those areas of the world where we have real concerns about the spread of nuclear weapons. A policy of denial toward countries with excellent nonproliferation credentials would be arbitrary as well as counterproductive. On the other hand, we are determined to maintain stringent controls to ensure that our nuclear cooperation is not misused. We recognize, in particular, a clear need to restrict sensitive nuclear activities in regions of instability and proliferation concern, like the Middle East and South Asia.

At the same time, we are striving to reduce the motivation of some states to acquire nuclear explosives by working with them to improve regional and global stability. Our $3.2-billion package of economic and security assistance to Pakistan is a case in point.

Closer Consultation and Cooperation   In light of the earlier criticism by our nuclear partners, and the recognition that America is no longer dominant in the field, we have sought to restore an emphasis on cooperation. It is not always possible, of course, to obtain full agreement on controversial issues. But we have tried, at least, to implement our nonproliferation policy with a maximum of consultation and agreement with other nations. Our approach is designed to give our closest nuclear-trading partners a firmer and more predictable basis on which to plan their vital energy programs, while at the same time furthering our nonproliferation objectives.

President Reagan has stated that the United States will not inhibit civil reprocessing and breeder-reactor development in countries with advanced nuclear programs that do not constitute a proliferation risk. In keeping with this policy, the United States has been discussing with Japan and the European Atomic Energy Community long-term arrangements on reprocessing and plutonium use. We all believe that such long-term arrangements will be mutually beneficial and will enhance the global nonproliferation regime.

Our negotiations with the People's Republic of China regarding an agreement for cooperation in the peaceful uses of nuclear energy also have important implications for the strengthening of the worldwide nonproliferation regime. China's decision during the process of those negotiations to join the International Atomic Energy Agency was a significant step in this regard. Its determination to require IAEA safeguards on its future export commitments, and its strong statement that it would refrain from assisting any other nations to acquire nuclear explosives, are evidence of China's broadening commitment to the world's nonproliferation effort.

We are convinced that nuclear cooperation with China, grounded on an agreement that satisfies all the requirements of our law and policy, will advance our worldwide nonproliferation objectives, enhance our overall political relations with China, and benefit US economic interests.

Although we have major differences with the Soviet Union on a wide range of arms control issues, we have broad common interests in the nonproliferation area. In the fall of 1982, Foreign Minister Gromyko and I agreed to initiate bilateral consultations on nonproliferation. Since then, three rounds of useful discussions have taken place, with both sides finding more areas of agreement than disagreement. We expect to confer again on this subject later this month. It is clear that both countries consider the horizontal spread of nuclear explosives to be in no one's interest. Moreover, we agree that we both have major responsibilities in strengthening the nonproliferation regime.

Broadening the Dialogue   Some rapidly industrializing nations—such as Brazil, Argentina, and South Africa—also have active peaceful nuclear energy programs. Moreover, they are emerging as nuclear materials suppliers in their own right. We have restored a dialogue on the benefits of a strong nonproliferation regime with these countries, where our ties in the area of peaceful nuclear energy had been all but broken. We have sought their cooperation and support for our efforts to assure that nuclear exports are not misused for nonpeaceful purposes. At the same time, we have stressed that regional stability would be enhanced if they would broaden the application of international safeguards in their own nuclear programs.

We are pleased to note that the government of South Africa has publicly undertaken to require IAEA safeguards on all of its future nuclear exports. South Africa has also reopened discussions with the IAEA on safeguarding a significant new semicommercial enrichment plant.

Our discussions with Brazil and Argentina, we believe, have led to an increased sensitivity on their part to our nonproliferation concerns. We attach great importance to the assurances of Brazil and Argentina that their nuclear programs are devoted solely to peaceful uses, and we look forward to continuing our dialogue both in multilateral fora and in bilateral discussions.

We continue to urge all of these countries to adhere to the Non-Proliferation Treaty and, in the case of the Western Hemisphere, the treaty of Tlatelolco, and to place *all* of their nuclear facilities under international safeguards.

Improving US Export Controls   I have talked mainly about this administration's diplomatic and policy initiatives, but we have not neglected the technical side of the problem. In his 1981 statement on nonproliferation policy, the President affirmed that the United States would continue to inhibit the transfer of sensitive nuclear material, equipment, and technology, particularly where the danger of proliferation required restraint.

We fully recognize the risks associated with reprocessing and other sensitive nuclear technologies because of their potential direct applicability to weapons production. We appreciate the need for great caution and restraint in dealing with these risks and the importance of limiting sensitive facilities and activities to as few locations as possible. Even then, reprocessing should only be done in places where no significant risk of proliferation exists.

A small but significant number of the world's states pose a real proliferation risk. In seeking to block these states—Libya, for example—from obtaining nuclear explosives, we have employed a range of political, economic, and security measures. And, of course, we have sought to persuade other suppliers to impose similar conditions and controls. This effort has been successful thus far in preventing acquisition of nuclear weapons by unstable and irresponsible regimes, in whose hands they could create a catastrophe. But unrelenting vigilance is necessary.

Strengthening International Safeguards   Our commitment to strengthened international safeguards remains constant and firm, for we recognize that this is one area in which we cannot allow inspection capabilities to be outpaced by advancing technology. Obviously, as advanced nuclear technologies come on line around the world, the International Atomic Energy Agency must have at its disposal the trained personnel and equipment required to apply adequate safeguards. Under our Program of Technical Assistance to IAEA Safeguards, we continue to contribute importantly to this effort.

In a major arms control speech last year, President Reagan called upon all nuclear suppliers to require recipient states to accept comprehensive safeguards on all their nuclear activities as a condition for any significant new nuclear supply commitments. Over the past three years we have worked through diplomatic channels to develop a favorable supplier consensus on this issue.

It was, for example, one of the topics discussed at the meeting of nuclear suppliers held earlier this year in Luxembourg. The nations represented there agreed that adoption of comprehensive safeguards remains a highly desirable nonproliferation goal. We are seeking to build on the Luxembourg results by examining concrete ways of persuading additional consumer states to accept comprehensive safeguards. As we pursue our dialogue with emerging suppliers, we will work to assure that they, too, come to understand and adopt the nonproliferation ethic that traditional suppliers have developed over the past quarter century.

Sharing Benefits with the Developing World   In our efforts to develop the atom for peaceful purposes—from medicine to nuclear power— we have not ignored the legitimate needs of those technologically less advanced nations that wish to share in the peaceful benefits of the atom. We will continue to ensure, bilaterally and through the IAEA, that those benefits are made available on a reliable basis to nations that have good nonproliferation credentials.

In East Asia and Latin America, the IAEA has recently sponsored initiatives to promote enhanced cooperation in nuclear research, development, and training. We support such regional initiatives and are examining the feasibility of broadening the Latin American effort to involve other nations of the Western Hemisphere, including the United States.

NPT Review Conference   Over the past several years, we have worked to strengthen the treaty that is at the heart of the international nonproliferation regime. Ten new countries have been persuaded to join in the last four years, making the Non-Proliferation Treaty, with 125 parties, the most widely adhered-to arms control agreement in history.

Preparations are now well under way for the 1985 conference to review the implementation of the NPT. For our part, we will work with all countries for a successful review conference in 1985. Indeed, we welcome a full debate, which, I am sure, will not overlook the treaty's critical contribution to international security and global peace.

The Continuing Priority of Preventing Proliferation

It is no exaggeration to say that controlling the spread of nuclear weapons is critical to world peace and, indeed, to human survival. It is a cause that deserves and receives a top priority in our foreign policy.

But as fateful as the stakes are, our efforts have not been widely noted. For the struggle we are waging is not on the battlefield. It goes on in the quiet of diplomatic chanceries, at meetings of technical experts, and in safeguards laboratories. Success is measured not in terms of territory liberated or new allies gained but rather in terms of confidence established, restraints voluntarily accepted, and destabilizing military options forgone.

By those measures, our nonproliferation policy has been a success. We have reestablished a spirit of confidence, both with other nuclear suppliers and with those customers of nuclear technology who share our nonproliferation goals; we have deepened our dialogues on practical cooperation; we have successfully encouraged some important countries to adopt new antiproliferation measures; and we have made significant progress toward the conclusion of new bilateral agreements that will further strengthen the international nonproliferation regime.

But these accomplishments, important as they are, must not lull us into complacency. Thus far, we have proven wrong the prophets of unchecked nuclear proliferation. But only with determination, realism, and unflagging effort can we continue to belie their gloomy prophecy and to ensure that the potential of the atom will be exploited not to threaten civilization but to serve it.

Nuclear Weapons, Arms Control, and the Future of Deterrence

Chicago, IL

November 17, 1986

Following is an address by Secretary Shultz before the International House of Chicago and the Chicago Sun-Times Forum at the University of Chicago, Chicago, Illinois, November 17, 1986.

I'm delighted to be back here at the pinnacle, and I come here to the University of Chicago to talk about nuclear weapons, arms control, and our national security. These issues have been given special timeliness by the President's recent meeting with Soviet General Secretary Gorbachev in Reykjavik. In years to come, we may look back at their discussions as a turning point in our strategy for deterring war and preserving peace. It has opened up new possibilities for the way in which we view nuclear weapons and their role in ensuring our security.

Questions for the Future

We now face a series of questions of fundamental importance for the future: how can we maintain peace through deterrence in the midst of a destabilizing growth of offensive nuclear weapons? How can we negotiate a more stable strategic balance at substantially lower levels of offensive forces? How can we use new defensive technologies to contribute to that stability? How can the West best seek to reduce its reliance on offensive nuclear weapons without running new risks of instability arising from conventional imbalances?

These are exceptionally difficult and complex issues. They go to the heart of our ability as a democratic nation to survive in a world threatened

United States Department of State, Bureau of Public Affairs, Washington, DC.

by totalitarianism and aggression. These questions should engage the best minds in American society, and, of course, they have to be treated at reasonable lengths so the best minds have to have a halfway decent attention span. So that's why I have come to speak to this particular audience at the University of Chicago. This isn't going to be an easy speech, or a short one. I'll ask that you listen carefully, and I hope that you'll reflect at greater length on the text of my remarks.

Forty-four years ago, and about 200 yards from where I am now standing, mankind generated its first self-sustained and controlled nuclear chain reaction. Enrico Fermi's crude atomic pile was the prototype for all that followed—both reactors to generate energy for peaceful uses and weapons of ever-increasing destructiveness. Seldom are we able to mark the beginning of a new era in human affairs so precisely.

I'm not here tonight to announce the end of that era. But I will suggest that we may be on the verge of important changes in our approach to the role of nuclear weapons in our defense. New technologies are compelling us to think in new ways about how to ensure our security and protect our freedoms. Reykjavik served as a catalyst in this process. The President has led us to think seriously about both the possible benefits—and the costs—of a safer strategic environment involving progressively less reliance on nuclear weapons. Much will now depend on whether we are far-sighted enough to proceed toward such a goal in a realistic way that enhances our security and that of our allies.

It may be that we have arrived at a true turning point. The nuclear age cannot be undone or abolished; it is a permanent reality. But we can glimpse now, for the first time, a world freed from the incessant and pervasive fear of nuclear devastation. The threat of nuclear conflict can never be wholly banished, but it can be vastly diminished—by careful but drastic reductions in the offensive nuclear arsenals each side possesses. It is just such reductions—not limitations in expansion but reductions— that constitute the vision President Reagan is working to make a reality.

Such reductions would add far greater stability to the US-Soviet nuclear relationship. Their achievement should make other diplomatic solutions obtainable and perhaps lessen the distrust and suspicion that have stimulated the felt need for such weapons. Many problems will accompany drastic reductions: problems of deployment, conventional balances, verification, multiple warheads, and chemical weapons. The task ahead is great but worth the greatest of efforts.

This will not be a task for Americans alone. We must engage the collective effort of all of the Western democracies. And as we do, we must also be prepared to explore cooperative approaches with the Soviet Union, when such cooperation is feasible and in our interests.

The Evolution of Our Thinking about Nuclear Weapons

Let me start by reviewing how our thinking has evolved about the role of nuclear weapons in our national security.

In the years immediately after Fermi's first chain reaction, our approach was relatively simple. The atomic bomb was created in the midst of a truly desperate struggle to preserve civilization against fascist aggression in Europe and Asia. There was a compelling rationale for its development and use.

But since 1945—and particularly since America lost its monopoly of such weapons a few years later—we have had to adapt our thinking to less clear-cut circumstances. We have been faced with the challenges and the ambiguities of a protracted global competition with the Soviet Union. Nuclear weapons have shaped, and at times restrained, that competition; but they have not enabled either side to achieve a decisive advantage.

Because of their awesome destructiveness, nuclear weapons have kept in check a direct US-Soviet clash. With the advent in the late 1950s of intercontinental-range ballistic missiles—a delivery system for large numbers of nuclear weapons at great speed and with increasing accuracy—both the United States and the Soviet Union came to possess the ability to mount a devastating attack on each other within minutes.

The disastrous implications of such massive attacks led us to realize, in the words of President Kennedy, that "total war makes no sense." And as President Reagan has reiterated many times, "A nuclear war cannot be won and must never be fought"—words that the President and General Secretary Gorbachev agreed on in their joint statement at Geneva a year ago.

Thus, it came to be accepted in the West that a major role of nuclear weapons was to deter their use by others—as well as to deter major conventional attacks—by the threat of their use in response to aggression. Over the years, we sought through a variety of means and rationales—beginning with "massive retaliation" in the 1950s up through "flexible response" and "selective nuclear options" in the 1970s—to maintain a credible strategy for that retaliatory threat.

At the same time, we also accepted a certain inevitability about our own nation's vulnerability to nuclear-armed ballistic missiles. When nuclear weapons were delivered by manned bombers, we maintained air defenses. But as the ballistic missile emerged as the basic nuclear delivery system, we virtually abandoned the effort to build defenses. After a spirited debate over antiballistic missile systems in the late 1960s, we concluded that—on the basis of technologies now 20 years old—such defenses would not be effective. So our security from nuclear attack came to rest on the threat of retaliation and a state of mutual vulnerability.

In the West, many assumed that the Soviets would logically see things this way as well. It was thought that once both sides believed that a state of mutual vulnerability had been achieved, there would be shared restraint on the further growth of our respective nuclear arsenals.

The Anti-Ballistic Missile (ABM) Treaty of 1972 reflected that assumption. It was seen by some as elevating mutual vulnerability from technical fact to the status of international law. That treaty established strict limitations on the deployment of defenses against ballistic missiles. Its companion Interim Agreement on strategic offensive arms was far more modest. SALT I [strategic arms limitation talks] was conceived of as an intermediate step toward more substantial future limits on offensive nuclear forces. It established only a cap on the further growth in the numbers of ballistic missile launchers then operational and under construction. The most important measures of the two sides' nuclear arsenals—numbers of actual warheads and missile throw-weight—were not restricted.

But controlling the number of launchers without limiting warheads actually encouraged deployment of multiple warheads—called multiple independently-targetable reentry vehicles (MIRVs)—on a single launcher. This eventually led to an erosion of strategic stability as the Soviets—by proliferating MIRVs—became able to threaten all of our intercontinental ballistic missiles with only a fraction of their own. Such an imbalance makes a decision to strike first seem all the more profitable.

During this postwar period, we and our allies hoped that American nuclear weapons would serve as a comparatively cheap offset to Soviet conventional military strength. The Soviet Union, through its geographic position and its massive mobilized conventional forces, has powerful advantages it can bring to bear against Western Europe, the Mideast, and East Asia—assets useful for political intimidation as well as for potential military aggression. The West's success or failure in countering these Soviet advantages has been, and will continue to be, one of the keys to stability in our postwar world.

Our effort to deter a major Soviet conventional attack through the existence of opposing nuclear forces has been successful over the past four decades. It gave the industrialized democracies devastated by the Second World War the necessary "breathing space" to recover and thrive. But there has also been recurring debate over the credibility of this strategy, as well as controversy about the hardware required for its implementation.

Over time, we and our allies came to agree that deterrence required a flexible strategy combining both conventional and nuclear forces. This combined strategy has been successful in avoiding war in Europe. But our reliance for so long on nuclear weapons has led some to forget that these arms are not an inexpensive substitute—mostly paid for by the United States—for fully facing up to the challenges of conventional defense and deterrence.

Sources of Strategic Instability

The United States and our allies will have to continue to rely upon nuclear weapons for deterrence far, far into the future. That fact, in turn, requires that we maintain credible and effective nuclear deterrent forces.

But a defense strategy that rests on the threat of escalation to a strategic nuclear conflict is, at best, an unwelcome solution to ensuring our national security. Nuclear weapons, when applied to the problem of preventing either a nuclear or conventional attack, present us with a major dilemma. They may appear a bargain—but a dangerous one. They make the outbreak of a Soviet-American war most unlikely; but they also ensure that should deterrence fail, the resulting conflict would be vastly more destructive, not just for our two countries but for mankind as a whole.

Moreover, we cannot assume that the stability of the present nuclear balance will continue indefinitely. It can deteriorate, and it has. We have come to realize that our adversary does not share all of our assumptions about strategic stability. Soviet military doctrine stresses warfighting and survival in a nuclear environment, the importance of numerical superiority, the contribution of active defense, and the advantages of preemption.

Over the past 15 years, the growth of Soviet strategic forces has continued unabated—and far beyond any reasonable assessment of what might be required for rough equivalency with US forces. As a result, the Soviet Union has acquired a capability to put at risk the fixed land-based missiles of the US strategic triad—as well as portions of our bomber and in-port submarine force and command-and-control systems—with only a fraction of their force, leaving many warheads to deter any retaliation.

To date, arms control agreements along traditional lines—such as SALT I and II—have failed to halt these destabilizing trends. They have not brought about significant reductions in offensive forces, particularly those systems that are the most threatening to stability. By the most important measure of destructive capability—ballistic missile warheads (the things that hit you)—Soviet strategic forces have grown by a factor of four since the SALT I Interim Agreement was signed. This problem has been exacerbated by a Soviet practice of stretching their implementation of such agreements to the edge of violation—and, sometimes, beyond. The evidence of Soviet actions contrary to SALT II, the ABM Treaty, and various other arms control agreements is clear and unmistakable.

At the same time, technology has not stood still. Research and technological innovation of the past decade now raise questions about whether the primacy of strategic offense over defense will continue indefinitely. For their part, the Soviets have never neglected strategic defenses. They developed and deployed them even when offensive systems seemed to have overwhelming advantages over any defense. As permitted by the

ABM Treaty of 1972, the Soviets constructed around Moscow the world's only operational system of ballistic missile defense. Soviet military planners apparently find that the modest benefits of this system justify its considerable cost, even though it would provide only a marginal level of protection against our overall strategic force. It could clearly be a base for the future expansion of their defenses.

For well over a decade—long before the President announced three years ago the American Strategic Defense Initiative (SDI)—the Soviet Union has been actively investigating much more advanced defense technologies, including directed energy systems. If the United States were to abandon this field of advanced defensive research to the Soviet Union, the results 10 years hence could be disastrous for the West.

The President's Approach: Seeking Greater Stability

President Reagan believes we can do better. He believes we can reverse the ever-increasing numbers and potency of nuclear weapons that are eroding stability. He believes we can and must find ways to keep the peace without basing our security so heavily on the threat of nuclear escalation. To those ends, he has set in motion a series of policies which have already brought major results.

First, this administration has taken much-needed steps to reverse dangerous trends in the military balance by strengthening our conventional and nuclear deterrent forces. We have gone forward with their necessary modernization.

Second, we have sought ambitious arms control measures—not agreements for their own sake but steps which could seriously contribute to the goal of stabilizing reductions in offensive forces. In 1981, the President proposed the global elimination of all Soviet and American longer-range INF [intermediate-range nuclear forces] nuclear missiles. Not a freeze or token reductions, as many urged at the time, but the complete elimination of this class of weapons.

The following year, at Eureka College, the President proposed major reductions in strategic offensive forces, calling for cuts by one-third to a level of 5,000 ballistic missile warheads on each side. Again, this was a major departure from previous negotiating approaches—both in the importance of the weapons to be reduced and in the magnitude of their reduction. Critics claimed he was unrealistic, that he was not really interested in arms control. But the President's call for dramatic reductions in nuclear warheads on the most destabilizing delivery systems has been at the core of our negotiating efforts. The Soviets have finally begun to respond to the President's approach and are now making similar proposals.

Finally, the President also set out to explore whether it would be possible to develop an effective defense against ballistic missiles, the central element of current strategic offensive arsenals. To find that answer, he initiated in 1983 the SDI program—a broad-based research effort to explore the defensive implications of new technologies. It is a program that is consistent with our obligations under the ABM Treaty. He set as a basic goal the protection of the United States and our allies against the ballistic missile threat.

Since then, we have been seeking both to negotiate deep reductions in the numbers of those missiles as well as to develop the knowledge necessary to construct a strategic defense against them. It is the President's particular innovation to seek to use these parallel efforts in a reinforcing way—to reduce the threat while exploring the potential for defense.

Reykjavik: A Potential Watershed in Nuclear Arms Control

All of these efforts will take time to develop, but we are already seeing their first fruits. Some became apparent at Reykjavik. Previously, the prospect of 30 percent, let alone 50 percent, reductions in Soviet and American offensive nuclear arsenals was considered an overly ambitious goal.

At Reykjavik, the President and General Secretary Gorbachev reached the basis for an agreement on a first step of 50 percent reductions in Soviet and American strategic nuclear offensive forces over a five-year period. We agreed upon some numbers and counting rules—that is, how different types of weapons would count against the reduced ceilings.

For INF nuclear missiles, we reached the basis for agreement on even more drastic reductions, down from a current Soviet total of over 1,400 warheads to only 100 on longer-range INF missiles worldwide on each side. This would represent a reduction of more than 90 percent of the Soviet

SS-20 nuclear warheads now targeted on our allies and friends in Europe and Asia. There would also have to be a ceiling on shorter-range INF missiles, the right for us to match the Soviets in this category, and follow-on negotiations aimed at the reduction in numbers of these weapons.

Right there is the basis for an arms control agreement that doesn't just limit the future growth of Soviet and American nuclear arsenals but which actually makes deep and early cuts in existing force levels. These cuts would reduce the numbers of heavy, accurate, multiple-warhead missiles that are the most threatening and the most destabilizing. These ideas discussed at Reykjavik flowed directly from the President's long-standing proposals. They are a direct result of his vision of major offensive reductions as a necessary step to greater stability.

At Reykjavik, the President and the General Secretary went on to discuss possible further steps toward enhanced stability. The President proposed to eliminate all ballistic missiles over the subsequent five years. Mr. Gorbachev proposed to eliminate all strategic offensive forces. They talked about these and other ideas, including the eventual elimination of all nuclear weapons. The very scope of their discussion was significant. The President and the General Secretary set a new arms control agenda at Reykjavik, one that will shape our discussions with the Soviets about matters of nuclear security for years to come.

Of course, make no mistake about it: tough, and probably drawn-out, negotiations will still be required if we are to nail down any formal agreement on offensive force reductions. For example, the Soviets are now linking agreement on anything with agreement on everything. But the fact that we now have such reductions clearly on the table has only been made possible by:

- Our steps to restore America's military strength;
- Our firm and patient negotiating efforts over the past five years;
- The sustained support of our allies; and, not the least,
- Our active investigation into strategic defenses.

The prospect of effective defenses and our determined force modernization program have given the Soviet Union an important incentive to agree to cut back and eventually to eliminate ballistic missiles. Within the SDI program, we judge defenses to be desirable only if they are survivable and cost effective at the margin. Defenses that meet these criteria—those which cannot be easily destroyed or overwhelmed—are precisely the sort which would lead Soviet military planners to consider reducing, rather than continuing to expand, their offensive missile force.

But only a dynamic and ongoing research program can play this role. And for their part, the Soviets are making every effort to cripple our program. Thus, there were major differences over strategic defenses at Reykjavik. The President responded to Soviet concerns by proposing that, for 10 years, both sides would not exercise their existing right of withdrawal from the ABM Treaty and would confine their strategic defense programs to research, development, and testing activities permitted by the ABM Treaty. This commitment would be in the context of reductions of strategic offensive forces by 50 percent in the first five years and elimination of the remaining ballistic missiles in the second five years, and with the understanding that at the end of this 10-year period, either side would have the right to deploy advanced defenses, unless otherwise agreed.

But at Reykjavik, the Soviet Union wanted to change existing ABM Treaty provisions to restrict research in a way that would cripple the American SDI program. This we cannot accept.

Even as we eliminate all ballistic missiles, we will need insurance policies to hedge against cheating or other contingencies. We don't know now what form this will take. An agreed-upon retention of a small nuclear ballistic missile force could be part of that insurance. What we do know is that the President's program for defenses against ballistic missiles can be a key part of our insurance. A vigorous research program will give the United States and our allies the options we will need to approach a world with far fewer nuclear weapons—a world with a safer and more stable strategic balance, one no longer dependent upon the threat of mutual annihilation.

Next Steps with the Soviets

In the short term, our task is to follow up on the progress arising out of the Reykjavik discussions. For our part, we are energetically seeking to do so. Our negotiators in Geneva have instructions to pick up where the two leaders' exchanges left off. We have formally tabled our proposals, based on the progress at Reykjavik, and we are ready to discuss them.

To give additional impetus to that process, I met with Soviet Foreign Minister Shevardnadze in Vienna at the beginning of this month to continue our exchanges—not just on arms control but on the full agenda of US-Soviet issues, including those regional and human rights problems which are so critical to building trust and confidence between our two nations.

Our negotiating efforts—and the President's own discussions with the General Secretary—have been based on years of analysis of these issues and on our frequent exchanges with the Soviets. The Reykjavik meeting, for instance, was preceded by extensive preliminary discussions with the Soviets at the expert level in Geneva, Moscow, and Washington. We have had our senior negotiators and best advisers at all of these sessions—as well as at our most recent encounter in Vienna.

So we have been well prepared to move. But whether we can achieve concrete results now depends on the Soviets. General Secretary Gorbachev has spoken positively of the need to capitalize on the "new situation," he called it, created by Reykjavik. But at Vienna two weeks ago, the Soviets seemed primarily interested in trying to characterize SDI in the public mind as the sole obstacle to agreement. Mr. Shevardnadze was quick to accuse us of backsliding from the Reykjavik results and to label our Vienna meeting "a failure" because of our unwillingness to accede to their demands to cripple SDI. We will doubtless hear more such accusations over the coming weeks.

So all of this will take time to work out. But that's to be expected in negotiating with the Soviets. We are serious about our objectives, and we are determined to hold firmly to them. We have a clear sense of how our two nations might be able to move toward greater strategic stability. We are ready to move quickly to that end, but we are also prepared to be patient.

The Challenges of a Less Nuclear World

The longer-term implications of the Reykjavik discussions may prove even more challenging for us. Thus far in the nuclear age, we have become accustomed to thinking of nuclear weapons in terms of "more bang for the buck" and of the high price for any possible substitute for these arms. But to my mind, that sort of bookkeeping approach risks obscuring our larger interests. We should begin by determining what is of value to us and then what costs we are prepared to pay to attain those ends.

The value of steps leading to a less nuclear world is clear—potentially enhanced stability and less chance of a nuclear catastrophe. Together with our allies, we could enjoy a safer, more secure strategic environment.

But we would not seek to reduce nuclear weapons only to increase the risks of conventional war or, more likely, of political intimidation through the threat of conventional attack. Therefore, a central task will be to establish a stable conventional balance as a necessary corollary for any less nuclear world.

How would a less nuclear world, one in which ballistic missiles have been eliminated, work? What would it mean? It would not be the end of nuclear deterrence for the West. With a large inventory of aircraft and cruise missiles, the United States and NATO would retain a powerful nuclear capability. In a sense, we would return to the situation of the 1950s, when strategic bombers served as our primary nuclear deterrent force. But there would be an important difference in the 1990s and beyond. Our aircraft would now be supplemented by a host of new and sophisticated technologies as well as cruise missiles launched from the air and sea. It would be a much more diverse and capable force than in previous decades.

In such circumstances, both the United States and the Soviet Union would lose the capability provided by ballistic missiles to deliver large numbers of nuclear weapons on each others' homelands in less than 30-minutes' time. But Western strategy is, in fact, defensive in nature, built upon the pledge that we will only use our weapons, nuclear and conventional, in self-defense. Therefore, the loss of this quick-kill capability—so suited to preemptive attack—will ease fears of a disarming first strike.

For our friends and allies in Europe and Asia, the elimination of Soviet ballistic missiles—including not just the Soviet Union's strategic ballistic missiles and its many SS-20s but also the shorter range missiles for which we currently have no deployed equivalent—would remove a significant nuclear threat.

But it would also have non-nuclear military benefits as well. Today, the Soviet Union has ballistic missiles with conventional and chemical warheads targeted on NATO airfields, ports, and bases. The elimination of ballistic missiles would thus be a significant plus for NATO in several respects.

The nuclear forces remaining—aircraft and cruise missiles—would be far less useful for first-strike attacks but would be more appropriate for retaliation. They would be more flexible in use than ballistic missiles. The slower flying aircraft can be recalled after launch. They can be retargeted in flight. They can be re-used for several misions. We currently have a major advantage in the relative sophistication of our aircraft and cruise missiles: the Soviets have greater numbers of these systems and are striving hard to catch up in quality. They have given far more attention to defense, where we have a lot of catching up to do. But our remaining nuclear forces would be capable of fulfilling the requirements of the Western alliance's deterrent strategy.

The West's Advantages in a Less Nuclear World

The prospect of a less nuclear world has caused concern in both Europe and America. Some fear that it would place the West at a grave disadvantage. I don't think so.

In any competition ultimately depending upon economic and political dynamism and innovation, the United States, Japan, and Western Europe have tremendous inherent advantage. Our three-to-one superiority in gross national product over the Warsaw Pact, our far greater population, and the Western lead in modern technologies—these are only partial measures of our advantages. The West's true strength lies in the fact that we are not an ideological or military bloc like the Warsaw Pact; we are an alliance of free nations, able to draw upon the best of the diverse and creative energies of our peoples.

But dramatic reductions in nuclear weapons and the establishment of stronger conventional defenses will require a united alliance effort. In light of the President's discussions in Reykjavik, we must join with our allies in a more systematic consideration of how to deal with a less nuclear world. To my mind, that sort of process of joint inquiry is healthy for the alliance, particularly since we remain firmly agreed on the basics—the alliance's fundamental principle of shared risks and shared burdens on behalf of the common defense.

All of these steps—deep reductions of nuclear weapons, a strong research program in strategic defense, improvements in conventional defenses, and negotiations with the Soviet Union and Warsaw Pact—will have to be closely synchronized. This will require a carefully coordinated political strategy on the part of the alliance to deal with these interrelated aspects of the larger problem of stability and Western security. We will begin a preliminary discussion of just such an approach during my next meeting with my NATO counterparts in Brussels at the December session of the North Atlantic Council.

Conclusion

This is a full and complex agenda for all of us to consider. Is it ambitious? Yes. Unrealistic? No. I think that, on the basis of the progress made at Reykjavik, substantial reductions in Soviet and American nuclear forces are possible, and they can be achieved in a phased and stabilizing way.

But we need to think hard about how to proceed. We are taking on a difficult task as we seek to create the conditions in which we can assure the freedom and security of our country and our allies without the constant threat of nuclear catastrophe.

And, of course, our work to achieve greater strategic stability at progressively lower levels of nuclear arms is only part of our larger effort to build a more realistic and constructive relationship with the Soviet Union. We cannot pursue arms control in isolation from other sources of tension. We will continue to seek a resolution of the more fundamental sources of political distrust between our nations, especially those in the areas of human rights and regional conflicts.

Progress—whether in science or foreign affairs—often has to do with the reinterpretation of fundamental ideas. That's no easy task. It requires challenging conventional wisdom. And often we find that gaining new benefits requires paying new costs.

Just as what happened 44 years ago in the squash court under old Stagg Field opened up both new horizons and new dangers, so we now see new possibilities for protecting our security, as well as new risks if we don't manage them well. So it is up to us—working together with both allies and adversaries—to ensure that we use these new opportunities to achieve a more stable and secure peace.

A World Free of Nuclear Weapons
George P. Shultz, William J. Perry, Henry A. Kissinger,
and Sam Nunn
January 4, 2007

Nuclear weapons today present tremendous dangers, but also an historic opportunity. US leadership will be required to take the world to the next stage—to a solid consensus for reversing reliance on nuclear weapons globally as a vital contribution to preventing their proliferation into potentially dangerous hands, and ultimately ending them as a threat to the world.

Nuclear weapons were essential to maintaining international security during the Cold War because they were a means of deterrence. The end of the Cold War made the doctrine of mutual Soviet-American deterrence obsolete. Deterrence continues to be a relevant consideration for many states with regard to threats from other states. But reliance on nuclear weapons for this purpose is becoming increasingly hazardous and decreasingly effective.

North Korea's recent nuclear test and Iran's refusal to stop its program to enrich uranium—potentially to weapons grade—highlight the fact that the world is now on the precipice of a new and dangerous nuclear era. Most alarmingly, the likelihood that non-state terrorists will get their hands on nuclear weaponry is increasing. In today's war waged on world order by terrorists, nuclear weapons are the ultimate means of mass devastation. And non-state terrorist groups with nuclear weapons are conceptually outside the bounds of a deterrent strategy and present difficult new security challenges.

Apart from the terrorist threat, unless urgent new actions are taken, the US soon will be compelled to enter a new nuclear era that will be more precarious, psychologically disorienting, and economically even more costly than was Cold War deterrence. It is far from certain that we can successfully replicate the old Soviet-American "mutually assured destruction" with an increasing number of potential nuclear enemies worldwide without dramatically increasing the risk that nuclear weapons will be used. New nuclear states do not have the benefit of years of step-by-step safeguards put in effect during the Cold War to prevent nuclear accidents, misjudgments or unauthorized launches. The United States and the Soviet Union learned from mistakes that were less than fatal. Both countries were diligent to ensure that no nuclear weapon was used during the Cold War by design or by accident. Will new nuclear nations and the world be as fortunate in the next 50 years as we were during the Cold War?

Leaders addressed this issue in earlier times. In his "Atoms for Peace" address to the United Nations in 1953, Dwight D. Eisenhower pledged America's "determination to help solve the fearful atomic dilemma—to devote its entire heart and mind to find the way by which the miraculous inventiveness of man shall not be dedicated to his death, but consecrated to his life." John F. Kennedy, seeking to break the logjam on nuclear disarmament, said, "The world was not meant to be a prison in which man awaits his execution."

Rajiv Gandhi, addressing the UN General Assembly on June 9, 1988, appealed, "Nuclear war will not mean the death of a hundred million people. Or even a thousand million. It will mean the extinction of four thousand million: the end of life as we know it on our planet earth. We come to the United Nations to seek your support. We seek your support to put a stop to this madness."

Ronald Reagan called for the abolishment of "all nuclear weapons," which he considered to be "totally irrational, totally inhumane, good for nothing but killing, possibly destructive of life on earth and civilization." Mikhail Gorbachev shared this vision, which had also been expressed by previous American presidents.

Although Reagan and Mr. Gorbachev failed at Reykjavik to achieve the goal of an agreement to get rid of all nuclear weapons, they did succeed in turning the arms race on its head. They initiated steps leading to significant reductions in deployed long- and intermediate-range nuclear forces, including the elimination of an entire class of threatening missiles.

What will it take to rekindle the vision shared by Reagan and Mr. Gorbachev? Can a worldwide consensus be forged that defines a series of practical steps leading to major reductions in the nuclear danger? There is an urgent need to address the challenge posed by these two questions.

The Non-Proliferation Treaty (NPT) envisioned the end of all nuclear weapons. It provides (a) that states that did not possess nuclear weapons as of 1967 agree not to obtain them, and (b) that states that do possess them agree to divest themselves of these weapons over time. Every president of both parties since Richard Nixon has reaffirmed these treaty obligations, but non-nuclear weapon states have grown increasingly skeptical of the sincerity of the nuclear powers.

Strong nonproliferation efforts are under way. The Cooperative Threat Reduction program, the Global Threat Reduction Initiative, the Proliferation Security Initiative and the Additional Protocols are innovative approaches that provide powerful new tools for detecting activities that violate the NPT and endanger world security. They deserve full implementation. The negotiations on proliferation of nuclear weapons by North Korea and Iran, involving all the permanent members of the Security Council plus Germany and Japan, are crucially important. They must be energetically pursued.

But by themselves, none of these steps are adequate to the danger. Reagan and General Secretary Gorbachev aspired to accomplish more at their meeting in Reykjavik 20 years ago—the elimination of nuclear weapons altogether. Their vision shocked experts in the doctrine of nuclear deterrence, but galvanized the hopes of people around the world. The leaders of the two countries with the largest arsenals of nuclear weapons discussed the abolition of their most powerful weapons.

What should be done? Can the promise of the NPT and the possibilities envisioned at Reykjavik be brought to fruition? We believe that a major effort should be launched by the United States to produce a positive answer through concrete stages.

First and foremost is intensive work with leaders of the countries in possession of nuclear weapons to turn the goal of a world without nuclear weapons into a joint enterprise. Such a joint enterprise, by involving changes in the disposition of the states possessing nuclear weapons, would lend additional weight to efforts already under way to avoid the emergence of a nuclear-armed North Korea and Iran.

The program on which agreements should be sought would constitute a series of agreed and urgent steps that would lay the groundwork for a world free of the nuclear threat. Steps would include:

- Changing the Cold War posture of deployed nuclear weapons to increase warning time and thereby reduce the danger of an accidental or unauthorized use of a nuclear weapon.
- Continuing to reduce substantially the size of nuclear forces in all states that possess them.
- Eliminating short-range nuclear weapons designed to be forward-deployed.
- Initiating a bipartisan process with the Senate, including understandings to increase confidence and provide for periodic review, to achieve ratification of the Comprehensive Test Ban Treaty, taking advantage of recent technical advances, and working to secure ratification by other key states.
- Providing the highest possible standards of security for all stocks of weapons, weapons-usable plutonium, and highly enriched uranium everywhere in the world.
- Getting control of the uranium enrichment process, combined with the guarantee that uranium for nuclear power reactors could be obtained at a reasonable price, first from the Nuclear Suppliers Group and then from the International Atomic Energy Agency (IAEA) or other controlled international reserves. It will also be necessary to deal with proliferation issues presented by spent fuel from reactors producing electricity.

- Halting the production of fissile material for weapons globally; phasing out the use of highly enriched uranium in civil commerce and removing weapons-usable uranium from research facilities around the world and rendering the materials safe.
- Redoubling our efforts to resolve regional confrontations and conflicts that give rise to new nuclear powers.

Achieving the goal of a world free of nuclear weapons will also require effective measures to impede or counter any nuclear-related conduct that is potentially threatening to the security of any state or peoples.

Reassertion of the vision of a world free of nuclear weapons and practical measures toward achieving that goal would be, and would be perceived as, a bold initiative consistent with America's moral heritage. The effort could have a profoundly positive impact on the security of future generations. Without the bold vision, the actions will not be perceived as fair or urgent. Without the actions, the vision will not be perceived as realistic or possible.

We endorse setting the goal of a world free of nuclear weapons and working energetically on the actions required to achieve that goal, beginning with the measures outlined above.

Toward a Nuclear-Free World

George P. Shultz, William J. Perry, Henry A. Kissinger,
and Sam Nunn

January 15, 2008

The accelerating spread of nuclear weapons, nuclear know-how and nuclear material has brought us to a nuclear tipping point. We face a very real possibility that the deadliest weapons ever invented could fall into dangerous hands.

The steps we are taking now to address these threats are not adequate to the danger. With nuclear weapons more widely available, deterrence is decreasingly effective and increasingly hazardous.

One year ago, in an essay in this paper, we called for a global effort to reduce reliance on nuclear weapons, to prevent their spread into potentially dangerous hands, and ultimately to end them as a threat to the world. The interest, momentum and growing political space that has been created to address these issues over the past year has been extraordinary, with strong positive responses from people all over the world.

Mikhail Gorbachev wrote in January 2007 that, as someone who signed the first treaties on real reductions in nuclear weapons, he thought it his duty to support our call for urgent action: "It is becoming clearer that nuclear weapons are no longer a means of achieving security; in fact, with every passing year they make our security more precarious."

In June, the United Kingdom's foreign secretary, Margaret Beckett, signaled her government's support, stating: "What we need is both a vision—a scenario for a world free of nuclear weapons—and action— progressive steps to reduce warhead numbers and to limit the role of nuclear weapons in security policy. These two strands are separate but they are mutually reinforcing. Both are necessary, but at the moment too weak."

We have also been encouraged by additional indications of general support for this project from other former US officials with extensive experience as secretaries of state and defense and national security advisors. These include: Madeleine Albright, Richard V. Allen, James A. Baker III, Samuel R. Berger, Zbigniew Brzezinski, Frank Carlucci, Warren Christopher, William Cohen, Lawrence Eagleburger, Melvin Laird, Anthony Lake, Robert McFarlane, Robert McNamara and Colin Powell.

Inspired by this reaction, in October 2007, we convened veterans of the past six administrations, along with a number of other experts on nuclear issues, for a conference at Stanford University's Hoover Institution. There was general agreement about the importance of the vision of a world free of nuclear weapons as a guide to our thinking about nuclear policies, and about the importance of a series of steps that will pull us back from the nuclear precipice.

The US and Russia, which possess close to 95 percent of the world's nuclear warheads, have a special responsibility, obligation and experience to demonstrate leadership, but other nations must join.

Some steps are already in progress, such as the ongoing reductions in the number of nuclear warheads deployed on long-range, or strategic, bombers and missiles. Other near-term steps that the US and Russia could take, beginning in 2008, can in and of themselves dramatically reduce nuclear dangers. They include:

- *Extend key provisions of the Strategic Arms Reduction Treaty of 1991.* Much has been learned about the vital task of verification from the application of these provisions. The treaty is scheduled to expire on Dec. 5, 2009. The key provisions of this treaty, including their essential monitoring and verification requirements, should be extended, and the further reductions agreed upon in the 2002 Moscow Treaty on Strategic Offensive Reductions should be completed as soon as possible.
- *Take steps to increase the warning and decision times for the launch of all nuclear-armed ballistic missiles, thereby reducing risks of acci-*

dental or unauthorized attacks. Reliance on launch procedures that deny command authorities sufficient time to make careful and prudent decisions is unnecessary and dangerous in today's environment. Furthermore, developments in cyber warfare pose new threats that could have disastrous consequences if the command-and-control systems of any nuclear-weapons state were compromised by mischievous or hostile hackers. Further steps could be implemented in time, as trust grows in the US-Russian relationship, by introducing mutually agreed and verified physical barriers in the command-and-control sequence.

• *Discard any existing operational plans for massive attacks that still remain from the Cold War days.* Interpreting deterrence as requiring mutual assured destruction (MAD) is an obsolete policy in today's world, with the US and Russia formally having declared that they are allied against terrorism and no longer perceive each other as enemies.

• *Undertake negotiations toward developing cooperative multilateral ballistic missile defense and early warning systems, as proposed by Presidents Bush and Putin at their 2002 Moscow summit meeting.* This should include agreement on plans for countering missile threats to Europe, Russia and the US from the Middle East, along with completion of work to establish the Joint Data Exchange Center in Moscow. Reducing tensions over missile defense will enhance the possibility of progress on the broader range of nuclear issues so essential to our security. Failure to do so will make broader nuclear cooperation much more difficult.

• *Dramatically accelerate work to provide the highest possible standards of security for nuclear weapons, as well as for nuclear materials everywhere in the world, to prevent terrorists from acquiring a nuclear bomb.* There are nuclear weapons materials in more than 40 countries around the world, and there are recent reports of alleged attempts to smuggle nuclear material in Eastern Europe and the Caucasus. The US, Russia and other nations that have worked with the Nunn-Lugar programs, in cooperation with the International Atomic Energy Agency (IAEA), should play a key role in helping to implement United Nations Security Council Resolution 1540 relating to improving nuclear security—by offering teams to assist jointly any nation in meeting its obligations under this resolution to provide for appropriate, effective security of these materials.

As Governor Arnold Schwarzenegger put it in his address at our October conference, "Mistakes are made in every other human endeavor. Why should nuclear weapons be exempt?" To underline the governor's point, on Aug. 29–30, 2007, six cruise missiles armed with nuclear warheads were loaded on a US Air Force plane, flown across the country and unloaded. For 36 hours, no one knew where the warheads were, or even that they were missing.

- *Start a dialogue, including within NATO and with Russia, on consolidating the nuclear weapons designed for forward deployment to enhance their security, and as a first step toward careful accounting for them and their eventual elimination.* These smaller and more portable nuclear weapons are, given their characteristics, inviting acquisition targets for terrorist groups.
- *Strengthen the means of monitoring compliance with the nuclear Non-Proliferation Treaty (NPT) as a counter to the global spread of advanced technologies.* More progress in this direction is urgent, and could be achieved through requiring the application of monitoring provisions (Additional Protocols) designed by the IAEA to all signatories of the NPT.
- *Adopt a process for bringing the Comprehensive Test Ban Treaty (CTBT) into effect, which would strengthen the NPT and aid international monitoring of nuclear activities.* This calls for a bipartisan review, first, to examine improvements over the past decade of the international monitoring system to identify and locate explosive underground nuclear tests in violation of the CTBT; and, second, to assess the technical progress made over the past decade in maintaining high confidence in the reliability, safety and effectiveness of the nation's nuclear arsenal under a test ban. The Comprehensive Test Ban Treaty Organization is putting in place new monitoring stations

to detect nuclear tests—an effort the US should urgently support even prior to ratification.

In parallel with these steps by the US and Russia, the dialogue must broaden on an international scale, including non-nuclear as well as nuclear nations.

Key subjects include turning the goal of a world without nuclear weapons into a practical enterprise among nations, by applying the necessary political will to build an international consensus on priorities. The government of Norway will sponsor a conference in February that will contribute to this process.

Another subject: Developing an international system to manage the risks of the nuclear fuel cycle. With the growing global interest in developing nuclear energy and the potential proliferation of nuclear enrichment capabilities, an international program should be created by advanced nuclear countries and a strengthened IAEA. The purpose should be to provide for reliable supplies of nuclear fuel, reserves of enriched uranium, infrastructure assistance, financing, and spent fuel management—to ensure that the means to make nuclear weapons materials isn't spread around the globe.

There should also be an agreement to undertake further substantial reductions in US and Russian nuclear forces beyond those recorded in the US-Russia Strategic Offensive Reductions Treaty. As the reductions proceed, other nuclear nations would become involved.

President Reagan's maxim of "trust but verify" should be reaffirmed. Completing a verifiable treaty to prevent nations from producing nuclear materials for weapons would contribute to a more rigorous system of accounting and security for nuclear materials.

We should also build an international consensus on ways to deter or, when required, to respond to, secret attempts by countries to break out of agreements.

Progress must be facilitated by a clear statement of our ultimate goal. Indeed, this is the only way to build the kind of international trust and broad cooperation that will be required to effectively address today's threats. Without the vision of moving toward zero, we will not find the essential cooperation required to stop our downward spiral.

In some respects, the goal of a world free of nuclear weapons is like the top of a very tall mountain. From the vantage point of our troubled world today, we can't even see the top of the mountain, and it is tempting and easy to say we can't get there from here. But the risks from continuing to go down the mountain or standing pat are too real to ignore. We must chart a course to higher ground where the mountaintop becomes more visible.

Deterrence in the Age of Nuclear Proliferation

George P. Shultz, William J. Perry, Henry A. Kissinger,
and Sam Nunn

March 7, 2011

The doctrine of mutual assured destruction is obsolete in the post–Cold War era.

As long as there has been war, there have been efforts to deter actions a nation considers threatening. Until fairly recently, this meant building a military establishment capable of intimidating the adversary, defeating him or making his victory more costly than the projected gains. This, with conventional weapons, took time. Deterrence and war strategy were identical.

The advent of the nuclear weapon introduced entirely new factors. It was possible, for the first time, to inflict at the beginning of a war the maximum casualties. The doctrine of mutual assured destruction represented this reality. Deterrence based on nuclear weapons, therefore, has three elements:

- It is importantly psychological, depending on calculations for which there is no historical experience. It is therefore precarious.
- It is devastating. An unrestrained nuclear exchange between superpowers could destroy civilized life as we know it in days.
- Mutual assured destruction raises enormous inhibitions against employing the weapons.

Since the first use of nuclear weapons against Japan, neither of the superpowers, nor any other country, has used nuclear weapons in a war.

A gap opened between the psychological element of deterrence and the risks most leaders were willing to incur. US defense leaders made serious efforts to give the president more flexible options for nuclear use short of global annihilation. They never solved the problem, and it was always recognized that Washington and Moscow both held the keys to unpredictable and potentially catastrophic escalations.

As a result, nuclear deterrence was useful in preventing only the most catastrophic scenarios that would have threatened our survival. But even with the deployment of thousands of nuclear weapons on both sides of the Iron Curtain, the Soviet moves into Hungary in 1956 and Czechoslovakia in 1968 were not deterred. Nor were the numerous crises involving Berlin, including the building of the Wall in 1961, or major wars in Korea and Vietnam, or the Soviet invasion of Afghanistan in 1979. In the case of the Soviet Union, nuclear weapons did not prevent collapse or regime change.

Today, the Cold War is almost 20 years behind us, but many leaders and publics cannot conceive of deterrence without a strategy of mutual assured destruction. We have written previously that reliance on this strategy is becoming increasingly hazardous. With the spread of nuclear weapons, technology, materials and know-how, there is an increasing risk that nuclear weapons will be used.

It is not possible to replicate the high-risk stability that prevailed between the two nuclear superpowers during the Cold War in such an environment. The growing number of nations with nuclear arms and differing motives, aims and ambitions poses very high and unpredictable risks and increased instability.

From 1945 to 1991, America and the Soviet Union were diligent, professional, but also lucky that nuclear weapons were never used. Does the world want to continue to bet its survival on continued good fortune with a growing number of nuclear nations and adversaries globally? Can we devise and successfully implement with other nations, including other nuclear powers, careful, cooperative concepts to safely dismount the nuclear tiger while strengthening the capacity to assure our security and that of allies and other countries considered essential to our national security?

Recently, the four of us met at the Hoover Institution with a group of policy experts to discuss the possibilities for establishing a safer and more comprehensive form of deterrence and prevention in a world where the roles and risks of nuclear weapons are reduced and ultimately eliminated. Our broad conclusion is that nations should move forward together with a series of conceptual and practical steps toward deterrence that do not rely primarily on nuclear weapons or nuclear threats to maintain international peace and security.

The first step is to recognize that there is a daunting new spectrum of global security threats. These threats include chemical, biological and radiological weapons, catastrophic terrorism and cyber warfare, as well as natural disasters resulting from climate change or other environmental problems, and health-related crises. For the United States and many other nations, existential threats relating to the very survival of the state have diminished, largely because of the end of the Cold War and the increasing realization that our common interests greatly exceed our differences. However, an accident or mistake involving nuclear weapons, or nuclear terrorism fueled by the spread of nuclear weapons, nuclear materials, and nuclear know-how, is still a very real risk. An effective strategy to deal with these dangers must be developed.

The second step is the realization that continued reliance on nuclear weapons as the principal element for deterrence is encouraging, or at least excusing, the spread of these weapons, and will inevitably erode the essential cooperation necessary to avoid proliferation, protect nuclear materials and deal effectively with new threats.

Third, the US and Russia have no basis for maintaining a structure of deterrence involving nuclear weapons deployed in ways that increase the danger of an accidental or unauthorized use of a nuclear weapon, or even a deliberate nuclear exchange based on a false warning. Reducing the number of operationally deployed strategic nuclear warheads and delivery vehicles with verification to the levels set by the New Start Treaty is an important step in reducing nuclear risks. Deeper nuclear reductions and changes in nuclear force posture involving the two nations should remain a priority. Further steps must include short-range tactical nuclear weapons.

Fourth, as long as nuclear weapons exist, America must retain a safe, secure and reliable nuclear stockpile primarily to deter a nuclear attack and to reassure our allies through extended deterrence. There is an inherent limit to US and Russian nuclear reductions if other nuclear weapon states build up their inventories or if new nuclear powers emerge.

It is clear, however, that the US and Russia—having led the nuclear buildup for decades—must continue to lead the build-down. The US and its NATO allies, together with Russia, must begin moving away from threatening force postures and deployments including the retention of thousands of short-range battlefield nuclear weapons. All conventional deployments should be reviewed from the aspect of provocation. This will make America, Russia and Europe more secure. It will also set an example for the world.

Fifth, we recognize that for some nations, nuclear weapons may continue to appear relevant to their immediate security. There are certain undeniable dynamics in play—for example, the emergence of a nuclear-armed neighbor, or the perception of inferiority in conventional forces—that if not addressed could lead to the further proliferation of nuclear weapons and an increased risk they will be used. Thus, while the four of us believe that reliance on nuclear weapons for deterrence is becoming increasingly hazardous and decreasingly effective, some nations will hesitate to draw or act on the same conclusion unless regional confrontations and conflicts are addressed. We must therefore redouble our efforts to resolve these issues.

Achieving deterrence with assured security will require work by leaders and citizens on a range of issues, beginning with a clearer understanding of existing and emerging security threats. The role of non-nuclear means of deterrence to effectively prevent conflict and increase stability in troubled regions is a vital issue. Changes to extended deterrence must be developed over time by the US and allies working closely together. Reconciling national perspectives on nuclear deterrence is a challenging problem, and comprehensive solutions must be developed. A world without nuclear weapons will not simply be today's world minus nuclear weapons.

Nations can, however, begin moving now together toward a safer and more stable form of deterrence. Progress must be made through a joint enterprise among nations, recognizing the need for greater cooperation, transparency and verification to create the global political environment for stability and enhanced mutual security. Ensuring that nuclear materials are protected globally in order to limit any country's ability to reconstitute nuclear weapons, and to prevent terrorists from acquiring the material to build a crude nuclear bomb, is a top priority.

Moving from mutual assured destruction toward a new and more stable form of deterrence with decreasing nuclear risks and an increasing measure of assured security for all nations could prevent our worst nightmare from becoming a reality, and it could have a profoundly positive impact on the security of future generations.

A World Free of Nuclear Weapons, An Idea Whose Time Has Come: Where We Are and Where We Need to Go[1]

Address at Global Zero World Summit, Paris
February 2, 2010

- New York City, September 24, 2009, UN Security Council Summit Meeting
- President Obama was joined by United Nations Secretary-General Ban Ki-moon, Presidents Óscar Arias Sánchez of Costa Rica, Stjepan Mesić of Croatia, Dmitry Medvedev of the Russian Federation, Felipe Calderón Hinojosa of Mexico, Heinz Fischer of Austria, Nguyen Minh Triet of Vietnam, Yoweri Kaguta Museveni of Uganda, Hu Jintao of China, Nicolas Sarkozy of France, Blaise Compaore of Burkina Faso, and Prime Ministers Gordon Brown of the United Kingdom, Yukio Hatoyama of Japan, and Recep Tayyip Erdoğan of Turkey.
- In its first comprehensive action on nuclear issues since the mid-1990s, the Security Council unanimously adopted Resolution 1887, which begins: "*Resolving* to seek a safer world for all and to create the conditions for a world without nuclear weapons. . . . "[2]

The resolution gains strength from the fact that it builds on a long history. Presidents Eisenhower and Kennedy spoke about this goal. Rajiv Gandhi urged its pursuit with eloquence and urgency before the United Nations General Assembly. I remember Ronald Reagan's dogged pursuit of this goal. I remember the evening of December 20, 1984, when Soviet

1. I have benefited enormously from the advice of my colleagues Sid Drell, Henry Kissinger, William Perry, and Sam Nunn.

2. United Nations Security Council SC/9746, Department of Public Information (New York, September 24, 2009), http://www.un.org/News/Press/docs/2009/sc9746 .doc.htm.

Ambassador Anatoly Dobrynin brought me a letter for Ronald Reagan from General Secretary Konstantin Chernenko, in which Chernenko said,

> Recently you have spoken on more than one occasion . . . in favor of moving along the road leading eventually to the liquidation of nuclear weapons, completely and everywhere.
>
> We, of course, welcome that. The Soviet Union, as is known, as far back as the dawn of the nuclear age, came out for prohibiting and liquidating such weapons. . . . But even today it is not yet too late to start practical movement toward this noble objective.[3]

Of course, there was the dramatic effort in Reykjavik by Presidents Reagan and Gorbachev to begin work toward a world free of nuclear weapons. The general reaction at that time was deeply hostile, but now the atmosphere has changed.

Both candidates in the 2009 US presidential election endorsed this goal in their campaigns. Now in office, President Obama has continued his advocacy of a world free of nuclear weapons, and Senator McCain has reaffirmed his commitment to the goal.

We can note that Foreign Minister Sergey Lavrov of Russia gave a speech in Geneva on March 7, 2009, that included a statement by President Medvedev:

> Today we are facing a pressing need to move further along the road of nuclear disarmament. In accordance with its obligations under the Treaty on the Non-Proliferation of Nuclear Weapons, Russia is fully committed to reaching the goal of a world free from these most deadly weapons.[4]

My first point is that these statements show that the idea of a world free of nuclear weapons has extraordinary staying power. Why this

---

3. Chernenko to Reagan, December 20, 1984, http://www.jasonebin.com/the reaganfiles/id44.html.

4. President Dmitry Medvedev, quoted by Russian Minister of Foreign Affairs Sergey Lavrov at the Plenary Meeting of the Conference on Disarmament, Geneva, March 7, 2009, http://www.acronym.org.uk/docs/0903/doc12.htm.

staying power? The answer is that we know all too well that these weapons are unique in their immense and inhumane destructive power, that the consequences of their use would be devastating, and that access to nuclear materials is in the process of proliferating.

UN Security Council Resolution 1887 shows something else, particularly when juxtaposed to numerous recent statements of support for this goal by the leaders of many countries. So my second point is that not only does this idea have staying power but we are also entitled to hope and believe that it is an idea whose time has come.

We now must consider ourselves charged with the task of helping to transform the vision of a nuclear-weapons-free world into reality. What does it take to get from here to there? The answer is a lot of hard work on many subjects. I don't see the merit of aiming for some all-encompassing treaty. We can build on the Nuclear Non-Proliferation Treaty.

More vigorous attention must be given to the proliferation threats from North Korea and Iran. These two countries present a test case for assessing the ability of key nations to act with cohesiveness and resolve. In both cases, it seems a propitious moment to use tough diplomacy that includes a sense of consequences and that leads the way toward a better future for the clearly disaffected populations within these countries.

Of course, Russia and the United States must lead the way in major reductions in nuclear arms. In their joint statement on April 1, 2009, Presidents Obama and Medvedev instructed their respective negotiators to get busy immediately to negotiate a follow-on agreement to the START Treaty. On April 5 in Prague, President Obama followed up powerfully with an ambitious agenda, including concrete steps toward a world without nuclear weapons. Even now, the US stockpile is about one-fourth of its size at the height of the Cold War in 1986. Russian numbers have also come down sharply. So my third point is that, based on evidence from the past, dramatic progress is possible.

Where do we go from here, and how? I believe we must proceed carefully, remembering that we are talking about the national security of each country and all of us collectively. President Obama has pledged that he "will always maintain a strong deterrent as long as nuclear weapons exist."[5] That is necessary for each country and for the non-nuclear states that depend on the deterrent capabilities of others.

As I said in a recent op-ed written with colleagues William Perry, Henry Kissinger, and Sam Nunn,

> We [in the United States must] recognize the necessity to maintain the safety, security, and reliability of our own weapons. They need to be safe so that they do not detonate unintentionally; secure so that they cannot be used by an unauthorized party; and reliable so that they can continue to provide the deterrent we need so long as other countries have these weapons. This is a solemn responsibility, given the extreme consequences of potential failure on any one of these counts.
>
> For the past fifteen years these tasks have been successfully performed by the engineers and scientists at the nation's nuclear-weapons production plants and at the three national laboratories (Lawrence Livermore in California, Los Alamos in New Mexico, and Sandia in New Mexico and California). Teams of gifted people, using increasingly powerful and sophisticated equipment, have produced methods of certifying that the stockpile meets the required high standards. . . .
>
> Yet there are potential problems ahead. . . . [We need] significant investments in a repaired and modernized nuclear weapons infrastructure and added resources for the three national laboratories. These investments are urgently needed to undo the adverse consequences of deep reductions over the past five years in the laboratories' budgets for the science, technology, and engineering programs that support and underwrite the nation's nuclear deterrent. . . . Beyond our concern about our own stockpile, we have a deep security interest in ensuring that all nuclear weapons everywhere are resistant to accidental detonation and to detonation by terrorists or other unauthorized users. [The United States] should seek a dialogue with other states that possess nuclear weapons and share our safety and security concepts and technologies consistent with our own national security.[6]

5. White House Web site, www.whitehouse.gov, January 2009.

6. George P. Shultz, William J. Perry, Henry A. Kissinger, and Sam Nunn, "How to Protect Our Nuclear Deterrent," *The Wall Street Journal*, January 19, 2010.

I say that we must go carefully, but being careful does not mean taking the attitude that time is irrelevant. Time is not on our side, so the key phrase must be "careful urgency." I much prefer this to the term "date certain," as a date that is too early risks appearing unrealistic and one that is too far in the future seems too relaxed. The process needs to advance by taking a series of steps that will pull us back from the nuclear precipice. The agenda is reasonably well known, and it is daunting.

Yes, there are steps that the United States and Russia must take because they currently have exceptionally large arsenals. I'm glad to observe that this essential process is under way in the negotiations to extend the Strategic Arms Reduction Treaty.

But there are numerous other necessary actions that involve many other countries, and some require global participation. In his stirring address in Prague, President Obama identified several of them: "A new international effort to secure all vulnerable nuclear material around the world within four years" and build "on our efforts to break up black markets, detect and intercept materials in transit, and use financial tools to disrupt this dangerous trade."[7]

We know that it is essential to be able to verify that agreements are kept. Then there are issues of enforcement: What to do when some country or group steps out of line? As President Obama put it in Prague, "Rules must be binding. Violations must be punished. Words must mean something."[8]

The G8 statement of July 8, 2009, in which "member states reiterate commitment to a world without nuclear weapons," sounded a similar note:

> We also agree that measures are needed to address non-compliance, to include real and immediate consequences for States that withdraw from the NPT while in violation of it, including appropriate action by the UN

7. President Barack Obama (remarks in Hradčany Square, Prague, Czech Republic, April 5, 2009).
8. Ibid.

Security Council, and full use of IAEA inspection authorities that provide for access to all relevant locations, information and people.[9]

President Obama and other G8 leaders are right to emphasize the importance of this issue since enforcement is central to the desired outcome. The reality is that words have not meant much in recent years. Security Council statements and declarations by government leaders have been ignored almost routinely, as after North Korea's test of its ballistic missile capability and a similar test by Iran after revelations of a previously secret additional nuclear facility. If the threat of proliferation is to be dealt with successfully, there must be consequences for violations.

I will not catalogue all of the steps that must be taken to reach the goal of a nuclear-free world, but my colleagues Bill Perry, Henry Kissinger, Sam Nunn, and I have identified several essential steps in our *Wall Street Journal* articles of the past couple of years. You in the Global Zero initiative have done important work to emphasize the necessary steps, and other significant efforts are being made, such as the recently concluded joint initiative of the Australian and Japanese governments. These combined efforts lead to establishing an agenda and creating a commitment to its implementation on a global basis.

We are on our way to the creation of a joint enterprise. Discussion of various alternatives for getting to the nuclear-free mountaintop is essential. Sam Nunn has compared the goal of a world free of nuclear weapons to the top of a very tall mountain. Today we are heading down, not up. We can see that we must turn around, that we must take paths leading to higher ground, and that we must convince others to move with us. Today, even if we cannot see the path to the top of the mountain—a world free of nuclear weapons—we can reach agreement on what a base camp might look like well on the way to the top. From there, our view of the mountaintop will be clearer to both governments and to the public.

Here are two additional pressing challenges:

9. "L'Aquila Statement on Non-Proliferation," July 8, 2009, http://www.g8 italia2009.it/static/G8_Allegato/2._LAquila_Statent_on_Non_proliferation.pdf.

- We need to square the circle between the world's increasing demand for energy—including nuclear energy—with the challenge of ending proliferation and the threat of nuclear weapons. This is a problem that must be solved if we are to reach the mountaintop. Fortunately, progress is being made in addressing the nuclear fuel cycle, but much more difficult work remains.
- We need to find a way to secure nuclear materials so that terrorists and rogue states cannot gain access to the fissile material necessary to build a bomb.

   This is one of the most pressing and urgent problems we face because we know there are terrorists who are seeking these materials today and who would not hesitate to use them in making a bomb that could kill hundreds of thousands.

Our agenda is truly extensive, so we must consider the immense diplomacy needed to take the steps that have been identified.

- The issues involved are of transcendent importance, so the heads of government must be the chief diplomats. This is their issue. A key task is helping them exercise their awesome responsibilities.
- Foreign ministers should expect to be at the center of organizing this effort, working in tandem with ministers of defense and others. Broad training is essential, particularly in order to work with technological issues and scientific people. Ways must be devised to retain seasoned officers and to engage senior people with political backgrounds. Young people should be encouraged to take careers in the foreign service.
- The principal diplomatic task is to ensure that key constituencies and the general public in each country—groups that have an impact on the body politic—are brought on board, kept informed, and made a part of this process.
- Scientists and diplomats must learn to work together on issues. When they do so successfully, they will experience the thrill of learning important things about areas with which they normally have little contact.

- Finally, work must be undertaken, right from the outset, on a global scale. When I was in office and dealing with members of Congress, I learned that one of the rules of the road is: If you want me with you on the landing, be sure I'm with you on the takeoff.

All of you who are participating in this Global Zero initiative have contributed by identifying the agenda, calling attention to the central importance of this effort, and, in your very name, keeping the vision prominently on display.

In 2006, Sid Drell and I gathered a small group at Stanford University's Hoover Institution on the twentieth anniversary of the Reykjavik Summit meeting to discuss the continuing relevance of the Reagan-Gorbachev vision of a world free of nuclear weapons. Out of this conference emerged the first of the op-eds that helped put this subject where it belongs: on the front burner. Ambassador Max Kampelman—who is here today—gave a stirring opening speech at that conference. Max spoke of the importance in America of the movement from the *is* of our present day to the *ought* to which we aspire, and how that movement has made our democracy the country we cherish today.

Our Declaration of Independence and our Constitution contained many *oughts,* but it has taken us many years to end slavery, grant voting rights to all our citizens, and guarantee civil rights, to give you just a few examples. Max said it very clearly then: We must work to establish a civilized *ought* for human beings—the abolition of nuclear weapons. Achieving a world free from the threat of nuclear weapons will require a willingness to be idealistic and realistic at the same time.

By combining realism with idealism, we can find a way to move through practical steps from what *is*—a world with a risk of increasing global disaster—to what *ought* to be: a world free from the threat of nuclear weapons. As Henry Kissinger put it, "Our age has stolen fire from the gods; can we confine it to peaceful purposes before it consumes us?"[10]

10. Henry A. Kissinger, "Our Nuclear Nightmare," *Newsweek,* February 16, 2009.

Issues and Opportunities in the Nuclear Enterprise
Sidney D. Drell, George P. Shultz, and Steven P. Andreasen
2012

Policy Overview

We live in dangerous times for many reasons. Prominent among them is the existence of a global nuclear enterprise made up of weapons that can cause damage of unimaginable proportions and power plants at which accidents can have severe, essentially unpredictable consequences for human life. For all of its utility and promise, the nuclear enterprise is unique in the enormity of the vast quantities of destructive energy that can be released through blast, heat, and radioactivity.

We addressed just this subject in a conference in October 2011 at Stanford University's Hoover Institution. The conference included experts on weapons, on power plants, on regulatory experience, and on the development of public perceptions and the ways in which these perceptions influence policy. The reassuring outcome of the conference was a general sense that the US nuclear enterprise currently meets very high standards in its commitment to safety and security.

That has not always been the case in all aspects of the nuclear enterprise. And the unsettling outcome of the conference was that it will not be the case globally unless governments, international organizations, industry, and media recognize and address the nuclear challenges and mounting risks posed by a rapidly changing world.

The acceptance of the nuclear enterprise is now being challenged by concerns about the questionable safety and security of programs primarily in countries relatively new to the nuclear enterprise, and the potential

The Nuclear Enterprise: High Consequence Accidents—How to Enhance Safety and Minimize Risks in Nuclear Weapons and Reactors (Hoover Institution Press, 2012), 1–10. Copyright 2012 by the Board of Trustees of the Leland Stanford Junior University.

loss of control to terrorist or criminal gangs of fissile material that exists in such abundance around the world. In a number of countries, confidence in nuclear energy production was severely shaken in the spring of 2011 by the Fukushima nuclear reactor plant disaster. And in the military sphere, the doctrine of deterrence that remains primarily dependent on nuclear weapons is seen in decline due to the importance of non-state actors such as al Qaeda and terrorist affiliates that seek destruction for destruction's sake. We have two nuclear tigers by the tail.

When risks and consequences are unknown, undervalued, or ignored, our nation and the world are dangerously vulnerable. Nowhere is this risk-consequence equation more relevant than with respect to the nucleus of the atom.

The nuclear enterprise was introduced to the world by the shock of the devastation produced by two atomic bombs hitting Hiroshima and Nagasaki. Modern nuclear weapons are far more powerful than those early bombs, which presented their own hazards. Early research depended on a program of atmospheric testing of nuclear weapons. In the early years following World War II, the impact and the amount of radioactive fallout in the atmosphere generated by above-ground nuclear explosions was not fully appreciated. During those years, the United States and also the Soviet Union conducted several hundred tests in the atmosphere that created fallout. The recent Stanford conference focused on a regulatory weak point from that time that exists in many places today, as the Fukushima disaster clearly indicates. The US Atomic Energy Commission (AEC) was initially assigned conflicting responsibilities: to create an arsenal of nuclear weapons for the United States to confront a growing nuclear-armed Soviet threat; and, at the same time, to ensure public safety from the effects of radioactive fallout. The AEC was faced with the same conundrum with regard to civilian nuclear power generation. It was charged with promoting civilian nuclear power and simultaneously protecting the public.

Progress came in 1963 with the negotiation and signing of the Limited Test Ban Treaty (LTBT) banning all nuclear explosive testing in the atmosphere (initially by the United States, the Soviet Union, and the United Kingdom). With the successful safety record of the US nuclear weapons program, domestic anxiety about nuclear weapons receded somewhat. Meanwhile, public attitudes toward nuclear weapons reflected recognition of their key role in establishing a more stable nuclear deterrent posture in the confrontation with the Soviet Union.

The positive record on safety of the nuclear weapons enterprise in the United States—there have been accidents involving nuclear weapons, but none that led to the release of nuclear energy—was the result of a strong effort and continuing commitment to include safety as a primary criterion in new weapons designs, as well as careful production, handling, and deployment procedures. The key to the health of today's nuclear weapons enterprise is confidence in the safety of its operations and in the protection of special nuclear materials against theft. One can imagine how different the situation would be today if there had been a recognized theft of material sufficient for a bomb, or if one of the two four-megaton bombs dropped from a disabled B-52 Strategic Air Command bomber overflying Goldsboro, North Carolina, in 1961 had detonated. In that event, just one switch in the arming sequence of one of the bombs, by remaining in its "off position" while the aircraft was disintegrating, was all that prevented a full-yield nuclear explosion. A close call indeed!

In the twenty-six years since Chernobyl, the nuclear power industry has strengthened its safety practices. Over the past decade, growing concerns about global warming and energy independence have actually strengthened support for nuclear energy in the United States and many nations around the world. Yet despite these trends, the civil nuclear enterprise remains fragile. Following Fukushima, opinion polls gave stark evidence of the public's deep fears of the invisible force of nuclear radiation, shown by public opposition to the construction of new nuclear power plants in close proximity. It is not simply a matter of getting better information to the public but of actually educating the public about the true nature of nuclear radiation and its risks. Of course, the immediate task of the nuclear power component of the enterprise is to strive for the best possible safety record with one overriding objective: no more Fukushimas.

Another issue that must be resolved involves the continued effectiveness of a policy of deterrence that remains primarily dependent upon nuclear weapons, and the hazards these weapons pose due to the spread of nuclear technology and material. There is growing apprehension about the determination of terrorists to get their hands on weapons or, for that matter, on the special nuclear material—plutonium and highly enriched uranium—that fuels them in the most challenging step toward developing a weapon.

The global effects of a regional war between nuclear-armed adversaries such as India and Pakistan would also wield an enormous impact, potentially involving radioactive fallout at large distances caused by a limited number of nuclear explosions.

This is true as well for nuclear radiation from a reactor explosion—fallout at large distances would have a serious societal impact on the nuclear enterprise. There is little understanding of the reality and potential danger of consequences if such an event were to occur halfway around the world. An effort should be made to prepare the public by providing information on how to respond to such an event.

An active nuclear diplomacy has grown out of the Cold War efforts to regulate testing and reduce superpower nuclear arsenals. There is now a welcome focus on rolling back nuclear weapons proliferation. Additional important measures include the Nunn-Lugar program, started in 1991 to reduce the nuclear arsenal of the former Soviet Union. These have led to greater investment by the US and other governments in better security for nuclear weapons and material globally, including billions of dollars through the G8 Global Partnership Against the Spread of Weapons and Materials of Mass Destruction. The commitment to improving security of all dangerous nuclear material on the globe within four years was made by forty-seven world leaders who met with President Obama in Washington, DC, in April 2010; this commitment was reconfirmed in March 2012 at the Nuclear Security Summit in Seoul, South Korea. Many specific commitments made in 2010 relating to the removal of nuclear materials and conversion of nuclear research reactors from highly enriched uranium to low-enriched uranium fuel have already been accomplished, along with increasing levels of voluntary commitments from a diverse set of states, improving prospects for achieving the four-year goal.

The nuclear enterprise faces new and increasingly difficult challenges. Successful leadership in national security policy will require a continuous, diligent, and multinational assessment of these newly emerging risks and consequences.

The Stanford conference examined the risks and potentially deadly consequences associated with nuclear weapons and nuclear power, and identified three guiding principles for efforts to reduce those risks globally:

First, the calculations used to assess nuclear risks in both the military and the civil sectors are fallible. Accurately analyzing events where we have little data, identifying every variable associated with risk, and the possibility of a single variable that goes dangerously wrong are all factors that complicate risk calculations. Governments, industry, and concerned citizens must constantly re-examine the assumptions on which safety and security measures, emergency preparations, and nuclear energy production are based. When dealing with very low-probability and high-consequence operations, we typically have little data as a basis for making quantitative analyses. It is therefore difficult to assess the risk of a nuclear accident and what would contribute to it, and to identify effective steps to reduce that risk.

In this context, it is possible that a single variable could exceed expectations, go dangerously wrong, and simply overwhelm safety systems and the risk assessments on which those systems were built. This is what happened in 2011 when an earthquake, followed by a tsunami—both of which exceeded expectations based on history—overwhelmed the Fukushima complex, breaching a number of safeguards that had been built into the plant and triggering reactor core meltdowns and radiation leaks. This in turn exposed the human factor, which is hard to assess and can dramatically change the risk equation. Cultural habits and regulatory inadequacy inhibited rapid decision-making and crisis management in the Fukushima disaster. A more nefarious example of the human factor would be a determined nuclear terrorist attack specifically targeting either the military or civilian component of the nuclear enterprise.

Second, risks associated with nuclear weapons and nuclear power will likely grow substantially as nuclear weapons and civilian nuclear energy production technology spread in unstable regions of the world where the potential for conflict is high. States that are new to the nuclear enterprise may not have effective nuclear safeguards to secure nuclear weapons and materials—including a developed fabric of early warning systems and nuclear confidence-building measures that could increase warning and decision time for leaders in a crisis—or the capability to safely manage and regulate the construction and operation of new civilian reactors. Hence there is a growing risk of accidents, mistakes, or miscalculations involving nuclear weapons, and of regional wars or nuclear terrorism. The consequences would be horrific: a Hiroshima-size nuclear bomb detonated in a major city could kill a half-million people and result in $1 trillion in direct economic damage.

On the civil side of the nuclear ledger, the sobering paradox identified at the Stanford conference is this: while an accident would be considerably less devastating than the detonation of a nuclear weapon, the risk of an accident occurring is probably higher. Currently, 1.4 billion people live without electricity, and by 2030 the global demand for energy is projected to rise by about 25 percent. With the added need to minimize carbon emissions, nuclear power reactors will become increasingly attractive alternative sources for electric power, especially for developing nations. These countries, in turn, will need to meet the challenge of developing appropriate governmental institutions and the infrastructure, expertise, and experience to support nuclear power efforts with a suitably high standard of safety. As the world witnessed in Fukushima, a nuclear power plant accident can lead to the spread of dangerous radiation, massive civil dislocations, and billions of dollars in cleanup costs. Such an event can also fuel widespread public skepticism about nuclear institutions and technology.

Some developed nations—notably Germany—have interpreted the Fukushima accident as proof that they should abandon nuclear power altogether, primarily by prolonging the life of existing nuclear reactors while phasing out nuclear-produced electricity and developing alternative energy sources.

Third, we need to understand that no nation is immune from risks involving nuclear weapons and nuclear power within their borders. There were 32 so-called "Broken Arrow" accidents involving US nuclear weapons between 1950 and 1980, mostly involving US Strategic Air

Command bombers and earlier bomb designs not yet incorporating modern nuclear detonation safety designs. The US no longer maintains a nuclear-armed in-air strategic bomber force and the record of incidents is greatly reduced. In several cases, accidents such as the North Carolina bomber incident came dangerously close to triggering catastrophes, with disaster averted simply by luck.

The United States has had an admirable safety record in the area of civil nuclear power since the 1979 Three Mile Island accident in Pennsylvania, yet safety concerns persist. One of the critical assumptions in the design of the Fukushima reactor complex was that, if electrical power were lost at the plant and its backup generators, it could be restored within a few hours. The combined one-two punch of the earthquake and tsunami, however, made such repair impossible. In the United States today, some nuclear power reactors are designed with a comparably short window for restoring power. After Fukushima, this is an issue that deserves action—especially in light of our own Hurricane Katrina experience, which rendered many affected areas inaccessible for days in 2005, and the August 2011 East Coast earthquake that shook the North Anna nuclear power plant in Mineral, Virginia, beyond expectations based on previous geological activity.

To reduce these nuclear risks, the conference arrived at four related recommendations that should be adopted by the nuclear enterprise, both military and civilian, in the United States and abroad.

First, the reduction of nuclear risks requires every level of the nuclear enterprise and related military and civilian organizations to embrace the importance of safety and security as an overarching operating rule. This is not as easy as it sounds. To a war fighter, more safety and control can mean less reliability and availability and greater costs. For a company or utility involved in the construction or operation of a nuclear power plant, more safety and security can mean greater regulation and higher costs.

But the absence of a culture of safety and security, in which priorities and meaningful standards are set and rigorous discipline and accountability are enforced, is perhaps the most reliable indicator of an impending disaster. In August 2007, after a B-52 bomber loaded with six nuclear-tipped cruise missiles flew from North Dakota to Louisiana without anyone realizing there were live weapons on board, then Secretary of Defense Robert Gates fired both the military and civilian heads of the US Air Force. His action was an example of setting the right priorities and enforcing accountability, but the reality of the incident shows that greater incorporation of a safety and security culture is needed.

Second, independent regulation of the nuclear enterprise is crucial to setting and enforcing the safety and security rule. In the United States today, the nuclear regulatory system—in particular, the Nuclear Regulatory Commission (NRC)—is credited with setting a uniquely high standard for independent regulation of the civil nuclear power sector. This is one of the keys to a successful and safe nuclear program. Effective regulation is even more crucial when there are strong incentives to keep operating costs down and keep an aging nuclear reactor fleet in operation, a combination that could create conditions for a catastrophic nuclear power plant failure. Careful attention is required to protect the NRC from regulatory capture by vested interests in government and industry, the latter of which funds a high percentage of the NRC'S budget.

Strong, independent regulatory agencies are not the norm in many countries. The independent watchdog organization advising the Japanese government was working with Japanese utilities to influence public opinion in favor of nuclear power. Strengthening the International Atomic Energy Agency (IAEA) so that it can play a greater role in civil nuclear safety and security would also help reduce risks, and will require substantially greater authorities to address both safety and security, and most importantly resources for an agency whose budget is only 333 million Euros, with only 1/10th of that total going to nuclear safety and security. In addition, exporting "best practices" of the NRC—that is, lessons of nuclear regulation, oversight, and safety learned over many decades—to other countries would pay a huge safety dividend.

Third, independent peer review should be incorporated into all aspects of the nuclear enterprise. On the weapons side, independent experts in the United States—both within and outside the organization—are relied on to review, or "red team," each other, rigorously challenge and discuss weapons and systems safety, and communicate these points up and down the line. The Institute of Nuclear Power Operations (INPO) provides strong peer review and oversight of the civil nuclear sector in the United States. Its global counterpart, the World Association of Nuclear Operators (WANO), should give a higher priority to further strengthening its safety operations, in particular its peer review process, learning from the experiences of the United States and other nations. Strong outside peer review—combined with an enhanced capacity to arrange fines based on incidents occurring in far distant countries—would help states entering into the world of high-consequence operations to develop a culture and standard needed to achieve a high safety record.

Beyond these recommendations, the military and civilian nuclear communities can and should learn from each other. A periodic dialogue structured around assessing and reducing the risks surrounding the nuclear enterprise would be valuable, both in the United States and abroad, and could be organized by governments or academia (as was done in the conference at Stanford). An analysis of the probabilities of undesired events and ways to minimize them, including lessons learned from accidents such as Fukushima as well as "close call" incidents, should be put on the front burner along with consequence management—that is, what to do if a nuclear incident were to occur.

An informed public is also an essential element in responding to a nuclear crisis. Greater public awareness and understanding of nuclear risks and consequences can lead to greater public preparation to handle post-disaster challenges.

Fourth, progress on all aspects of nuclear threat reduction should be organized around a clear goal: a global effort to reduce reliance on nuclear weapons, prevent their spread into potentially dangerous hands, and ultimately end them as a threat to the world. A step-by-step process—along lines proposed by George Shultz, William Perry, Henry Kissinger, and Sam Nunn in a series of *Wall Street Journal* essays[1]—and

---

1. George P. Shultz, William J. Perry, Henry A. Kissinger, and Sam Nunn, "A World Free of Nuclear Weapons," *The Wall Street Journal* (January 4, 2007); George P. Shultz, William J. Perry, Henry A. Kissinger, and Sam Nunn, "Toward a Nuclear-Free World," *The Wall Street Journal* (January 15, 2008); George P. Shultz, William J. Perry, Henry A. Kissinger, and Sam Nunn, "Deterrence in the Age of Nuclear Proliferation," *The Wall Street Journal* (March 7, 2011).

demonstrated progress toward realizing the vision of a world free of nuclear weapons will build the kind of international trust and broad cooperation required to effectively address today's threats—and prevent tomorrow's catastrophe.

Our bottom line: Since the risks posed by the nuclear enterprise are so high, no reasonable effort should be spared to ensure safety and security. That must be the rule in dealing with events of very low probability but potentially catastrophic consequences.

Next Steps in Reducing Nuclear Risks

George P. Shultz, William J. Perry, Henry A. Kissinger,
and Sam Nunn

March 5, 2013

The pace of nonproliferation work today doesn't match the urgency of the threat.

Every American president since the end of World War II has sought to come to grips with the unique security risks and challenges associated with nuclear weapons. The specter of a nuclear war, accident, proliferation or terrorism has led to serious and sustained efforts to control, reduce and eliminate nuclear risks. Over the decades, progress has been made in reducing nuclear weapons, and bringing about international agreements on nonproliferation.

Recently, the four of us have supported two major policy initiatives: the 2010 New Start Treaty with Russia, which verifiably reduced bilateral nuclear stockpiles; and the Nuclear Security Summits of 2010 and 2012, which have energized global efforts to secure nuclear weapons and materials. Both initiatives are significant and hopeful steps that add to a solid foundation of bipartisan accomplishment over many decades. Most notably, the number of nuclear weapons in the world today is less than one-third of the total in 1986 at the time of the Reagan-Gorbachev Reykjavik summit.

Despite these considerable efforts, nuclear dangers remain all too real. Technological progress and the proliferation of nuclear weapons to additional states are compounded by dangerous complacency. Bilateral relations between the two largest nuclear powers, the United States and Russia, are frayed, and there are continuing difficulties in effectively addressing emerging nuclear threats in North Korea and Iran, punctuated recently by a test explosion in North Korea. Combined with the dangers of suicidal terrorist groups, the growing number of nations with nuclear arms and differing motives, aims and ambitions poses very high and unpredictable risks.

It is far from certain that today's world can successfully replicate the Cold War Soviet-American deterrence by "mutually assured destruction"—the threat of imposing unacceptable damage on the adversary. That was based essentially on a bipolar world. But when a large and growing number of nuclear adversaries confront multiple perceived threats, the relative restraint of the Cold War will be difficult to sustain. The risk that deterrence will fail and that nuclear weapons will be used increases dramatically.

Global leaders owe it to their publics to reduce, and eventually to eliminate, these risks. Even during the Cold War, the leaders of the two superpowers sought to reduce the risk of nuclear war. What was possible among declared enemies is imperative in a world of increasing nuclear stockpiles in some nations, multiple nuclear military powers and growing diffusion of nuclear energy. A global effort is needed to reduce reliance on nuclear weapons, prevent their spread, and ultimately end them as a threat to the world. It will take leadership, creative approaches and thoughtful understanding of the perils of inaction. Near-term results would lay the foundation for transforming global security policies over the medium and long term. We suggest four areas requiring urgent consideration:

1. *Securing nuclear materials to prevent catastrophic nuclear terrorism.* Materials necessary for building a nuclear bomb today are stored at hundreds of sites in 28 countries—down from over 40 countries just 10 years ago. But many of these sites aren't well secured, leaving the materials vulnerable to theft or sale on the black market. Important commitments were undertaken to secure nuclear materials and improve cooperation during the 2010 and 2012 Nuclear Security Summits. These could improve security for generations to come. Yet no global system is in place for tracking, accounting for, managing and securing all weapons-usable nuclear materials.

At the next Nuclear Security Summit, planned for 2014 in the Netherlands, world leaders should commit to develop a comprehensive global materials security system—including procedures for international assurances—to ensure that all weapons-usable nuclear materials are secure from unauthorized access and theft.

2. *Changes in the deployment patterns of the two largest nuclear powers to increase decision time for leaders.* In the 2008 campaign, then-Senator Obama said: "Keeping nuclear weapons ready to launch on a moment's notice is a dangerous relic of the Cold War. Such policies increase the risk of catastrophic accidents or miscalculation. I will work with Russia to end such outdated Cold War policies in a mutual and verifiable way." The US should work with nuclear-armed nations worldwide to remove all nuclear weapons from the prompt-launch status in which nuclear-armed ballistic missiles are deployed to be launched in minutes. To jump-start this initiative, the US and Russia should agree to take a percentage of their nuclear warheads off prompt-launch status—remembering Ronald Reagan's admonition to "trust but verify."

3. *Actions following New Start. The progress in the strategic field has been considerable.* Washington should carefully examine going below New Start levels of warheads and launchers, including the possibility of coordinated mutual actions. Such a course has the following prerequisites:

a) strict reciprocity; b) demonstrable verification; and c) providing adequate and stable funding for the long-term investments required to maintain high confidence in our nuclear arsenal.

Consolidating and reducing US and Russian tactical nuclear weapons not covered under New Start should also be a high priority. It must be recognized that as some other nuclear-armed states are building up their inventories, or if new nuclear powers emerge, US and Russian nuclear reductions face an inherent limit. The nuclear programs of North Korea and Iran undermine the Non-Proliferation Treaty and pose a direct threat to regional and global stability. Unless these two states are brought into compliance with their international obligations, their continued nuclear programs will erode support for non-proliferation and further nuclear reductions.

4. *Without verification and transparency, nuclear-security agreements cannot be completed with confidence.* The US should launch a "verification initiative" that involves the US nuclear weapons laboratories and global scientific experts in developing essential technologies and innovations for reducing and controlling nuclear weapons and materials. The principle of enhanced transparency could also be applied to missile defense so long as it doesn't risk capabilities. Taking the lead in fostering greater transparency sets an important baseline for all nations and can facilitate future verification of nuclear materials and weapons.

This strategy focused on immediate steps would give leaders greater confidence to take measures to improve security in the nearterm. It would boost prospects for support by legislatures. Close consultations with Congress are crucial.

We also need a new dialogue. In our January 2007 op-ed on these pages, we identified practical steps toward the goal of a world free of nuclear weapons. These steps will involve many nations, not just those currently in possession of nuclear weapons. Progress will require greater cooperation. The US must work with other key states to establish a joint enterprise with common objectives to achieve near-term results. Russia and the US, with the largest nuclear stockpiles, have a special responsibility in this regard.

- *A coalition of the willing.* The Nuclear Security Summits could provide a model for leaders working together to create a joint enterprise that would generate a coalition of willing states to establish priorities and achieve progress on specific steps. Essential subjects should be identified in which many nations have a stake, and to which many must make a contribution. A timetable for meetings between heads of government would help build a diplomatic structure for engagement, within which foreign ministers, defense ministers and others can work together between the meetings of government leaders.

- *Regional dialogues.* Such a joint enterprise should include and be reinforced by regional dialogues. Top political, defense and military leaders
  should explore with their counterparts a range of practical steps on
  core security issues. The Euro-Atlantic region—an area that includes
  Europe, Russia and the US, four nuclear weapon states and over 90 percent of global nuclear inventories—will need to play a central role.
  China and other key states will need to be engaged both on multilateral
  issues and within their own regions.

The continuing risk posed by nuclear weapons remains an overarching
strategic problem, but the pace of work doesn't now match the urgency
of the threat. The consequences of inaction are potentially catastrophic,
and we must continue to ask: How will citizens react to the chaos and suffering of a nuclear attack? Won't they demand to know what could have
been done to prevent this? Our age has stolen fire from the gods. Can we
confine this awesome power to peaceful purposes before it consumes us?

About the Author

GEORGE P. SHULTZ, a native of New York City, attended Princeton University, served in the US Marine Corps, and earned a PhD in industrial economics from the Massachusetts Institute of Technology (MIT) in 1949. From 1948 to 1957 he taught at MIT. In 1955 he served as a senior staff economist on President Eisenhower's Council of Economic Advisers.

In 1957 Shultz joined the faculty of the University of Chicago's Graduate School of Business as a professor of industrial relations, becoming dean in 1962. From 1968 to 1969 he was a fellow at the Center for Advanced Study in the Behavioral Sciences at Stanford University.

He was appointed secretary of labor by President Nixon in 1969. In 1970 he became director of the Office of Management and Budget; in 1972 he was named secretary of the treasury. In 1974 he became president of Bechtel Group and joined the faculty of Stanford University. Shultz was chairman of President Reagan's Economic Policy Advisory Board from 1981 to 1982 and secretary of state from 1982 to 1989.

Shultz's publications include *Ideas & Action, Featuring 10 Commandments for Negotiations* (2010); *Ending Government Bailouts as We Know Them*, coedited with Kenneth E. Scott and John B. Taylor (2010); *Putting Our House in Order: A Citizen's Guide to Social Security and Health Care Reform*, with John B. Shoven (2008); *Turmoil and Triumph: My Years as Secretary of State* (1993); *Economic Policy Beyond the Headlines*, with Kenneth Dam (1977); *Workers and Wages in the Urban Labor Market*, with Albert Rees (1970); *Guidelines, Informal Controls, and the Marketplace*, with Robert Aliber (1966); *Strategies for the Displaced Worker: Confronting Economic Change*, with Arnold Weber (1966); *Management Organization and the Computer*, with Thomas Whisler (Eds.) (1960); *Labor Problems: Cases and Readings*, with John Coleman (1959); *The Dynamics of a Labor Market*, with Charles Myers (1951); *Pressures on Wage Decisions* (1951); *Causes of Industrial Peace Under Collective*

Bargaining, Case Study No. 10, with Robert P. Crisara (1951); and *Causes of Industrial Peace Under Collective Bargaining,* Case Study No. 7, with Charles A. Myers (1950).

Shultz is the Thomas W. and Susan B. Ford Distinguished Fellow at the Hoover Institution, Stanford University. He is honorary chairman of the Stanford Institute for Economic Policy Research, Advisory Council chair of the Precourt Institute for Energy Efficiency at Stanford University, chair of the MIT Energy Initiative External Advisory Board, and chair of the Hoover Institution Task Force on Energy Policy.

Index

Photo Credits

George P. Shultz: 1 (top and bottom), 2, 3 (top and bottom), 5, 6 (top), 7 (top and bottom), 8 (top and center), 9 (bottom), 10 (top left and right), 11 (all), 12 (top and center), 13 (bottom) concept and execution by Nancy Carroll, 14 (top), 16 (top and bottom)

United States Department of Labor: 4 (top)

Associated Press (AP Photo): 4 (bottom)

The Ronald Reagan Presidential Foundation and Library: 6 (bottom), 9 (top), 12 (bottom), 14 (bottom), 15

The Richard Nixon Presidential Library and Museum: 8 (bottom)

Conrad Estate: 10 (bottom), reprinted with permission.

J. R. Garappolo and C. G. Pease: 13 (top) © 2013, Light at 11B.